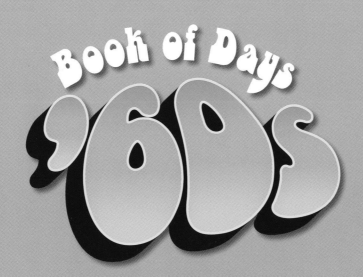

Book of Days

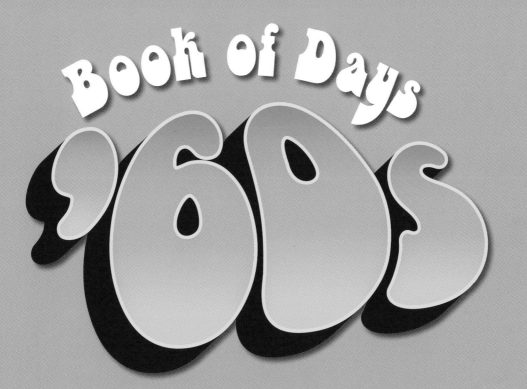

'60s

A Day-by-Day Look at the
Pop Culture Moments
That Made History

HARVEY SOLOMON & RICH APPEL

METRO BOOKS
NEW YORK

Dedication

To Rachel and Sarah: born too late to remember the '60s,
*but absolutely perfect in every other r-e-s-p-e-c-t. **(HS)***

To Melody and Jordan, who at 10 and 14 are already more prolific writers
*than I'll ever be. And to Jane—ahead of these 366, the best date of all. **(RA)***

© 2009 by Tell Tale Press, Inc.

This 2009 edition published by Metro Books,
by arrangement with Tell Tale Press, Inc.

Cover design: Jim Sarfati
Interior concept design: Charles Kreloff
Interior layout and design: Suraiya Hossain

Metro Books
122 Fifth Avenue
New York, NY 10011

ISBN: 978-1-4351-0472-3

Printed and bound in China

10 9 8 7 6 5 4 3 2 1

CD Track Listing

1. White Rabbit—Jefferson Airplane (Grace Slick). Originally Released 1967 Sony Music Entertainment

2. The Ballad Of The Green Berets—SSgt. Barry Sadler, US Army Special Forces (SSgt. Barry Sadler / Robin Moore). Originally Released 1966 Sony Music Entertainment

3. The Good, The Bad and The Ugly—Hugo Montenegro and His Orchestra and Chorus (Ennio Morricone). Originally Released 1968 Sony Music Entertainment

4. Somewhere from West Side Story—Jim Bryant and Marni Nixon (Leonard Bernstein). Originally Released 1961 Sony Music Entertainment

5. Only The Lonely—Roy Orbison (Roy Orbison / Joe Melson). Originally Released 1960 Sony Music Entertainment

6. Mellow Yellow—Donovan (Donovan Leitch). Originally Released 1966 Sony Music Entertainment

7. Folsom Prison Blues (Live)—Johnny Cash (J.R. Cash). Originally Released 1968 Sony Music Entertainment

Sony Music
CUSTOM MARKETING GROUP

Contents

Introduction

Reversing the old adage about the month of March, the 1960s came in like a lamb and went out like a lion. What began as a continuation of the conservative, complacent 1950s ended in a storm of dissent and disorder. It all started very promisingly, though, with the inauguration of America's youngest president, John F. Kennedy, whose election gave rise to a new generation of hope, of promise, and of change. "And so, my fellow Americans," spoke Kennedy in his 1961 inaugural address, "ask not what your country can do for you. Ask what you can do for your country."

Americans, especially young Americans, responded enthusiastically. Thousands joined the newly formed Peace Corps, which dispatched more than 7,000 volunteers to forty-four countries within two years. The race for space began in April 1961 when the USSR put the first cosmonaut into outer space. American Alan Shepard followed three weeks later, and the following year John Glenn orbited the Earth and returned to a hero's welcome and tickertape parades. Kennedy had already committed America to "landing a man on the moon and returning him safely" before the end of the decade, an accomplishment achieved in 1969.

By then, Kennedy's short-lived presidency seemed but a distant, perhaps wistful memory as the country was besieged by political division and social unrest. Triggered largely by the escalating Vietnam War, the nation faced unprecedented agitation and action on a far-reaching range of issues, including civil rights, environmentalism, and women's and gay rights, all embodying a slogan popular on buttons and bumper stickers: "Question Authority." Ironically, the man Kennedy had defeated, Richard M. Nixon, had by then been elected president—but America in 1969 was a far different place than it had been when the decade began.

For a vivid illustration of just how radical the change, thumb through any college yearbook from the early '60s and compare it to one from '68 or '69. (For high schools, the change isn't so apparent until the '70s.) In more than any other decade in twentieth-century America, the changes are obvious and overwhelming— from the buttoned-down, well-groomed, obedient faces of the postwar Eisenhower era to the tie-dyed, long-haired, radical faces of a nation immersed in controversy and conflict. "There's a battle outside and it is ragin'. It'll soon shake your windows and rattle your walls, for the times they are a-changin'," succinctly summed up folksinger Bob Dylan in 1964 before his contentious conversion to rock 'n' roll the following year.

Revolution on Main Street

One of America's quintessential retail chains, Woolworth's—the archetypical five and dime—became the unlikely site of one of the decade's earliest civil rights protests. A 1960 sit-in by four black students trying to integrate a segregated lunch counter at one of its stores in Greensboro, North Carolina, presaged a nationwide civil rights movement. Three years and many demonstrations (peaceful and otherwise) later, the March on Washington for Jobs and Freedom drew 200,000 Americans and culminated in Dr. Martin Luther King, Jr.'s legendary speech. "I have a dream," he said, "that one day this nation will rise up and live out the true meaning of its creed: 'We hold these truths to be self-evident, that all men are created equal.'"

As the burgeoning civil rights movement ignited passions on all sides, other socially conscious movements became emboldened to rise up and attack the status quo and the powers that be, popularly referred to as "The Establishment." The escalation of the Vietnam War triggered demonstrations of unprecedented scope, size, and ferocity. Black Power encapsulated the confrontational stance of many African Americans hungry for more than incremental civil rights. The feminist movement, inspired by Betty Friedan's *The Feminine Mystique*, led to the formation of the National Organization for Women (NOW) and a newfound focus on changing women's place in society.

Rachel Carson's *Silent Spring* revealed the dangers of pesticides like DDT, launching an environmental movement that led to the first Earth Day in 1970. Opposition to corporate America arose from a consumer advocacy movement led by crusader

Ralph Nader, whose book *Unsafe at Any Speed* accused automakers of putting profits before safety. By decade's end the gay rights movement erupted with unexpected fervor during the Stonewall riots in Greenwich Village, and "the love that dared not speak its name" became visible and viable seemingly overnight.

"During the 1960s, American society fractured in ways it never had before," wrote Stanford University professor Clayborne Carson. "Voices that were once silenced or ignored could no longer be excluded from discussions about the nation's destiny."

Popular culture, both the voice of the people and a force that shapes society, underwent cataclysmic change in the '60s. And rock music not only provided the soundtrack—it drove and defined the decade. Rock drew a social conscience from the resurgence of folk music in the late '50s and early '60s, with troubadours like Dylan, Joan Baez, Phil Ochs, and Pete Seeger stirring the nation's consciousness. Mainstream success came with the crossover appeal of more commercial, less confrontational acts like the Kingston Trio and Peter, Paul and Mary.

Beatlemania, The Rebirth of Soul, & Expanding Musical Boundaries

Less than three months after the assassination of JFK, a musical force arrived in America that pushed folk and pop music out of the spotlight. More importantly, it provided a welcome diversion from those devastating, dark days in Dallas and triggered a revolution that helped redefine pop culture worldwide.

Instantly the fresh-faced, mop-topped Beatles upended the musical scene. Their landmark appearances on three straight weeks of *The Ed Sullivan Show* in February 1964 drew record audiences and captivated America. The Establishment, however, predicted a short-lived reign. "The only thing that's different is the hair," said the show's musical director. "As far as I can see, I give them a year."

Though the screaming, teeming young fans (reminiscent of Elvis devotees from a few years earlier) subsided, Beatlemania didn't. The British Invasion overwhelmed the soft sounds of

American pop as the Beatles led a wave of bands onto the airways. Six different UK groups delivered songs that topped the US pop charts before the second most influential group, the Rolling Stones, managed their first #1: "(I Can't Get No) Satisfaction," 1965's biggest hit.

This infusion of imported talent vied with homegrown sounds to drive music to new heights. Dick Clark's *American Bandstand* solidified its status as *the* must-see show that launched careers and new dances. The Twist, popularized by Chubby Checker, paved the way for dances with increasingly outlandish names like the Frug, the Hully Gully, the Jerk, the Mashed Potato, and many more. Even primetime TV got an unusual youthful infusion with shows like *Shindig* and *Hullabaloo*.

Soul music, too, enjoyed a renaissance. Black artists had previously received little attention in mainstream America, with their songs often overshadowed by white artists' cover versions. However, the originals found eager audiences in England. Singers like Chuck Berry received newfound prominence after bands like the Beatles and Stones introduced US audiences to rockier, R&B-tinged versions like "Roll Over Beethoven."

The steady but small niche occupied by soul music in the pop ranks skyrocketed thanks to the efforts of one man— Berry Gordy. An entrepreneurial Detroit producer, he envisioned "the sound of young America" and single-handedly formed Motown Records (a.k.a. Hitsville, USA) in 1959. Amassing a wealth of writing, producing, and performing talent, Gordy created an empire that introduced black music to mainstream America. Ghettoized "race music" gave way to an avalanche of smartly choreographed, catchy hits that introduced budding black stars like Smokey Robinson, Little Stevie Wonder, Diana Ross,

Marvin Gaye, and Michael Jackson. On other labels, black artists like James Brown, Aretha Franklin, and Otis Redding shone.

As the decade progressed, musical boundaries continued to expand. The Beatles moved from innocent love songs to edgier, more experimental sounds that broke new ground with every album and raised the bar for everyone else. Their landmark concept album *Sgt. Pepper's Lonely Hearts Club Band* incorporated new kaleidoscopic, psychedelic sounds. The counterculture emerged, blossoming most vividly in San Francisco, birthplace of 1967's Summer of Love with the Jefferson Airplane and the Grateful Dead.

Musicians, poets, artists, and social activists coalesced around its famed Haight-Ashbury district. Hippie culture, lifestyles, and fashions arose; and drug use—especially marijuana and LSD—flourished. "What I have to say can be summed up in six words," said acid guru Timothy Leary at the first "Be-In" in Golden Gate Park in 1967. "Turn on, tune in, drop out."

Psychedelic, mind-altering music exploded with a fury as a new pantheon of rock talent emerged with the likes of Janis Joplin, Jim Morrison of the Doors, Jimi Hendrix, and the Velvet Underground. An amalgamated folk/rock sound appeared with The Byrds. "Acid among the youth culture was not a tool of resistance," David Haugen and Matthew Box would write in *The 1960s: Examining Pop Culture*. "It was a path of escape…from the bland conformity of the middle class, the supposed limitations of institutional education, and the national predilections for war and consumerism."

Yet consumerism and capitalism ultimately triumphed. Free-form FM radio arose to embrace the eclectic and experimental sounds that didn't fit into rigorously programmed AM. Rebellious rock 'n' roll went commercial, just like Beatlemania had previously inspired a glut of licensed products from action figures to wigs. Entertainment executives manufactured the Monkees,

I LOVE the "BEATLES"

assiduously assembling a perfect pop group they could efficiently market to the masses. The fashion industry co-opted and marketed the trends of the counterculture, with hippie-inspired anti-fashion supplanting the mod mini-skirts and peacock fashions of London's Carnaby Street.

The decade culminated with the landmark Woodstock Music and Art Fair in August 1969, the epitome of the sex, drugs, and rock 'n' roll generation. More than a half million hippies, freaks, and longhairs gathered to celebrate four days of great music and good vibes. Ironically, the song that has come to symbolize the festival—Joni Mitchell's "Woodstock"—was sung by an artist who passed on the event so as not to miss a scheduled TV talk show appearance.

The archetypical musical *Hair* similarly came to represent the peak of flower power, though those good vibes died hard at year's end when Woodstock's evil doppelganger, the Rolling Stones' concert at Altamont, resulted in four deaths and the realization that hard times lay ahead. Within a year Hendrix and Joplin would be dead of drug overdoses, followed by Morrison the year after. But the vibrancy of the rock scene lived on with current and new artists emerging to expand its horizons.

Reflections on the Silver Screen

Like music, American cinema underwent extraordinary changes in the '60s. In 1960 the #1 box office star was Doris Day, "America's Sweetheart," who starred in fluffy comedies like *Lover Come Back* and *That Touch of Mink* opposite Rock Hudson and Cary Grant. Those handsome leading men ranked second and third, followed by Elizabeth Taylor and Debbie Reynolds—all studio-system stars. By decade's end Day's star had been firmly eclipsed, with the top five exclusively a men's club: Paul Newman at #1, followed by John Wayne, Steve McQueen, Dustin Hoffman, and Clint Eastwood. Rougher, realistic fare ruled the box office, with an X-rated film, *Midnight Cowboy,* winning the 1969 Oscar for best picture for the first and only time in history.

At the decade's outset, movie audiences were plummeting as television offered stiff stay-at-home competition. Average weekly theater attendance had fallen from fifty-five million in 1950 to thirty million in 1960. Hollywood opened the Walk of Fame to try to rekindle the magic, but far greater changes were needed on screen. One film especially exemplified the excesses of old Hollywood: *Cleopatra* (1963). The 20th Century Fox epic was an epic blunder with a famously moody and overpaid star, Elizabeth Taylor; an ever-lengthening shooting schedule; and a skyrocketing budget. Savaged when it finally opened, the film nearly bankrupted the studio, signaling Hollywood's desperate need for a more economic approach.

So the movie capitol looked east, enticing and enlisting members of its competition. New York veterans of the stage and/or live telecasts from television's "golden years" revived cinema with some of the decade's most provocative hits: Arthur Penn's *Bonnie and Clyde*, Mike Nichols' *The Graduate*, Mel Brooks' *The Producers*, John Frankenheimer's *The Manchurian Candidate* and *Seven Days in May*, and Norman Jewison's *In the Heat of the Night*.

Hollywood received another jolt from a local producer who proved that big budgets did not a hit make. Maverick independent Roger Corman pioneered the B movie, a drive-in quickie shot fast and cheap that was aimed squarely at the young. Films like *The Wild Angels* and *The Trip* mirrored youth culture and generated sizeable returns, a lesson not lost on the major studios. The Beatles also showed the power of youth with their fast-paced but low budget hits *A Hard Day's Night* and *Help!* Following suit, Columbia put up a relatively modest $800,000 and greenlit what became the decade's quintessential road movie, *Easy Rider*. Its overwhelming success confirmed that the movies' future lay in catering to youngsters, typified by 1969 hits like *Bullitt, Butch Cassidy and the Sundance Kid,* and *Romeo and Juliet*.

Nevertheless, as in music, the decade's most influential screen figure came from Great Britain. Novelist Ian Fleming's James Bond did for film what it had done for publishing, with moviegoers preferring the 007 escapist fare of *From Russia With Love, Goldfinger,* and *Thunderball* to the more realistic adventures of *The Spy Who Came in From the Cold*. Secret agent wannabes flooded the screen, from James Coburn as Derek Flint to Dean Martin as Matt Helm.

Television mined the Cold War spy craze that dominated cinema but ignored other topical timely issues that the movies embraced such as nuclear fears (*Fail-Safe*), space exploration (*2001: A Space Odyssey*), and racial tension (*Guess Who's Coming to Dinner*, *To Kill a Mockingbird*).

The Oblivious Medium: Television

Meanwhile, pure escapism reigned on the small screen. Westerns (*Gunsmoke, Bonanza*) presented morality tales (black hats versus white hats), with good inevitably triumphing over evil. Variety shows (*The Ed Sullivan Show*, *The Red Skelton Show*) presented lowest-common-denominator programming like acrobats, plate-spinners, and ventriloquists, giving only the occasional nod to youthful tastes with groups like the Beatles. Even here, Ed opted to go the safest route: the British band that appeared more times on his show than any other was the squeaky clean Dave Clark Five. Sitcoms went with fantastical themes (*Bewitched, I Dream of Jeannie*); old-fashioned Americana (*The Andy Griffith Show*); goofy, feel-good fare (*Gomer Pyle, U.S.M.C.; The Beverly Hillbillies; Green Acres*); lightweight escapism (*My Favorite Martian, Gilligan's Island*); and ghoulish family fun (*The Munsters, The Addams Family*).

Despite its glaring obliviousness to the changes roiling society, primetime television had little incentive to transform itself.

Business was booming, with a big boost from technology. Television began broadcasting in color, triggering an unparalleled explosion of creativity in advertising. Revenues poured into the three major networks' coffers as viewers with virtually no other home entertainment choices (cable television was a decade away, video even further) embraced broadcast fare, however inane. "I invite you to sit down in front of your television set when your station goes on the air," FCC Chairman Newton Minow told an audience of television executives in 1961, "and stay there without a book, magazine, or newspaper, profit-and-loss sheet, or rating book to distract you, and keep your eyes glued to that set, until the station signs off. I can assure you that you will observe a vast wasteland."

His famed broadside had no impact as the networks instead hewed to the bottom line: if it ain't broke, don't fix it. Several years later a congressional investigation into sex and violence on television similarly produced fleeting headlines but no measurable results. "A producer who deliberately employs violence and brutality to attract an audience is unscrupulous," wrote a senatorial advisor. "A network which encourages such material, even by default, is irresponsible, and a sponsor which accepts such sadism if it produces sales is unethical."

As the decade progressed, the cinematic success of James Bond inspired a spate of spy shows like *Mission: Impossible*,

> **❝Turn onto the scene, tune into what is happening, and drop out—of high school, college, grade school, junior executive, senior executive—and follow me, the hard way.❞**
>
> —Timothy Leary

The Avengers, Get Smart, The Man From U.N.C.L.E., The Wild, Wild West (incorporating a period Western setting), Honey West, and more. Star Trek made a low-rated debut and disappeared after three seasons, its impact delayed for nearly a decade until its first feature film opened in late 1979. Television did gradually move a bit towards topicality, with the Brits at the helm once again. The sketch show That Was the Week That Was, based on an English series, enjoyed a short satirical run and presaged a late-'60s breakout hit, Rowan & Martin's Laugh-In. Its energetic mix of skits, pratfalls, blackouts, and one-liners broke the stale mold of variety shows and propelled it to TV's #1 spot for two seasons. The politically controversial The Smothers Brothers Comedy Hour had a popular but con-tentious run before its cancellation by a nervous network that later lost a lawsuit over prematurely pulling the plug.

Television did excel in one area: news. The medium's immediacy helped kill off theatrical newsreels, a primary source of information for Americans during the pre-vious forty years. The landmark televised presidential debates between Kennedy and Nixon in 1960 vividly demonstrated the power of the small screen. On TV the handsome, articulate senator triumphed over the sweaty vice president with a five o'clock shadow, though radio listeners judged the debate a tie. Television's subsequent coverage of JFK's assassination, civil rights protests and riots, and anti–Vietnam War protests like those outside the 1968 Democratic National Convention in Chicago, provided unprecedented immediacy. The impact rever-berated in living rooms across the nation.

News anchors like NBC's Chet Huntley and David Brinkley, and CBS's Walter Cronkite grew in stature, the latter dubbed "the most trusted man in America." When Cronkite later reported that Vietnam had become a stalemate, President Johnson privately lamented, "If I've lost Cronkite, I've lost America."

Ready, Steady—Heady!

From agonizing, violent lows to dizzying, sweet-smelling highs, the '60s were many things to many people. The decade's countercultural shift changed America radically and permanently, though not in ways many hoped or expected. "It was a time of intense conflict and millennial expectations," wrote Maurice Isserman and Michael Kazin in America Divided: The Civil War of the 1960s. "The most profound and lasting effects of the 1960s are to be found in the realm of 'the personal' rather than 'the political.'"

The larger, overarching issues of the changin' times can often obscure their finer points. So if the devil is indeed in the details, then please allow us to introduce ourselves. We may not be men of wealth, but we do like to think we have taste. We've assembled a flavorful day-by-day recounting of the '60's greatest hits—as well as a generous help-ing of more obscure yet revealing incidents and tidbits. Together they provide a glimpse into a decade that was giddy and groovy, hip and happening, sad and silly. And never boring. Whether you were there, or simply wish you were, we hope you'll enjoy the ride.

Harvey Solomon and Rich Appel

JANUARY

PAUL McCARTNEY

JANUARY
1

1962 On this frigid New Year's Day, after an icy ten-hour drive from Liverpool the day before, the Beatles nervously record fifteen songs at a studio a scant couple miles from competitor EMI's Abbey Road. Inexperienced but driven Brian Epstein, a young record retailer turned band manager, had secured the band an audition for Decca Records in London. Later they get the bad news. "The boys won't go, Mr. Epstein," says Decca's Dick Rowe. "We know these things. You have a good record business in Liverpool. Stick to that." Successively the Pye, Phillips, Columbia, and HMV labels also turn down the band until a persistent Epstein arranges *the* meeting with EMI's George Martin from which Beatlemania emerges. Rowe later wakes up and signs the Rolling Stones.

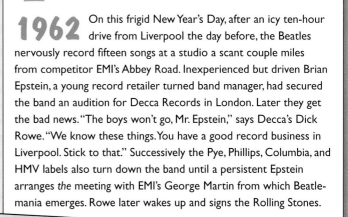

"I have really never considered myself a TV star. I always thought I was a neighbor who just came in for a visit." —Fred Rogers

IN THE NEIGHBORHOOD

On January 2, 1967, a beautiful day dawned in the neighborhood as Fred Rogers, a minister trained in child psychology and music, debuted his new show, *Mister Rogers' Neighborhood*. The genial, gentle Rogers had returned to his native Pennsylvania from Toronto, where he had moved three years earlier to host a fifteen-minute CBC children's program. His show on Pittsburgh's WQED and other eastern educational stations was even more of a hit than his CBC show, thanks to his friendly, folksy way of talking with—not to—children (and didn't those cardigan sweaters look awfully comfy?). The next year, the program was picked up by PBS, where it ran nationally for thirty-three years.

JANUARY 2

1963 The Magic Castle, private club of the magical arts and magnet for the world's finest practitioners, opens today in the Hollywood Hills. Built by a real estate magnate in 1908, the ornate Victorian mansion had served as a multi-family home, then as a home for the elderly, and, finally, as apartments. Milt Larsen, a writer on NBC's *Truth or Consequences*, worked in an office overlooking the building. He bought the dilapidated mansion and enlisted friends and volunteers to return it to its more elegant past—but this time as a luxe home for the Academy of Magical Arts. Entry is restricted to members and invited guests only. Pick a card.

JANUARY 3

1962 The earth moves in Houston, presaging a new era in sports stadiums. After breaking ground today, construction begins on the world's first domed, air-conditioned ballpark. The Astrodome will host the city's new home team, the Houston Colt .45s, which along with the New York Mets joined the National League this year. "When we Texans put things up," says one fan, "we put them up right big." The stadium opens on schedule with the newly renamed Astros playing an exhibition game on April 10, 1965. President Lyndon Johnson and Lady Bird attend, and the Yankees' Mickey Mantle hits the dome's first home run. But daytime glare off its clear Lucite roof panels blinds ballplayers, so the league tries using orange baseballs. This experiment flops, so the panels are painted black. That blocks out sunlight and kills the grass. Teams are forced to play on dirt and dead grass painted green until a year later when the Monsanto Company invents an artificial grass—eventually dubbed AstroTurf.

JANUARY 4

"**David Lean is at once the most prestigious and most mysterious British film director.**"

—Adrian Turner

1965 Fresh off *Lawrence of Arabia*, director David Lean begins filming author Boris Pasternak's epic *Doctor Zhivago* in Madrid. With an ensemble cast topped by Omar Sharif and Julie Christie, the tumultuous Russian drama proceeds lavishly through on-location shooting in Spain, Finland, and Canada. Opening the following Christmas, the film does big business despite withering critical disdain. It misses top honors but still rakes in five Oscars, most notably for adapted screenplay (Robert Bolt) and soundtrack (Maurice Jarré). The latter delivers "Lara's Theme," an eternal song that makes the charts in both the original instrumental version (by pianist Roger Williams) and, with lyrics, as "Somewhere, My Love"—a Top 10 hit for those old smoothies, the Ray Conniff Singers.

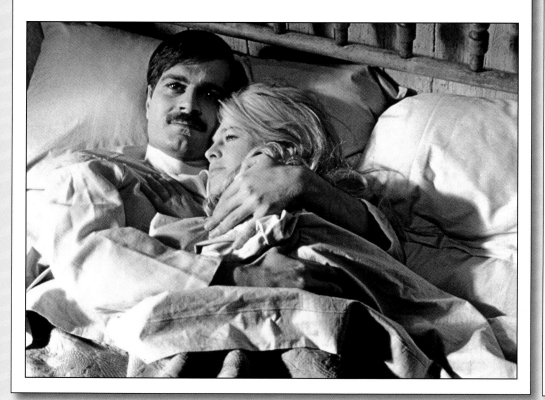

JANUARY 5

1960 Cold War jitters roil America. Some citizens build underground fallout shelters they hope will protect themselves and their families in case of nuclear attack. "Survival Under Atomic Attack" is the title of a popular government booklet. But when Hollywood gets into the act, politicians strike back. Today Senator Wallace Bennett (R-Utah) of the Joint Congressional Atomic Energy Committee lambastes the film *On the Beach* as "unscientific, unrealistic, and dangerously misleading." Based on a bestseller by Nevil Shute, the bleak movie starring Gregory Peck, Ava Gardner, and Fred Astaire (in his first dramatic role) explores mankind's final days following nuclear Armageddon. The director is Stanley Kramer, known for his "message movies" like *Judgment at Nuremberg* and *Guess Who's Coming to Dinner*.

The young, raw Rolling Stones kick off their second UK tour, the band's first as headliners. It's a smash ("fever pitch excitement," raves one paper), playing to packed houses teeming with screaming girls. A typical set includes covers of American R&B nuggets like Chuck Berry's "Roll Over Beethoven" and "Memphis," plus Lennon and McCartney's "I Wanna Be Your Man"—the Stones' second UK single (never released stateside) and one they'd sung four days earlier on the premiere broadcast of the BBC's pop music showcase, *Top of the Pops*. But out on the wild road, with opening acts the Ronettes (from America) and other Brit bands, not all the press is kind. One paper calls the Stones a "caveman-like quintet."

JANUARY 7

1966 Consummate showman Sammy Davis, Jr., is ridin' high with fellow Rat Packers Frank Sinatra, Dean Martin, Peter Lawford, and Joey Bishop. Today the multi-hyphenate singer, dancer, musician, impressionist, and comedian first appears as host of NBC's *The Sammy Davis Show*. But the small screen has cooled to the musical variety hour. Judy Garland's CBS show made a quick exit despite her duets with a who's who of entertainment, including Lena Horne, Ethel Merman, Peggy Lee, Mel Tormé, Barbra Streisand, Bobby Darin, and Vic Damone. (Being slotted opposite *Bonanza* on Sunday nights didn't help her either.) Sammy's shot lasts just one season, though it does manage to enlist three impressive, disparate guest hosts: Johnny Carson, Sean Connery, and Jerry Lewis. A rare misstep for the pint-sized, ever-perky Sammy in a long, successful career.

JANUARY 8

1968 In the late nineteenth century, French writer Jules Verne brought a wondrous world to life in his sci-fi classic, *20,000 Leagues Under the Sea*. Almost exactly a hundred years later, the medium of television delivers unprecedented access to the sights and sounds of the sea, accompanied by a soft French accent. Today the wiry, bespectacled marine explorer Jacques Cousteau debuts "Sharks," the first in a series of ABC documentary specials (initially narrated by *The Twilight Zone* creator/writer Rod Serling) under the umbrella title *The Undersea World of Jacques Cousteau*. A resistance fighter during World War II, he had co-created the Aqua-Lung and later converted a former minesweeper, the *Calypso*, into a floating, mobile laboratory. The unassuming man whose name becomes synonymous with underwater exploration likes to call himself an "oceanographic technician."

JANUARY 9

1964 Discovered busking for train fare by blues rocker Long John Baldry, raspy Rod Stewart (turning twenty tomorrow) makes his stage debut tonight with Baldry and His Hoochie Coochie Men at a London club, the Marquee. Their first single, "Good Morning Little Schoolgirl," fails to chart despite the group's appearance on the popular television series *Ready Steady Go!* The band splits and re-forms with others as Steampacket, later opening for a Rolling Stones tour. But things don't jell for Rod 'til several years later, when a now-solo Stewart joins the Jeff Beck Group. His vocals explode amidst the searing guitar riffs and plunking piano on their seminal album *Truth*—especially on Willie Dixon's "You Shook Me." A rift erupts between Beck and Jimmy Page when Led Zeppelin lifts the tune for their debut album, coming only a few months after *Truth*.

> **Probably the rudest sounds ever recorded, intended for listening to whilst angry or stoned.**
>
> —Jeff Beck, on "You Shook Me"

JANUARY
10

1964 Biting political satire *That Was the Week That Was* (a.k.a. *TW3*), debuts on NBC with a blend of skewering songs by writer/composer Tom Lehrer and comedy sketches. Patterned after a British series, it gleefully tackles topical issues from race relations to politics to religion. An instant watercooler show, it grabs an Emmy nomination for best comedy amidst four sitcoms, losing to *The Dick Van Dyke Show*. Often preempted during the presidential campaign of '64, the show will lose momentum and end its run after a brief sixteen months. But *TW3* sets the bar high for future satiric shows from *The Smothers Brothers Comedy Hour* to *Saturday Night Live* and introduces several future stars in its largely unknown cast, including Alan Alda (*M*A*S*H*), Tom Bosley (*Happy Days*), and Buck Henry (*Get Smart* co-creator and *Saturday Night Live* guest host).

JANUARY
11

1964 Shake shake shake! At a corner of Sunset Boulevard, the nation's first discotheque, the Whisky-a-Go-Go, opens tonight. Its caged, booted dancers ignite a craze that singer Johnny Rivers capitalizes on with live albums like *Johnny Rivers at the Whisky-a-Go-Go*, delivering a #2 hit with his version of Chuck Berry's "Memphis." Live bands start packing the dank but white-hot club on the site of a former bank, its lineup reading like a who's who of the budding West Coast rock scene: the Rascals, Love, the Grass Roots, the Beau Brummels, Buffalo Springfield. Otis Redding records a live album here in April, and in May the Doors start a three-month stint as the house band. Jimi Hendrix stops by to jam with Sam & Dave, and raucous sets by Frank Zappa and the Mothers of Invention lead to their first recording contract.

JANUARY
12

1960 In the entertainment biz, a bit of hyperbole never hurts. So the promos for *Scent of Mystery*, opening today, scream: "First they moved (1895)! Then they talked (1927)! Now they smell!" That latter sensory assault comes via "Smell-O-Vision," a movie theater technology hyped by showy producer Mike Todd, Jr., whose father had pioneered *This Is Cinerama* and *Around the World in 80 Days*. But technical snafus cause the emitted scents to reach different sections of movie theaters at different times, or not at all, and the adventure/comedy *Scent of Mystery*—featuring Denholm Elliot and Peter Lorre—is dubbed a stinker. "This business of using smells with pictures," sniffs Bosley Crowther (see Oct. 3) of the *New York Times*, "is a fetching but ineffective stunt."

JANUARY 13 **1962** Chubby Checker's "The Twist" returns for an unusual second stop at #1, having first topped the charts eighteen months earlier. While not the first recording to pull this off—Bing Crosby's "White Christmas" hit the top on three separate occasions—its return to #1 today reflects the dance's newfound popularity among adults. That's right: moms and dads, who'd decried rock 'n' roll when Elvis Presley shook his hips on national TV just a few years earlier, are now twistin' the night away—as doctors who treat a rash of knee and hip injuries will readily attest. Chubby's return touches off a wave of "twist" records, from Gary U.S. Bonds' "Dear Lady Twist" to Billy Joe & the Checkmates' "Percolator (Twist)," based on a Maxwell House coffee commercial.

"The Twist happens to be a contortion for children which got taken up by adults."
—*The New York Times*

SHORTLIST

HOLY ONOMATOPOEIA, BATMAN!

In January 1966, ABC scored big—*KAPOW!*—with *Batman*, a silly spoof with colorful costumes, plentiful bad puns, and exaggerated fight sequences complete with words flashed onscreen to show us all the punches. Everyone remembers "pow" and "zap," but here are some of the lesser-used fightin' words from the show.

BLURP!

Ker-sploosh!

VRONK!

Zgruppp!

JANUARY 14

1967 Some twenty-five thousand hippies—a term coined by San Francisco journalist Herb Caen—gather in Golden Gate Park for the first "Human Be-In." This peaceful prelude to the looming Summer of Love features beat poets Allen Ginsberg and Lawrence Ferlinghetti, plus LSD guru Timothy Leary, who famously invites the tie-dyed, flower-powered, dope-smoking, and/or tripping crowd to "turn on, tune in, drop out." Jefferson Airplane, the Grateful Dead, and Quicksilver Messenger Service provide suitable sounds, while the Hells Angels handle security. The mainstream media is agog, with one local paper calling it a "huge invasion" and gonzo journalist Hunter S. Thompson dubbing the Haight-Ashbury district "Hashbury." Welcome to the dawning of the Age of Aquarius.

JANUARY
15

1962 Celebrated as the savior of French couture, Yves Saint Laurent today opens his own fashion house in Paris. Born in Algeria, Saint Laurent had left home at seventeen to begin working for Christian Dior. At twenty-one, he had become head of the famed house after his mentor died. On his own, he introduces masculine styling for women with his now-classic "le smoking" tuxedo suit, pioneering long, minimalist, androgynous styles for women. Elegant, tasteful, and sophisticated, Saint Laurent quickly becomes a major directional force in fashion. He moves into ready-to-wear, opens a chain of franchised boutiques—and soon the initials YSL become a fashion must. A fashion writer later calls him "the most consistently celebrated and influential designer of the past twenty-five years."

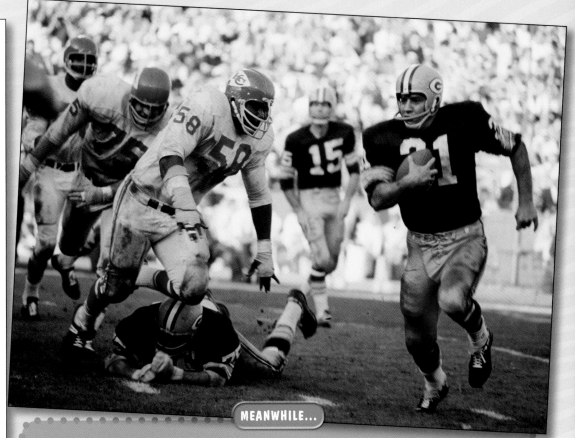

MEANWHILE...

LET THE GAME BEGIN!

One of the most eagerly awaited (and heavily hyped) football clashes in history kicked off on January 15, 1967, before sixty-one thousand fans at the Los Angeles Coliseum—the first Super Bowl. The NFL powerhouse Green Bay Packers faced the upstart AFL's Kansas City Chiefs for unprecedented supremacy. Many felt that the Chiefs didn't belong on the same field as the Vince Lombardi–led Packers, and the event proved them right. After a close first half, the Pack pulled away en route to a 35-10 shellacking, with quarterback and eventual MVP Bart Starr passing for 250 yards and two touchdowns. Several other rivalries unfolded this afternoon, too: Wilson (NFL) versus Spalding (AFL), as each league used its own regulation football while on offense. For the first and last time, two networks—CBS and NBC—broadcasted the game, and the gridiron contest scored the highest ratings of any show in history, a record that was surpassed a decade later by *Roots*.

JANUARY
16

1963 Yes, Virginia, there was a time when film studios actually made movies from new, not recycled, ideas. But today Walt Disney revisits and revives last year's hit comedy *The Absent-Minded Professor* by introducing *Son of Flubber*. Again co-starring Fred McMurray, Nancy Olson, and Tommy Kirk, this first sequel to a major motion picture is "fun, and indeed a bit of a satire on the weird inventions of the new atomic age" (*New York Times*). It's also a box-office hit that announces the arrival of a new phenomenon in movie-making: the sequel—a practice that shows no signs of abating as a proven, potent moneymaker.

The Professor's on the loose again...and FUN EXPLODES all over the Place!

Walt Disney presents SON of FLUBBER

HE PUTS A HALFBACK INTO ORBIT!

HE'S THE LAFF OF THE PARTY!

HE BLOWS UP A STORM!

STARRING FRED MACMURRAY · NANCY OLSON · KEENAN WYNN

CO-STARRING TOMMY KIRK · JOANNA MOORE · LEON AMES · ED WYNN · CHARLIE RUGGLES · KEN MURRAY · WILLIAM DEMAREST · PAUL LYNDE · BOB SWEENEY FEATURING ELLIOTT REID EDWARD ANDREWS · Screenplay by BILL WALSH and DON DaGRADI · Co-Producer BILL WALSH

JANUARY
17

1966 Six years in the writing, Truman Capote's eagerly awaited *In Cold Blood* finally comes to bookstores. The "nonfiction novel" published by Random House tells of the brutal murders of the four-member Clutter family in tiny Holcomb, Kansas, in 1959, and the subsequent trial of two accused killers. Previously known best for the sprightly *Breakfast at Tiffany's*, diminutive, bespectacled Capote had conducted extensive interviews with the pair and amassed two trunks of paperwork. "I thank God I won't have to lug those trunks all over the world any longer," says Capote, who did much of the writing at a house in the Swiss Alps and received a staggering $2 million in book, magazine, and movie rights. A stark, documentary-style film adaptation starring Robert Blake opens the following year to strong reviews. But this year, Truman's got time and money on his hands, and begins plotting the party of the century (see Nov. 28).

JANUARY 18

1964

Towering achievement: New York Governor Nelson Rockefeller and various city officials lead a press conference at the New York Hilton Hotel unveiling plans for a massive new complex: the World Trade Center. Dominated by signature twin towers that at 1,300+ feet will surpass the Empire State Building as the world's tallest, the project consists of seven buildings on a 16-acre site in lower Manhattan. Outside the hotel, fifty picketers protest that hundreds of businesses now on the site will be forced out, threatening the livelihoods of 30,000 owners, employees, and family members. Originally slated to cost $350 million, construction of the World Trade Center begins two years later and eventually approaches $1.5 billion. The towers open on April 4, 1973.

JANUARY 19

1960

California native and inveterate surfer John Severson shot some of the earliest surfing movies (*Surf* and *Surf Safari*) while stationed with the Army in Hawaii. Today, after returning home, he publishes the first issue of *The Surfer* magazine to promote his third film, *Surf Fever*. Consisting of stills and screen shots, it quickly sells out its 10,000-copy run and helps popularize the budding sport while paving the way for musical groups like the Beach Boys that elevate surfing to international prominence. What *The Surfer* does for print, *The Endless Summer* does for movies. Director Bruce Brown's 1965 documentary introduces the sport to the larger world, which is exactly where he shoots: "On any day of the year it's summer somewhere in the world," explains its poster, and surfer dudes promptly adventure in search thereof.

JANUARY 20

1967

Two years after the popular Woody Allen–penned movie and Tom Jones song "What's New Pussycat?", singer Lesley Gore portrays Pussycat, Catwoman's henchgirl, on *Batman*. The petite, big-voiced gal debuted in '63 with the chart-topping "It's My Party," the first #1 single for producer Quincy Jones and engineer Phil Ramone. "I was one of those little kids that you put up on a cocktail table and didn't have to bother winding up," she says. "I just loved to sing." Tonight on *Batman* she proves another of her hits, "You Don't Own Me," by putting Robin under the spell of a drug that turns him into one of Catwoman's henchmen. On the show, she performs "California Nights," which in the coming weeks becomes her final Top 40 hit.

FIRST FASHION

At the inauguration of President John F. Kennedy in 1961, his wife Jacqueline set a new standard of sophisticated style that reshaped and revolutionized the world of fashion. Her exclusive couturier, Oleg Cassini, had been a surprise choice to many in haute-fashion circles who didn't consider him top-shelf talent. But after winning the most visible client on Earth, Cassini delivered in high style. At one of the many inaugural balls in wintry Washington, DC, Jackie removed a coat of leopard pelts to reveal a stunning ivory satin gown. (Her father-in-law, Joseph P. Kennedy, Sr., paid for both creations.) But an even bigger craze inspired by the First Lady was still to come: the pillbox hat.

JANUARY 21

1964 Rock 'n' roll is shaking, rattling, and roiling America, led by the Kingsmen's controversial "Louie Louie." A burning and yearning question divides the nation: Are its slurred lyrics a graphic description of a sailor and his girl having sex? Today, an Indiana teenager complains to that state's governor, Matthew Welsh, who says that his ears "tingled" when he heard the song. He suggests that the state's radio stations stop playing it, triggering a controversy over censorship. "Few people dump trash in the living room," says an editorial in the *Indianapolis Star*. "There should be little place for musical garbage in the American home." The FBI conducts a lengthy investigation, eventually concluding that it is "unable to interpret any of the wording in the record." That doesn't matter to the kids who turn "Louie Louie" into one of the country's hottest discs. It hits #2 and becomes a staple for garage bands nationwide, who are about to get even more inspiration from a British group that will touch down in America two weeks later (see Feb. 9).

JANUARY
22

1968 Sock it to us! Today, two nightclub comedians dust off the age-old sketch comedy format and strike TV gold. *Rowan and Martin's Laugh-In*, produced by comedy vet George Schlatter, becomes an overnight sensation with a blitz of sketches, pratfalls, blackouts, and one-liners by a relatively unknown cast (including future stars Goldie Hawn—see Dec. 16—and Lily Tomlin). "A genuine phenomenon of the 1960s, breaking the stale old mold of the standard host-guest-comic-choreography variety show," writes *TV Guide*. Famous cameos include presidential candidate Richard Nixon uttering one of the show's catchphrases, "Sock it to me!" Other instantaneous additions to the country's vernacular: "You bet your bippy," "Verrry interesting," and "Here come de judge."

JANUARY
23

1965 Today Petula Clark's melodic "Downtown" hits #1, becoming the first single by a British female vocalist to top the US charts in thirteen years, and the first of fifteen consecutive Top 40 hits for the versatile, sweet-sounding singer. Long before heading downtown, the lights were already bright for Clark. In her native England she'd begun on BBC Radio at age nine, starred in her own television show at eleven, and appeared in more than twenty movies before "Downtown" made her an international sensation. Next year Clark hits #1 again with "My Love," her first song recorded in the US. She soon segues to a respectable Hollywood career with roles in films including *Finian's Rainbow* and *Goodbye Mr. Chips*.

JANUARY
24

1962 A Senate subcommittee studying juvenile delinquency holds its first hearing on television violence and its possible effect on juvenile behavior. Chairman Thomas Dodd (D-Conn.) accuses the networks of ordering more sex and violence to increase ratings, a charge the networks refute. "A producer who deliberately employs violence and brutality to attract an audience is unscrupulous," writes one of Dodd's advisors. "A network which encourages such material, even by default, is irresponsible, and a sponsor which accepts such sadism if it produces sales is unethical." Despite this well-intentioned investigation, violence on television only accelerates. As one unnamed television executive later remarks, "When ratings go up, sex and violence become love and adventure."

JANUARY 25

1961 Kids swarm toward downtown and Main Street as theater lines wrap around blocks for the debut of Walt Disney's latest animated adventure, *101 Dalmatians*. Told from a doggie's point of view, the enchanting cartoon tells the tale of the villainous Cruella De Vil, who aspires to make a coat out of puppy pelts. In addition to becoming the year's top-grossing film, it also pioneers a new Xerox process that saves time and money by allowing faster transfer of artists' illustrations to cels. Costing an estimated $4 million, the movie grosses $14 million at the box office; re-issues in subsequent years push its all-time gross to nearly $150 million.

JANUARY 26

1963 Baby, let your hair hang down. Listening to an old album by an obscure jug band, longtime folkie Erik Darling was mesmerized by one particular cut. He quickly formed a trio, the Rooftop Singers, and today their cover of "Walk Right In" tops the charts. It isn't Darling's first hit or his first trio: back in 1956, he'd led the Tarriers to back-to-back Top 10 hits. The group had disbanded when member Alan Arkin left to pursue his acting career, and Darling later replaced Pete Seeger in the Weavers, an influential quartet whose protest songs inspired a folk revival. Two of the most popular folk acts are Peter, Paul and Mary ("If I Had a Hammer," "Puff the Magic Dragon"), whose look one exec described as "two rabbis and a hooker," and the scrubbed, square Kingston Trio ("Tom Dooley"), who at one point placed an incredible four albums in the Top 10 in one week. But one of the revival's biggest winners is the seventy-nine-year-old writer of "Walk Right In," Gus Cannon, who was almost penniless until Darling scooped up the song. He not only received welcome royalties, but a recording contract, too.

JANUARY
27

1961 An awful half-hour of television? Big deal. A half-hour spent apologizing for said crap? Big deal! Tonight Jackie Gleason does just that, ripping into his new panel show, *You're in the Picture*, which had premiered the previous week. On the show, guest panelists had stuck their heads though holes in a picture, then asked Gleason questions to try to determine what the image was of. Tonight, the big man is alone on a bare stage, and he's in rare form, giving an unscripted, unprecedented television performance as he sips from a mug that he says contains new coffee brand "Chock Full o'Booze" (and it does appear to be). The apology gets much better raves than the original show, which was such a bomb that Gleason cracks, "it would make the H-bomb look like a two-inch salute."

JANUARY 28

1968

On an Australian tour dubbed the "Big Show," today the Who and the Small Faces ("Itchycoo Park") are escorted from a plane upon arrival in Melbourne. Their offense? Drinking beer onboard, generally rowdy behavior, and using "filthy" language—all of which reportedly reduces several stewardesses to tears. "Crackdown on Pop Show Louts" screams one newspaper headline, reporting that the "garishly dressed singers and musicians" waited in a reception lounge patrolled by police until arrangements were made to fly them to Sydney. Prime Minister John Gorton later orders the two bands never to return to Australia.

JANUARY 29

1966

Riding high as suave spy Napoleon Solo in NBC's *The Man from U.N.C.L.E.*, Robert Vaughn ignites a furor tonight by lambasting President Johnson at a Democratic fundraiser in Indianapolis. The first major actor to come out against the war, he aims to "debate, argue, discuss, implore, provoke, and agitate people to think and educate themselves about how the US got into Vietnam." He later debates conservative William F. Buckley on *Firing Line* and earns a PhD at USC with a dissertation on blacklisting in the US theater. Singer Eartha Kitt similarly blasts the war several years later at a most unlikely venue: a White House conference on juvenile delinquency, hosted by Lady Bird Johnson. "You send the best of this country off to be shot and maimed," exclaims Kitt to her stunned lunch mates, later adding, "I see nothing wrong with the way I handled myself. I can only hope it will do some good." Newspapers don't see it that way, and Kitt's career suffers as a result of the negative publicity.

TRENDSETTER

NUCLEAR NERVES

As the Cold War intensified, three major Hollywood directors delivered pulse-pounding, topical thrillers in 1964. Released on January 29, Stanley Kubrick's *Dr. Strangelove, or How I Learned to Stop Worrying and Love the Bomb* told a cynical tale of advancing technology, man's stupidity, and nuclear insanity. Peter Sellers played the title role and two others. "I'm not saying we wouldn't get our hair mussed," says George C. Scott as gung-ho General "Buck" Turgidson, "but I do say no more than ten to twenty million people killed, tops, depending on the breaks." In John Frankenheimer's *Seven Days in May*, released the next week, a tangled subversive plan threatens to topple the government. Adapted by Rod Serling (*The Twilight Zone*) from a bestseller, its top-notch ensemble cast included Burt Lancaster, Kirk Douglas, Fredric March, and Ava Gardner. In Sidney Lumet's *Fail-Safe*, which opened in October, an accidental order to bomb Moscow brings the US and the USSR to the brink of nuclear annihilation. Shot in a stark documentary style, the film's manly mix included Henry Fonda, Walter Matthau, and Fritz Weaver.

JANUARY 30

1967 Today *Publishers Weekly* reports that America's bestselling mass-market paperback in 1966 was J.R.R. Tolkien's *The Fellowship of the Ring,* the first in the enduring *Lord of the Rings* trilogy. Written over a span of more than ten years before and after World War II, Tolkien's epic, three-volume *Lord of the Rings* had first published in 1954. Reviews were mixed, but word gradually spread until American sci-fi publisher Ace Books spotted what it thought was a copyright loophole and published the first paperback edition. British author/professor Tolkien fought back, signing with Ballantine Books for an authorized edition and warning people to boycott the pirated Ace edition. The boycott worked—Ace conceded, paid out royalties to the author, and let its *Rings* paperbacks go out of print.

JANUARY 31

1967 While shooting a short promotional film for "Strawberry Fields Forever," John Lennon visits an antiques shop in Kent and purchases an 1843 circus poster proclaiming "Being for the Benefit of Mr. Kite!" Transcribing its vintage wording into verse, he and Paul McCartney quickly pen what later becomes the closing song on side one of the Beatles' crowning achievement, *Sgt. Pepper's Lonely Hearts Club Band.* During the recording, producers are unable to locate an authentic hand-operated steam organ necessary to create the circus-like atmosphere. So they chop up old calliope tapes of Sousa marches, toss the pieces into the air, and reassemble them at random to help form its eerie instrumental breaks.

TRENDSETTER

BAD FASHION

Before the '60s, the press wrote only slavish, puffy pieces about the elegance of fashion. But when Mr. Blackwell's tart-tongued list of the worst-dressed celebrities appeared in the LA *Examiner* in January 1960, he pulled no punches. "As a designer," he said, "I found that the over-pampered, over-puffed, over-perfumed, over-publicized, and over-dressed ladies of the silver screen knew as much about fashion as King Kong. And I said so." Did he ever! His list—which was so popular that it expanded to an annual affair in national syndication in 1961—has given us tidbits like Elizabeth Taylor in tight clothes "looks like a chain of link sausages" ever since.

FEBRUARY

FEBRUARY

1

1961 "How do you find your way back in the dark?" asks Marilyn Monroe. "Just head for the big star straight on—the highway's under it, and it'll take us right home," replies Clark Gable. These final lines of *The Misfits*, opening today, sadly represent the end of two storied careers—one long and successful, the other short and troubled. The film boasts a strong pedigree: the potent pairing of its box office stars, noted director John Huston (*The Maltese Falcon*, *The Treasure of the Sierra Madre*), and screenwriter Arthur Miller, whose rocky marriage to Monroe is soon to end. Though the black-and-white film didn't live up to its high expectations, it has since attained cult status, especially for Gable's role as a brooder struggling to find his place in life. He died of a heart attack several weeks after the strenuous shoot, just short of his sixtieth birthday, also today. Monroe never completes another film.

1961 After taking heat for its negative portrayal of Italian-Americans, Desilu Productions, led by Desi Arnaz, today agrees to make ethnic changes on its mobster shoot-'em-up *The Untouchables*. The program follows Eliot Ness (played by Robert Stack) and his incorruptible men as they battle organized crime on the mean streets of Chicago. Critics had blasted the show for its stereotyping, and Italian-American groups even threatened to boycott its sponsors. "It has got so bad," says lawyer Dominic Frinzi, "that people have started referring to *The Untouchables* as 'The Italian Hour.'" Others object to its blood-spattering violence, threatening Congressional investigation. James Bennett, director of the US Bureau of Prisons, piles on with a plot critique: "To picture honorable and courageous officers as venal, and a public institution like the Atlanta Penitentiary as toadying to a character like [mobster Al] Capone is an unforgivable public disservice." Desilu concedes by increasing the role of an Italian "good guy," Ness's right-hand man Nick Rossi (Nick Georgiade), and promising that no new fictional criminals on the program will have Italian names.

1968 Rock 'n' roll: it'll rot your brain—and now your teeth, as bubblegum music ascends to #1 in the form of the Lemon Pipers' "Green Tambourine." Though many hits before have appealed to a mostly pre-teen audience and easily qualified as "bubblegum"—like Shirley Ellis's "The Name Game" and Len Barry's "1-2-3"—"Green Tambourine" is the first chart-topper for the Buddah record label, which for the next year may as well be run by Bazooka Joe. Following the Lemon Pipers up the charts are the label's aptly named 1910 Fruitgum Co. ("Simon Says," "1, 2, 3, Red Light") and Ohio Express, with back-to-back hits "Yummy Yummy Yummy" and "Chewy Chewy." Small wonder that it takes a group of comic book characters to beat Buddah at its own sticky-sweet game: producer Don Kirshner's Archies make "Sugar, Sugar" next year's top single.

FEBRUARY
4

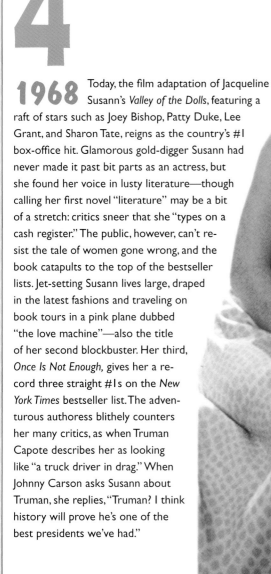

1968 Today, the film adaptation of Jacqueline Susann's *Valley of the Dolls*, featuring a raft of stars such as Joey Bishop, Patty Duke, Lee Grant, and Sharon Tate, reigns as the country's #1 box-office hit. Glamorous gold-digger Susann had never made it past bit parts as an actress, but she found her voice in lusty literature—though calling her first novel "literature" may be a bit of a stretch: critics sneer that she "types on a cash register." The public, however, can't resist the tale of women gone wrong, and the book catapults to the top of the bestseller lists. Jet-setting Susann lives large, draped in the latest fashions and traveling on book tours in a pink plane dubbed "the love machine"—also the title of her second blockbuster. Her third, *Once Is Not Enough,* gives her a record three straight #1s on the *New York Times* bestseller list. The adventurous authoress blithely counters her many critics, as when Truman Capote describes her as looking like "a truck driver in drag." When Johnny Carson asks Susann about Truman, she replies, "Truman? I think history will prove he's one of the best presidents we've had."

FEBRUARY 5

1966 With patriotism at its early peak during the Vietnam War, Staff Sgt. Barry Sadler scores a hit today with his uplifting tune "The Ballad of the Green Berets." The antiwar movement has yet to gain steam, and the media is still flush with positive stories about our boys overseas. For kids, there are G.I. Joe dolls and the comic strip *Tales of the Green Beret*, which focuses on the Special Forces unit known for its distinctive headgear. Sadler, a vet recovering from wounds suffered in the war, soon sees his song climb to #1, where it stays for a five-week reign. Co-written by author Robin Moore, an ex-WWII soldier and Harvard classmate of then Attorney General Robert Kennedy, the patriotic smash hit makes an unlikely star of Sadler. Popular not only in the US but overseas, the song is banned from the radio in East Germany.

FEBRUARY 6

1965 At an early live performance of Southern Californian duo Bill Medley and Bobby Hatfield, a black fan's enthusiastic reaction to their blue-eyed soul—"That was righteous, brothers!"—prompted a new stage name. Today, the Righteous Brothers top the charts with a lush Phil Spector–produced ballad, "You've Lost That Lovin' Feelin'." The pop masterpiece endures through the decades, sparking covers by dozens of artists (Cilla Black takes her version to #2 in her native England) and reviving yet again in the '80s when it's featured in the Tom Cruise movie *Top Gun*. The song kicks off a two-year string of hits for the scrubbed, handsome twosome, including "Ebb Tide" and "Unchained Melody." The latter also enjoys a cinematic revival a quarter century later when it's featured in *Ghost* with Patrick Swayze and Demi Moore.

FEBRUARY 7

1963 An off-duty Brooklyn cabbie who arrived at 6:00 a.m. heads an early-morning line stretching down the steps of New York's famed Metropolitan Museum of Art and well down Fifth Avenue. By day's end, nearly sixteen thousand people have entered to view Leonardo da Vinci's *Mona Lisa*, on loan from the Louvre in Paris. Even behind bulletproof glass, the haunting lady, completed in 1506, still casts a mocking yet tender spell befitting the most famous painting on Earth. More than a million visitors will attend the month-long display, prompting the *New York Times* to note that "the old enchantress is making new conquests."

FEBRUARY 8

"Take your stinking paws off me, you damned dirty ape!" snarls stranded astronaut Charlton Heston. And so man speaks to his domineering captors in the role-reversing, minor sci-fi classic *Planet of the Apes*, which opens today. Boasting a record one-million-dollar budget for makeup, it wins an honorary Oscar for its designer, John Chambers. Based on a French novel, the script had undergone many drafts, with early, notable contributions by sci-fi master Rod Serling (*The Twilight Zone*). He devised its breathtaking twist ending: the discovery of a shattered Statue of Liberty, revealing that the nightmarish planet is actually Earth. The film generates massive media attention, spawning many sequels, live action and animated TV series, and documentaries—and earning an eternal place in pop culture kitsch.

FEBRUARY 9

1964 We saw them standing there. But we couldn't hear them. Savvy showman Ed Sullivan features the Beatles in their first live US performance. The band (with a flu-stricken George) performs five songs—"All My Loving," "Till There Was You," "She Loves You," "I Saw Her Standing There," and "I Want to Hold Your Hand"—all barely audible amidst an audience predominated by screaming, swooning girls. Though the studio holds only 728 fans (selected from more than 50,000 requests), an estimated seventy-three million viewers tune in from home. Also featured on this landmark edition of *The Ed Sullivan Show* is the children's chorus from the Broadway show *Oliver!*, which includes future Monkee Davy Jones. A week later, the Fab Four perform an encore live from Miami's Deauville Hotel (their third appearance for Ed Sullivan that month is pre-recorded). Beatlemania engulfs America, now and forever.

> **"So this is America—they all seem out of their minds."**
> —Ringo Starr

FEBRUARY 10

1968 Conductor/arranger Paul Mauriat tops the charts with the instrumental "Love is Blue," the only #1 US single ever to originate in France. While it's Mauriat's only US hit as a recording artist, it's actually his second credit on a #1 song in America. His first? As co-writer of "Chariot," a big hit in France for Petula Clark earlier in the decade—the English version of which was Little Peggy March's 1963 chart-topper "I Will Follow Him."

FEBRUARY 11

> **"I was thirty-two when I started cooking—up until then, I just ate."**
> —Julia Child

1963

Bon Appetit! In her cheery warble, Julia Child demonstrates how to prepare *boeuf bourguigon* when *The French Chef* premieres today on Boston's public television station WGBH. Overnight, the entertaining, effervescent authoress turned on-screen chef and unlikely fifty-year-old celebrity becomes a household name. The series runs for a decade, winning Emmy and Peabody awards, and Child later stars in another half-dozen PBS series. Her original kitchen from Cambridge, Massachusetts, including its pegboard wall with outlines for the hanging pots and pans stenciled by her husband Paul, can now be seen on display at the Smithsonian National Museum of American History.

MEANWHILE...

A WALK ON THE CELEBRITY SIDE

Conceived to reinvigorate a celebrated but fading neighborhood, the Hollywood Walk of Fame unveiled its first star—in honor of actress Joanne Woodward—in a glittery Tinseltown event on February 9, 1960. To date, more than 2,300 entertainment figures—from comedic legend Bud Abbott to film mogul Adolph Zukor, cartoon family the Simpsons to television icon Bob Barker—have received the star treatment. Only one, Muhammad Ali, has a star that is not on the sidewalks aside Hollywood Boulevard, but on the wall of the Kodak Theater—because the boxing great didn't want it tread upon.

FEBRUARY 12

1968

Searing guitarist Jimi Hendrix returns to his hometown nine years after dropping out of high school to headline a standing-room-only concert at the Seattle Center Arena. The fast-rising star, who had quit school and his native city at sixteen after running afoul of the law, wants a triumphant return to his alma mater, and so he arrives early at Garfield High School the next morning. But thanks to a post-show night of drinking bourbon with friends and family, he's hungover, disheveled, and exhausted; plans for a free concert are quickly scrapped. In a packed gymnasium, Hendrix nervously mumbles a couple answers to students' questions: "How long have you been gone from Garfield?" someone asks. "Oh, about 2,000 years." Some students don't even know who he is, and heckle him. After five minutes, Hendrix walks out, never receiving his honorary diploma.

> **"Blues is easy to play but hard to feel."**
> —Jimi Hendrix

FEBRUARY

13

1965 Making quite a name for themselves, rising UK band Them breaks into the Top 10 in England with an R&B-tinged version of an old blues chestnut, "Baby Please Don't Go." Though the label says "Them," it mostly represents driving force Van Morrison, backed by session players including guitarist Jimmy Page. Little noticed at the time is the flip side, a jam-driven, galvanizing tune called "Gloria" that'll eventually find its way into every garage band repertoire alongside "Louie Louie" (see Jan. 21) and achieve future anthemic status. A couple of years later, songwriter/singer Morrison cracks the US Top 10 his first time out on his own, with "Brown Eyed Girl," destined to become one of rock's most recognizable signature songs.

FEBRUARY
14

1962 Having just completed her landmark redecoration of the White House, First Lady Jackie Kennedy gives CBS's Charles Collingwood—along with millions of other Americans—a televised tour. Dressed in a simple wool suit and three strands of pearls, she gets rave reviews for her sense of both decor and history, along with her confident screen presence. The *New York Times* calls her "an art critic of subtlety and standard...an antiquarian relishing pursuit of the elusive treasure...and a poised TV narrator." In an unusually cooperative gesture, CBS offers the hour-long program to NBC, which airs it simultaneously. ABC sticks with police drama *The Naked City*.

FEBRUARY
15

1961 Today, R&B superstar Jackie Wilson is shot in the stomach in his New York City apartment by Juanita Jones, a purported ex-lover. An energetic, charismatic tenor (and quite the womanizer), Wilson had first made the charts in the late '50s with several tunes penned by unknown songwriter Berry Gordy (soon to found Motown). Known as Mr. Excitement, Wilson had become a major force in the R&B scene, scoring a Top 10 hit with "Lonely Teardrops" and being named "Entertainer of the Year" by *Cash Box* magazine. His management covers up the shooting incident by claiming Jones was a deranged fan, and the deception works. Wilson recovers and is soon back touring. He appears on *The Ed Sullivan Show*, records an album at NYC's prestigious Copacabana nightclub, and re-enters the Top 10 with "Baby Workout" and "(Your Love Keeps Lifting Me) Higher and Higher."

FEBRUARY
16

1964 Until now, the toaster had been used primarily for one thing: toast. Today, food company Post diversifies its culinary offerings by introducing Country Squares, fruit-filled pastries made for heating in the toaster. But since the name sounds rural and unhip—not unlike television's high-rated sitcom rubes *The Beverly Hillbillies*—people don't warm to its new product. Meanwhile, rival Kellogg's, fearing a serious threat to its bottom-line breakfast champion—cereal—quickly develops its own fruit-filled snack, Pop Tarts, whose name cleverly echoes two of the nation's hottest trends: pop music and pop art. Post changes its product's name to Toast 'Em Pop Ups, but they've lost the war. First in, first out—four years later Post discontinues its fruity failure while Kellogg's expands and now rules the multi-million-dollar toaster pastry category.

FEBRUARY 17

1965

Can we talk? Today, Joan Rivers makes her first appearance on *The Tonight Show Starring Johnny Carson*, and the famed host immediately takes a shine to the loud, gruff New Yawk comedienne. Over the next twenty years, she'll guest host the show nearly a hundred times (Johnny did like his vacation time). In 1983 she begins serving as his permanent guest host, but leaves abruptly without saying goodbye to star in Fox's new *The Late Show Starring Joan Rivers*. It flops, and a piqued Johnny never invites her back to his late-night chat fest.

"The first time I see a jogger smiling, I'll consider it."
—Joan Rivers

FEBRUARY 18

1967

With smartly cut moptops and matching tailored outfits, the five lads who make up the Buckinghams look for all the world like another sharp British Invasion band. Actually, they're Chicagoans. Formerly known as the Pulsations, they'd auditioned for a local variety show at WGN, and the station asked them to come up with a more British-sounding moniker. A janitor suggested the Buckinghams, and the name stuck. Today their melodic "Kind of a Drag" knocks the Monkees' "I'm a Believer" out of the #1 spot, where it had resided for seven weeks straight. Their commercial sound clicks with two more Top Ten hits, "Don't You Care" and a vocal version of Cannonball Adderly's instrumental hit, "Mercy, Mercy, Mercy."

FEBRUARY 19

1962

Chuck Berry, the pioneering blues rocker who'd catapulted to fame in the mid-'50s with such hits as "Maybellene," "Sweet Little Sixteen," and "Johnny B. Goode," begins serving a three-year prison sentence today. Convicted of violating the Mann Act—transporting a minor across state lines for immoral purposes—Berry had hired a sixteen-year-old Apache girl from Mexico to work in his St. Louis nightclub, and after he fired her she was arrested for prostitution. Upon his release nearly two years later, he began a comeback boosted by fast-rising British bands like the Beatles and the Rolling Stones, who covered his songs like "Roll Over Beethoven," "Carol," and "You Can't Catch Me." Unfortunately for Berry, the latter wasn't true.

HAS ANYBODY HERE SEEN MY OLD FRIEND...

The '60s reverberated with three of the most infamous assassinations in American history: President John F. Kennedy (Nov. 22, 1963), Reverend Martin Luther King, Jr. (April 4, 1968), and Senator Robert F. Kennedy (June 6, 1968). But they weren't the only leaders struck down during the decade.

On February 21, 1966, gunmen assassinate fiery Black Muslim leader Malcolm X at a ballroom assembly in Harlem. Back on June 12, 1963, a Ku Klux Klan sniper killed NAACP leader Medgar Evers on the doorstep of his home in Jackson, Mississippi.

FEBRUARY 20

1962 Glued to their television sets (or radios) for twelve hours of nonstop coverage, Americans anxiously follow the journey of astronaut John Glenn aboard *Friendship 7*. The first American to orbit the Earth, he faces an especially harrowing complication during reentry. When an automatic control malfunctions, the resulting heat disrupts communications for seven agonizing minutes. Glenn manually fires the retrorockets and makes a successful splashdown. He receives a triumphant hero's welcome home, with a ticker-tape parade in New York City two weeks later that draws an estimated four million jubilant fans.

FEBRUARY
21

1966 A mediocre film, a break-out star. Today, buxom beauty Raquel Welch busts out in a British fantasy/adventure film, *One Million Years B.C.* The poster of her in skimpy prehistoric garb becomes more famous than the movie itself, selling more than a million copies and igniting her cinematic career. A frequent beauty pageant winner growing up, she had held previous odd jobs including cocktail waitress, model, and local TV weathergirl. After *One Million Years*, she segues to a sci-fi flick, *Fantastic Voyage*, in which being shrunk to miniature size fortunately doesn't affect her proportions. Then it's on to *Bedazzled*, playing one of the seven deadly sins (Lust—surprised?) opposite Dudley Moore.

FEBRUARY 22 1960 A word to all those parents unnerved by rock 'n' roll's ascendancy: have faith. Specifically, Percy Faith, whose orchestra today claims the #1 song with the theme from *A Summer Place*, a sudsy, steamy romance flick co-starring Sandra Dee and Troy Donahue. As rock 'n' roll is rocked by the payola scandal (see Aug. 30), "easy listening" music thrives with several gentle instrumentals led by "Theme From 'A Summer Place.'" Lovers of those soothing strings keep Faith at the top of the charts for nine straight weeks, making it the year's biggest song—and Columbia Records' biggest-selling single of the decade. It's the first title theme from a motion picture to enjoy such a lengthy stay atop the singles chart since 1953's "Song from 'Moulin Rouge,'" recorded by...Percy Faith.

FEBRUARY 23 1964 James Bond may get the girls and the glamour, but John le Carré gets the goods. Today, the ex-spy turned novelist tops the bestseller lists with *The Spy Who Came in From the Cold*, a realistic portrait of the gritty world of Cold War espionage. Le Carré, the pen name of David Cornwell, had seen his career as a secret agent destroyed in the '50s by infamous British double agent Kim Philby, but he later downplays the past. "In the old days it was convenient to bill me as a spy turned writer," he says. "I was nothing of the kind. I am a writer who, when I was very young, spent a few ineffectual but extremely formative years in British Intelligence." Hollywood rushes out a feature film version, featuring Richard Burton and Claire Bloom, and le Carré's off on a long, fruitful career exposing and exploring the netherworld of covert operations.

"A desk is a dangerous place from which to view the world."

—John le Carré

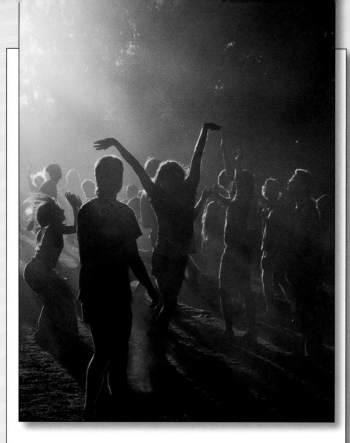

FEBRUARY 24

1967

Acid rock/psychedelic pioneers the Grateful Dead open at San Francisco's Fillmore Auditorium alongside Otis Rush and Canned Heat. Local icons, they deliver legendarily long, freeform concerts that generate a fanatical following. Mainstays of the "love-in" and "flower child" movements of the day in Haight-Ashbury, the Dead produce a relaxed sound that is a hybrid of country and acid rock. Unlike most every other band, their success is not measured in record sales but in never-ending sold-out tours and shows. Their forthcoming Live/Dead album tries capturing their captivating live presence, though diehard fans prefer (and copy, and re-copy, and circulate) countless live bootlegs. More mainstream acceptance comes through later studio albums Workingman's Dead and American Beauty.

SHORTLIST

SAN FRANCISCO GIANTS

The Grateful Dead played 122 concerts in 1967, and almost half of them were in their hometown of San Francisco. Though the Fillmore (in its new incarnation as the Fillmore West) would later become the setting for the Dead's landmark Live/Dead album, the band spread the love throughout the city in 1967. Here are their favorite Frisco haunts, along with the number of shows they played there that year.

- **Fillmore Auditorium (11).** The first concert hall that the group ever played as "The Grateful Dead," this legendary venue was owned and operated by renowned promoter Bill Graham (see May 17) and hosted the decade's biggest acts.

- **Whisky-a-Go-Go (7).** An offshoot of the famous West Hollywood hot spot, this club's 1967 headliners included the Doors.

- **Avalon Ballroom (6).** This two-story club drew audiences in with their psychedelic posters by artists who went on to design Grateful Dead album covers.

- **The Rock Garden (6).** This short-lived venue regularly hosted rock artists that included the Dead and Janis Joplin.

- **Winterland Arena (6).** Also owned by Graham, this skating rink was sometimes used for concerts the Fillmore couldn't accommodate, until it was converted to music-only use in 1971.

- **Golden Gate Park (6).** The Dead played in San Francisco's most famous park for the Human Be-In (see Jan. 14) as well as concerts with Joplin.

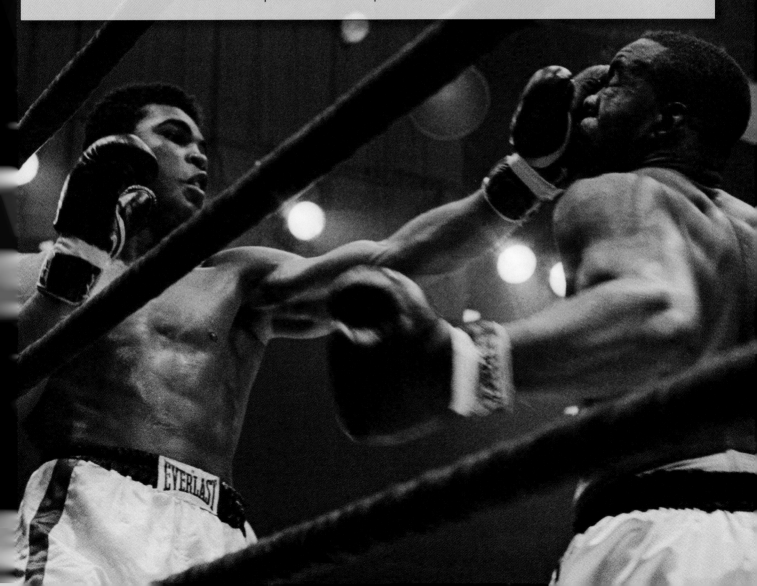

FEBRUARY 25

1964

Most people remember his shocking first-round TKO of Sonny Liston in remote Lewiston, Maine, in 1965. But that was the rematch. Tonight in Miami Beach, former Olympic gold medalist Cassius Clay defeats Liston to become world heavyweight champion. Reveling as a 7-1 underdog, the twenty-two-year-old Clay had boasted, "If you wanna lose your money, then bet on Sonny." But few sportswriters or fans expected him to beat the persistent, powerful champion, a tough ex-con who'd dethroned Floyd Patterson. So it's to a half-full arena that Clay demonstrates his soon-to-be-legendary, graceful "float like a butterfly, sting like a bee" style. Inflicting his lightning-fast jab, the challenger grabs the title when a spent Liston declines to answer the bell for the seventh round. Clay soon joins the Nation of Islam, denouncing his "slave name" and becoming Muhammad Ali, a.k.a. The Greatest.

FEBRUARY
26

1966 It's been awhile since anyone with the surname Sinatra has scored a major hit: Frank's last big one, "Witchcraft," came in 1958. Today, his eldest daughter Nancy strides to #1 with the sultry "These Boots Are Made for Walkin'," thanks to adept writer/producer Lee Hazelwood. Its lyrics are inspired by a western movie, but Hazelwood later reveals that he overheard its kicker line—"one of these days these boots are gonna walk all over you"—in a bar. He masterminds more hits for Nancy, even sharing vocals on "Some Velvet Morning," while she branches out to add B movies like *The Wild Angels* to her credits. A scant four months later, papa Frank hits #1 with "Strangers in the Night"—and, to complete the double-edged family assault, Hazelwood co-produces a father/daughter duet, "Something Stupid," that tops the charts the following year. Try as he might, pale sibling Frank Sinatra, Jr., never comes close. His biggest career news is his brief kidnapping in Lake Tahoe in 1963, for which the perpetrators are quickly caught.

> **"I wasn't allowed to grow as an artist. My albums were nicer to look at than to listen to."**
>
> —Nancy Sinatra

GRAMMYS FACE THE MUSIC

Begun in 1957 by the National Academy of Recording Arts and Sciences, the Grammy Awards had always favored safe, middle-of-the-road pop music over rock 'n' roll—early winners included Tony Bennett, Bobby Darin, Ella Fitzgerald, and Frank Sinatra. In 1965, when the Grammy for best performance by a vocal group went to the Anita Kerr Singers (*We Dig Mancini*) over the Beatles (*Help!*), howls erupted. The organization begrudgingly faced the music: rock 'n' roll was here to stay. So at 1967's ceremony, held at New York's swanky Waldorf-Astoria Hotel, the board did an astonishing about-face by including a performance by Frank Zappa and the Mothers of Invention (*Freak Out, We're Only in It For the Money*). Zappa, one of the counterculture's freakiest forces, delivered a trademark tasteless performance—a nightmare for the well-coifed, well-connected exec set that was in attendance. Frank Zappa wasn't invited back. Frank Sinatra was.

FEBRUARY 27

1961 Everyone's seen them in movies and on television, but rarely does anyone recognize their names—or even their faces, for that matter. They're stunt men: those agile, anonymous athletes who jump and fight, drive and crash cars, and perform myriad feats of derring-do day in and day out. Today the Stuntmen's Association of Motion Pictures forms in Hollywood (followed six years later by the Stuntwomen's Association). Its co-founders are Loren Jones, who's doubled for superstars like Steve McQueen and Paul Newman (and even Debbie Reynolds in *How the West Was Won*), and Dick Geary, whose credits include *The Great Race* and *Bullitt*.

FEBRUARY 28

1967

Visionary but reclusive artist/illustrator R. Crumb began publishing his outrageous sex- and drug-draped comics in underground papers like *Yarrowstalks* and *The East Village Other*. Today he and his pregnant wife Dana peddle the first copies of his now legendary *Zap Comix* out of a baby stroller on the streets of San Francisco. Classic creations like Mr. Natural, Flakey Foont, and the legendary "Keep on Truckin'" and "Stoned Again" illustrations make him a creepy-ish cult favorite, and he soon snags his most commercial gig to date: the cover of *Cheap Thrills* for Big Brother and the Holding Company, featuring Janis Joplin. "Crumb succeeds at making you see through his eyes," says the *New Yorker*, "The experience is so magical that you forget you do not want to be R. Crumb, an anxiety-ridden perpetual loser, any more than he does."

INSTRUMENTAL BREAKS

As rock 'n' roll took control of pop music in the '60s, instrumentals kept pace. Throughout the decade, some of the biggest artists were men of few, if any, words: The Ventures, Booker T. & the MG's (guitarist Steve Cropper, pictured), and especially Herb Alpert & the Tijuana Brass ("The Lonely Bull"), who at one point placed a phenomenal four albums in the Top 10. Here are some other notable lyricless tunes from the decade.

- The first British group to reach #1 in America wasn't the Beatles, but the Tornadoes, with their futuristic instrumental "Telstar" (see July 10).

- When the surf rolled in, so did the genre's archetypical classic, the Surfaris' "Wipe Out."

- Cliff Nobles & Co.'s "The Horse" was a lyric-free B-side of the less-successful single "Love Is All Right." Though Nobles himself doesn't perform on the B-side, the horn section would later go on to become MFSB, who recorded the hit theme to *Soul Train*.

- The only song keeping "The Horse" at #2 was the #1 "Grazing in the Grass" by jazz instrumentalist Hugh Masekela.

- Guitarist extraordinaire Dick Dale would later enjoy a revival when his "Misirlou" appeared on the *Pulp Fiction* soundtrack. But in the '60s, it was the twangy sound of "Let's Go Trippin'" that earned him fame.

- "Classical Gas" won three Grammys for its composer/performer Mason Williams, who was a writer for *The Smothers Brothers Comedy Hour* when it was released.

- Before they became Young-Holt Unlimited, Eldee Young and Red Holt were part of the Ramsey Lewis Trio, best known for their version of "Hang On Sloopy." In 1968, they hit it big with the instrumental "Soulful Strut."

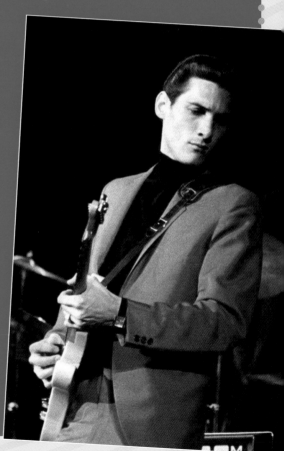

FEBRUARY 29

1960

In morally upright (and uptight) times, and with little money and no backing, Hugh Hefner had taken a gamble by launching *Playboy* magazine in 1953, defying Eisenhower-era conservative public morals to become a huge success. Pretenders inevitably follow, most notably Bob Guccione with *Penthouse* in 1965 and Larry Flynt with his more explicit *Hustler* in 1974. Today, Hefner expands his empire with his next big idea: the Playboy Club. The original downtown Chicago club clicks, and dozens more open in some thirty cities worldwide. Cardholders revel in the permissive atmosphere while sipping drinks served by buxom Playmates. Some of Hef's bunnies go on to future fame, including actresses Sherilyn Fenn and Lauren Hutton and rock star Deborah Harry. Radio and television forays soon enhance the lusty, busty Playboy empire, overseen by Hef (called Ner by Woody Allen) at his legendary Playboy Mansion in the Hollywood Hills.

MARCH

MARCH

1

1969

Born to be wild, Doors front man Jim Morrison begins a string of run-ins with the law when he's arrested after a gig in Miami for exposing himself onstage. Before the year is out, he's arrested on charges of public drunkenness and interfering with an airplane flight. Meanwhile, the group, bolstered by #1 singles "Light My Fire" and "Hello, I Love You," celebrates its growing reputation as fiery, anti-establishment warriors. "I'm interested in anything about revolt, disorder, chaos," says Morrison, son of a career naval officer. "It seems to me to be the road toward freedom." He later bolts for Paris, where he writes poetry and dies a mysterious death, supposedly in his bathtub, on July 3, 1971. Forty-five years later a former nightclub manager writes in a book that Morrison actually overdosed on heroin in a club's toilet, and drug dealers carted his body back to his apartment. Conspiracy theories still abound.

MEANWHILE...

THE MEDIA ACCORDING TO MCLUHAN

Media theory may seem like a rather esoteric field to many, but no writer brought it more pop culture prominence than Marshall McLuhan. Leaping from academia to celebrity, he coined now-ubiquitous phrases like "global village" and "the medium is the message." The latter was the title of his book that was released on March 1, 1967, which in its initial run was misspelled as *The Medium Is the Massage.* Though McLuhan noticed the mistake in proofing, he deliberately left it in. "All media exist to invest our lives with artificial perceptions and arbitrary values," said McLuhan, who continued to be confrontational and confounding with his controversial theories on media and mores. Becoming such a fixture on media discourse, he got perhaps the ultimate recognition: a cartoon about him in the *New Yorker.*

A HIGH CENTURY MARK

On March 2, 1962, the 4,124 spectators attending an insignificant contest between the Philadelphia Warriors and the last-place New York Knicks were about to witness NBA history. When towering Warriors' center Wilt "the Stilt" Chamberlain slam-dunked with forty-six seconds left, he netted a record-shattering 100 points. The seven-foot-one athlete went on to become the first player named both MVP and Rookie of the Year in the same season, play thirteen seasons with more than 1,000 re-bounds, and set many more basketball records. But it's a personal record that he will be best-remembered for: his claim to have slept with 20,000 women. "I was just doing what was natural," said Wilt, "chasing good-lookin' ladies, whoever they were and wherever they were available."

MARCH 2

1969 Marked by its distinct cone-shaped nose, the Concorde makes its first trial run today. Bankrolled by the British and French governments, the first supersonic airliner flies a short run from Toulouse, France. "Finally the big bird flies," says pilot André Turcat, "and I can say now that it flies pretty well." With an average cruising speed of 1,330 m.p.h.—more than twice that of conventional aircraft—the Concorde begins passenger service in 1976. Over the next twenty-seven years, it flies regularly between Europe and the US and sets many records, including a 1996 flight from London to New York that lasted just less than three hours.

MARCH
3

1960 After years of playing the bickering couple on *I Love Lucy*, the honeymoon's over. America's most famous on- and off-screen lovebirds, Lucille Ball and Desi Arnaz, announce their separation and pending divorce. For nearly ten years their sitcom has reigned as television's biggest—their second child Desi (Ricky on the show) even graced the cover of *TV Guide*'s first issue. *I Love Lucy* had literally invented the sitcom, shooting on film before a live audience in Los Angeles. Lucy and Desi were also shrewd businesspeople. Before anyone else, they'd recognized the value of reruns, buying the rights from CBS and becoming mega-rich pioneers in television syndication. Their empire, Desilu Productions, began back in 1950 when the B movie gal and her bongo-playing Cuban husband put up $5,000 of their own money to shoot the pilot of a series that soon wrote television history— leaving her with absolutely no 'splaining to do.

MARCH 4

1960 Comedy star Jerry Lewis has a film, *Cinderfella* (a gender-bending take on *Cinderella*), shot and ready for release, but wants to debut it at Christmastime. Paramount agrees, so long as he makes another movie to be released in the summer. Doing double duty, the funnyman performs his regular stage act at night and films *The Bellboy* by day. Today, he wraps shooting at Miami Beach's Fountainbleau Hotel. As bumbling bellboy Stanley, Lewis is mostly mute throughout the movie, which is basically a series of highly improvised sketches. Though he'll later be remembered for his starring roles in such films as *The Nutty Professor* and for his work with the Muscular Dystrophy Association, Lewis also leaves a lasting legacy by way of a groundbreaking technology he pioneers as a director—he attaches a TV camera to the film camera and has the video images sent to a monitor, so he can make sure he's getting the shots he wants right on the scene.

MARCH
5

1963 After performing at a benefit concert in Kansas City, quintessential torch singer Patsy Cline and fellow Opry stars Hawkshaw Hawkins and Cowboy Copas die when their single-engine plane crashes in Tennessee. The iconic, incomparable Cline had broken barriers at every turn. Dressing in elegant designer gowns instead of calico and gingham, she was a country music star at a time when female country singers were mostly regarded as pretty window dressings. She was the first county singer to headline at Carnegie Hall and the Hollywood Bowl, and most importantly, she crossed over into the pop charts like no other country star, with heartbreakers like "Walkin' After Midnight," "I Fall to Pieces," and "Crazy," which was penned by Willie Nelson. Thirty when she died, Cline's posthumous signature song becomes "Sweet Dreams (of You)."

The greatest compliment I could pay Patsy Cline is that she was one of the guys.

—Roger Miller

MARCH
6

1965 From preaching the gospel to singing gospel, Solomon Burke now gravitates to a more secular sound. His effortless swings between smooth crooner and gruff soul shouter score him continuous hits on both the R&B and country charts. Today Burke releases "Got to Get You Off My Mind," his biggest double shot: his sole #1 soul tune and highest charting pop song (at #22). It's based on two tragedies—his pending divorce, and the untimely death of soul singer Sam Cooke, whom he'd seen shortly before Cooke's killing at an LA motel under mysterious circumstances. Dubbed "the King of Rock and Soul," singer/songwriter Burke delivers vocals "of rare prowess and remarkable range," says pioneering producer Jerry Wexler—high praise from a man who's worked with such timeless talent as Ray Charles, Bob Dylan, and Dusty Springfield.

MARCH
7

1967 Two-and-a-half years in the making, a special *CBS Reports* episode premieres tonight. Boycotted by advertisers, the commercial breaks contain only public-service announcements due to its controversial subject matter: homosexuality. Hosted by Mike Wallace, "The Homosexuals" provides a sober, non-sensationalistic narrative featuring a handful of interviews (with mostly hidden faces), blurry footage of gay bars, shots of longtime activists like Frank Kameny picketing the White House, and a debate between Gore Vidal and Columbia professor Albert Goldman about the role of homosexuals in the arts. Mostly emphasizing the traditional view of homosexuality as an illness, the documentary "might have been better," writes the *New York Times*, "to give the minority viewpoint that homosexuals are just as normal as anyone else."

MARCH 8

1967 Twentieth Century Fox had high hopes for *Bloomer Girl*, a movie version of a 1944 Broadway musical featuring Celeste Holm that led to her film career (and an Oscar for *Gentleman's Agreement*). It signed Shirley MacLaine, a perky, popular actress with recent successes such as *Irma la Deuce* opposite Jack Lemmon and *Gambit* with Michael Caine. But when the studio pulled the plug shortly before filming was to begin, it offered her a role in a western, *Big Country, Big Man*, at the same salary. MacLaine declines and today files a breach of contract suit. Three years later, in a much-anticipated decision, the California Supreme Court rules in her favor. MacLaine wins an $800,000 decision and a spot in law students' casebooks forever.

MARCH 9

1967 The Broadway version of the ambitious musical *How to Succeed in Business Without Really Trying* not only won seven Tony awards but also a Pulitzer Prize for drama. So the rollicking farce, featuring young Robert Morse as a fast-climbing window washer and crooner Rudy Vallee as his crusty boss, cried out for the big screen. Today the United Artists movie opens, featuring the male co-stars reprising their Tony-winning performances plus Michele Lee in her movie debut (more than a decade before her career-making turn in *Knots Landing*). Bob Fosse (*Sweet Charity, Chicago*) handles the choreography, just as he did on stage.

MARCH 10

1964 From their pop roots in the late '50s as a duo called Tom & Jerry, Paul Simon and Art Garfunkel move to a folk music sound today when they record their debut Columbia album, *Wednesday Morning 3 A.M.*, with folk standards like "Go Tell It on the Mountain." The album languishes, the duo breaks up. A year later producer Tom Wilson, mindful of the folk/rock success of Bob Dylan and the Byrds, overdubs one of its acoustic cuts— "The Sounds of Silence"—with electric guitars, percussion, and drums. Released as a single, it soars to #1 in early 1966, almost two years after today's original recording. A string of successful singles and albums follows, capped by their soundtrack for director Mike Nichols' film *The Graduate*, whose "Mrs. Robinson" catapults them to international fame.

MARCH 11

1969 Back in the fifties, a US Army colonel at a base in Germany banned military wives from wearing blue jeans, saying they reflected badly on America. But jeans, originally sturdy trousers favored by workers of all stripes, gradually become a teenage favorite. Screen idols like James Dean and Marlon Brando made wearing them unquestionably cool. And not just any jeans—despite also-rans like Lee and Wrangler, it's Levi's that emerges as the overwhelming brand of choice among young Americans. In 1963, the San Francisco–based company had introduced pre-shrunk jeans; in 1967, they'd tapped groups like Jefferson Airplane for radio commercials. Today, Levi's introduces groovy bell-bottomed jeans. Forget the flares—the bigger the bell, the cooler the wearer.

MARCH 12

1962 First popularized in the US by First Lady Jackie Kennedy, the bouffant hairstyle rose in popularity—and height. Fifties' pixie cuts and ponytails gave way to puffed-up piles that required enormous amounts of time, energy, and aerosol. "We have tenth graders who find it hard to get through a doorway," notes a Detroit high school guidance counselor in an article in today's issue of *Newsweek*. Classmates dread getting seated behind a towering 'do. Trend-grabbing gals and Hollywood starlets alike adopt the large, lacquered look, but by the mid-'60s, the fad fades. Years later the cult director John Waters reignites the era with multiple incarnations of *Hairspray*—first as a movie in 1988, then on stage and in a second screen version.

MARCH 13

1964 Late at night in a quiet Queens, New York, neighborhood, twenty-eight-year-old Kitty Genovese returns from work. Walking to her apartment, she's brutally assaulted by an attacker. Her screams rouse neighbors, but no one calls the police. "Leave that girl alone" is the most one calls from a window. The assailant leaves, returns, rapes, and kills Genovese. "Thirty-Eight Who Saw Murder Didn't Call the Police" blares a headline in the *New York Times* two weeks later. "I didn't want to get involved," says one unnamed neighbor, crystallizing the apathy and anonymity of modern urban life. Further investigation shows that the reporting had been inaccurate—the attack continued out of sight of most neighbors—but the shame and outrage remained. The brutal murder and callous response shakes an already shaken America, still traumatized by the assassination of President Kennedy four months earlier.

MARCH 14

1969 Desperately needing a program to dent the ratings of NBC's Sunday night blockbuster *Bonanza*, CBS launches the irreverent *The Smothers Brothers Comedy Hour*. Maybe a bit too irreverent, as the anti–Vietnam War, pro–civil rights siblings battle network censors again and again. Even still, it's renewed today, and continues to contain many controversial and/or censored skits, plus the presidential parody campaign of Pat Paulsen. Several weeks later, CBS President William Paley abruptly reverses course and cancels the series in spite of solid ratings. A lengthy breach of contract lawsuit ensues, and four years later a jury awards Tom and Dick Smothers $776,300 in damages. Mom never liked CBS anyway.

MARCH 15

1967 Initially part of Andy Warhol's ultra-hip, multi-media live show, the Exploding Plastic Inevitable, the Velvet Underground releases its debut album: *The Velvet Underground and Nico*. The iconoclastic, influential rock band features the streetwise sounds of Lou Reed ("Heroin"), the classically trained talents of John Cale, breathy vocals by Nico, and a hardcore and often nihilistic view. With a famous banana cover designed by Warhol (who also produced it), the album is encapsulated by musician Brian Eno's later summation: "Hardly anybody bought it, but everyone who did formed a band." Three years and three albums later, the Velvet Underground splits up, with Reed ("Walk on the Wild Side") going on to the most successful solo career.

MARCH 16

1968 In the early morning hours, American soldiers enter a tiny Vietnamese hamlet in search of Viet Cong. Finding none, they still suspect the village of harboring the enemy, and a bloodbath erupts. "Soldiers went berserk, gunning down unarmed men, women, children, and babies," the BBC later reports. "By late morning word had got back to higher authorities and a cease-fire was ordered. My Lai was in a state of carnage. Bodies were strewn through the village." News of the My Lai Massacre doesn't emerge until more than a year later when investigative reporter Seymour Hersh writes an exposé that triggers worldwide shock and outrage. The story becomes a political football, with endless rounds of recriminations, investigations, and court proceedings. Eventually one participant, Lieutenant William Calley, Jr., is convicted of the premeditated murder of twenty-two civilians. He comes to personify the tragedy, but since none of his superiors are convicted, many see him as a scapegoat. Calley serves three and a half years for his crime.

MARCH 17

1966 For the only time ever, a former #1 recording artist portrays another former #1 recording artist—on film. Stumped? Welcome to the strange saga of *The Singing Nun*. Belgian nun Jeanine Deckers, who'd entertained her fellow sisters at their monastery, had recorded a few songs at a local studio. One upbeat number, "Dominique," improbably got wide airplay in Europe, prompting an American release. Stateside, its popularity rose so quickly that both the single and album by Soeur Sourire (Sister Smile, Deckers' stage name) hit #1 simultaneously. This nun's run prompts the motion picture version, which debuts today starring perky Debbie Reynolds (she of the #1 tune "Tammy" in 1957) as Deckers—one of the most unlikely chart-toppers in pop music history.

MARCH
18

1963

In a New York studio, jazz saxophonist Stan Getz is recording an album with Brazilian singer/guitarist Joao Gilberto. On one cut, they invite Gilberto's wife Astrud to sing in English. Her light, breathy vocals transform "The Girl from Ipanema" from just another album cut into an international sensation. The song, released today, rises to #5 on the pop charts and wins a Grammy for Record of the Year. The album also wins three Grammy awards, igniting a craze (with help from Eydie Gorme's "Blame It on the Bossa Nova") for the samba, bossa nova, and all things Brazilian. With a very limited but smooth voice, the winsome Astrud embarks on a career that includes a short American run but long-term Latin success. Her signature song identifies her forever as that lovely girl from Ipanema. Aahhh.

MARCH
19

1966

With all sorts of sweet smells in the air, Paul Revere & the Raiders today release "Kicks," which becomes the first major chart hit with an antidrug message: "Before you find out it's too late, girl, you better get straight." (Its songwriters, hubby and wife Barry Mann and Cynthia Weil, show incredible versatility from Jay and the Americans' "Only in America" to the Animals' "We Gotta Get Out of This Place.") The group quickly gains extraordinary exposure by becoming the house band on Dick Clark's daytime variety show, *Where the Action Is*. Hits ("Hungry," "Good Thing") keep a-comin', and cute lead singer Mark Lindsay becomes a pinup teenybopper heartthrob. After a couple years, the luster fades and personnel changes. The later-renamed Raiders manage only one #1: yet another "message" song, "Indian Reservation" in 1971.

MARCH
20

1967 From the moment she arrives at JFK airport, Twiggy mesmerizes America—just like she had Europe. No one has ever seen a model quite like her: a rail-thin, tiny, androgynous waif. An overnight phenomenon and polar opposite of the conventional buxom model, she earns multimillions modeling and via a line of licensed products, including clothes, cosmetics, dolls, and posters. It's all planned and superbly executed by her boyfriend, Nigel Davis, who'd discovered Twiggy (then Leslie Hornby) working as a shampoo girl in a hair salon. Blessed with a high metabolism, she could (and did) eat lots of ice cream and never gain a pound. Amidst the hoopla, Twiggy maintains an endearing sense of humor. "It's not what you'd call a figure," she says, "is it?"

MARCH
21

1962 America's insatiable appetite for roadside fast food drives new restaurateurs into the business. While '50s pioneers McDonald's, Burger Chef, and Burger King had concentrated on all-American hamburgers, today a south-of-the-border flavor arrives when the first Taco Bell opens in Downey, California. Roast beef sandwiches join the party when Arby's opens its doors two years later, the same year that Colonel Harlan Sanders sells his famed Kentucky Fried Chicken chain. That deal boosts an expansion that soon puts the Colonel's robust, recognizable face on restaurants lining the highways from coast to coast. Other burger joints joining the mix in the '60s include Hardee's (1961) and Wendy's (1969), named after founder Dave Thomas's daughter.

MARCH
22

1962 After appearing in a series of off-off-Broadway productions, a nineteen-year-old New York City native finally catches that elusive big break—a role on Broadway! Tonight Barbra Streisand debuts in a small part in *I Can Get It for You Wholesale*, a musical comedy starring Elliott Gould (whom she later marries). Her career explodes when she wins a Tony nomination and signs a recording contract with Columbia later that year. Then come the hit songs like "People" and "Second Hand Rose," acting roles in *Funny Girl* (the play and the movie), and specials like CBS's *My Name is Barbra*, a stunning small-screen showcase. Over the years she becomes a multifaceted threat, adding producing, directing, and composing credits and amassing multiple Grammy, Emmy, and Oscar awards.

MARCH
23

1963 They'd begun at a high school talent show in 1961 as Carl & the Passions, but within a few months had settled on a more melodic name: the Beach Boys (which will conveniently place them just ahead, alphabetically, of arch rivals the Beatles). Led by mercurial Brian Wilson, the Beach Boys epitomize the southern California surf and hot-rod culture—although, ironically, only one member, Brian's brother Dennis, is a surfer. Today they release "Surfin' USA," the first of a dozen Top 10 hits that include three #1s in the '60s: "I Get Around," "Help Me, Rhonda," and "Good Vibrations." Several years later, Brian fashions their magnificently nuanced album *Pet Sounds*, featuring "God Only Knows" and "Sloop John B." Many consider the album not only the band's best, but one of the best LPs of all time.

MARCH 24

1962 Inexpensive to produce and shot in relatively small spaces, boxing had been a mainstay of programming from television's earliest days. But tonight, ABC's *Fight of the Week*, live from smoke-filled Madison Square Garden, changes everything. In a welterweight grudge match between Emile Griffith and Benny "The Kid" Paret, Griffith beats his opponent mercilessly. The referee is slow to stop the bout, and Paret is carted away on a stretcher. He undergoes emergency brain surgery but dies ten days later. Ironically, new replay equipment had allowed ABC to show repeated slow-motion takes of the bout's fatal blows, triggering renewed criticism of the "sweet science." Boxing gets a lot less airtime over the next decade until the rise of cable TV.

MARCH 25

1967 It's Saturday night and entrepreneurial deejay Murray the K's got the hottest show in town—the US debut of the Who and Cream. Over the next nine days at New York's RKO Radio Theater, an extraordinary assemblage including the Blues Project, Wilson Pickett, Smokey Robinson & the Miracles, and Mitch Ryder play a numbing five shows per day. The event, dubbed "Music in the Fifth Dimension," features the Who blasting out "Happy Jack" and "My Generation." Yet they demonstrate little understanding of the current American generation when lead singer Pete Townsend, despite escalating anti-war sentiments, records a radio jingle for the US Air Force. But their working-class roots peek through when the band, scheduled to play the prestigious *Ed Sullivan Show*, refuses to cross a picket line of striking CBS newsreaders.

MARCH 26 · 1964

Hollywood studios had been wary of big-budget epic films since the epic flop of 20th Century Fox's *Cleopatra* last year. Still, Paramount bravely soldiers on with *The Fall of the Roman Empire*, another sword-and-sandal entry that opens today. Producer Samuel Bronston had shown a deft touch with similar widescreen fare like *King of Kings* and *El Cid*. He films in Spain with nearly 10,000 extras and a blockbuster ensemble cast including Alec Guinness, James Mason, Christopher Plummer, Omar Sharif, and Sophia Loren (who received a million-dollar salary to match Liz Taylor's stratospheric pay on the ill-fated *Cleopatra*). "Darkness holds sway on the fringes of the Empire," writes *Time Out*, in this "superior example of the genre." Despite good reviews, the film's a flop. Romanian native Bronston loses his Spanish film studio and declares bankruptcy. A subsequent criminal prosecution for perjury devastates his film career.

MARCH 27 · 1960

Director Otto Preminger begins shooting his epic *Exodus*, based on a Leon Uris novel, in Israel. The star-studded ensemble production—including Peter Lawford, Sal Mineo, Paul Newman, and Eva Marie Saint—draws attention worldwide as it recreates on-location the tensions, turbulence, and violence that marked the creation of the state of Israel. Cameras arrive from Hollywood, period weaponry from England, and old British army trucks and other vehicles from Cyprus. Of the many animals rounded up, the camels are cooperative but their greedy owners aren't. Production is halted twice one night as Arab negotiators huddle to solve the problem over tiny cups of steaming Turkish coffee. The script isn't without controversy as well. In a gutsy, groundbreaking move, Preminger had hired writer Dalton Trumbo, who had been blacklisted due to Red Scare paranoia. "I think that to employ Trumbo and hide that fact under a fictitious name would constitute cheating the public," says Preminger.

MARCH 28 · 1966

James Bond shakes, not stirs, a secret agent fad in America, as stateside networks premiere a slew of shows that become of-the-moment hits like *The Man from U.N.C.L.E.* and *I Spy*. Today a stylish series from across the pond is smartly snapped up by ABC. *The Avengers* features a cool, collected crime-fighting duo: Patrick Macnee as dapper Englishman-slash-secret agent John Steed, and Diana Rigg as his lithe partner Emma Peel. Her name comes from the producers' desire for a character with "man appeal," shortened to m-appeal. "A golden jewel of an actress who alighted upon us like a glorious butterfly on a summer's day and proceeded to add gossamer to the show," says Macnee of his new co-star. Rigg filled big boots, er, shoes, following the departure of British actress Honor Blackman (stepping over to portray Pussy Galore in 007's *Goldfinger*). The Blackman episodes never air in the US but inspire ABC to pick up the show. Not to worry—Rigg becomes a knockout idol.

FINE FEATHERED FOES

After producing more than a dozen films during each of the two preceding decades, Alfred Hitchcock halved that in the '60s. He kicked off the era with the harrowing *Psycho* (see June 16), and in March 1963, unleashed his alarming avian adventure *The Birds*. Based on a short story by Daphne de Maurier, the film featured unknown Tippi Hedren ("a fascinating new personality," gushed its ads) as a young woman beset by birds turned into gashing, slashing attackers. Hitch masterfully heightened the film's portentous mood with an ingenious, musicless soundtrack of electronically simulated bird cries and flapping wings. The rest of the decade would see some of the director's least popular films— another Tippi Hedren picture, *Marnie*, Paul Newman vehicle *Torn Curtain*, and Cold War thriller *Topaz*—each of which failed to reach the prominence of *The Birds*, a film so talked-about it even landed on the cover of *Life* magazine. The diminutive director posed with three large, black birds perched ominously on his arms and head. "Remember," he teased, "the last scream you hear... may be your own."

MARCH
29

1969 Days before the Oscars, first-time nominee Liza Minelli (for *The Sterile Cuckoo*) separates from her openly gay husband, Peter Allen. Five years before, her mother Judy Garland had discovered Aussie Allen playing in a trio at the Hong Kong Hilton. She signed him to open for her, and he later married Minelli. A flamboyant showman, the charismatic Allen not only shined as a performer but as a songwriter, penning hits for Melissa Manchester ("Don't Cry Out Loud") and Olivia Newton-John ("I Honestly Love You"). Minelli wound up losing the Oscar to Goldie Hawn (see Dec. 16) for *Cactus Flower*, while Allen went on to huge international success. He won an Oscar for best song ("Arthur"), gave a performance for Queen Elizabeth II, and sold out New York's 6,000-seat Radio City Music Hall. Allen died of AIDS in 1992 at age forty-eight.

MARCH
30

1964 Merv Griffin had worn a lot of hats—singer, producer, talk show host—but discovers the proverbial pot of gold when he invents a game show that debuts today with Art Fleming as host. *Jeopardy!* becomes an instant hit, and when NBC unwisely cancels it a decade later, the savvy producer creates a syndicated version that later features a new host, Alex Trebek. The show grows into a powerhouse franchise, entering the lexicon of pop culture phenomena alongside its equally famous companion, *Wheel of Fortune,* another Griffin creation. "When Merv Griffin created *Jeopardy,*" says Roger King of distributor King World, "I think he created a format that will be around for a hundred years."

MARCH
31

1962 The most successful female artist of the times, raven-haired beauty Connie Francis today scores her third #1 hit with "Don't Break the Heart That Loves You." Like her first Top 10 song, "Who's Sorry Now," it's been selected by her domineering daddy who demonstrates the old adage that, indeed, Father knows best. But it's in movies that Connie finds a second career, co-starring in wholesome hits like *Where the Boys Are* and *Follow the Boys* (see April 14). Her music not only appeals to youngsters but adults, too, and she even sings at a prestigious command performance for Queen Elizabeth II the next year. Unfortunately for Connie, four of the Queen's mop-topped subjects are soon to launch a revolution that will make her achy ballads sound quite dated.

APRIL
1

1960 The wheel deal: *Motor Trend* heralds GM's sporty Chevrolet Corvair as its Car of the Year. In an era of behemoth American cars, the trim Corvair competes successfully against the Ford Mustang and Volkswagen Beetle. It sells more than 200,000 cars every year, expanding its market share by appealing to both sports and family car enthusiasts. Things screech to a halt in 1965 when consumer crusader Ralph Nader publishes *Unsafe at Any Speed*, which lambastes the auto industry and devotes a full chapter to the Corvair. His criticism of safety problems posed by its rear-mounted engine, steering column design, and other deficiencies dents sales irreparably. The Corvair slowly peters out, eventually replaced by Chevy's next sporty model, the Camaro.

APRIL
2

1967 With the Spencer Davis Group's "I'm a Man" still rising on the charts, Stevie Winwood—the band's eighteen-year-old creative force—bows out. Tapping friends Dave Mason, Jim Capaldi, and Chris Wood, he forms the rock-meets-blues outfit Traffic. Its members jell instantly, their instrumental and compositional dexterity producing a distinctive melodic sound. Soon they're a progressive FM radio mainstay with cuts like "Dear Mr. Fantasy" and "You Can All Join In." Pioneering rock journalist Lillian Roxon calls Winwood "one of the Renaissance men of rock—writer, arranger, performer." As personnel shifts, Winwood temporarily jumps to the supergroup Blind Faith with Eric Clapton, Ginger Baker, and Rich Grech. But Traffic reforms and delivers two master albums, *John Barleycorn Must Die* and *The Low Spark of High Heeled Boys*. When asked about the term "white soul," mega-producer Jerry Wexler, who'd worked with legends like Aretha Franklin, offers a two-word response: Steve Winwood.

APRIL

3

1965 Inspired by the James Bond spy craze, the British action/adventure series *Danger Man* debuts on CBS tonight as *Secret Agent*. Suave Patrick McGoohan stars as John Drake, who never carries a gun but is quite handy with his fists. The stylish import delivers an hour-long dose of good-versus-evil intrigue, well-captured in its stark black-and-white format. Though the show only lasts one year, its twangy, guitar-driven theme, "Secret Agent Man" by Johnny Rivers, is much more successful, hitting #3 on the pop charts. Three years later, McGoohan again plays a secret agent (and the title role) in CBS's Kafkaesque cult classic *The Prisoner* (see June 1), in which, as in Rivers' hit song, they've given him a number and taken 'way his name.

APRIL

4

1964 Records come and records go. But today the Beatles set one that may stand forever: they've got the top five songs in America. At #1 is "Can't Buy Me Love," followed by "Twist and Shout," "She Loves You," "I Want to Hold Your Hand," and "Please Please Me." They also claim an unprecedented twelve songs in the Top 100, a record they smash just a week later when that total rises to fourteen. This chart domination stems not only from their overwhelming talent but also from business vagaries. When Capitol Records in the US initially declined a deal from its sister label Parlophone in the UK to sign the Beatles, several small American indie labels (Swan, Tollie, Vee-Jay) licensed the rights to some songs. A legal ruling in the fall will require them to relinquish those rights, but for now the riches are spread around.

APRIL

5

1965 After opening to packed houses and critical acclaim in 1957, the Broadway production of *My Fair Lady* had gone on to win seven Tony awards. Turning the smash musical into a movie was a foregone conclusion, but it took a while. Opting for a bigger name, the producers nixed stage star (and Tony winner) Julie Andrews and selected ethereally elegant Audrey Hepburn. Critics vent, including one who blames the producers' "evil and rampantly lunatic force." But Hepburn's singing is deemed inadequate, so Marni Nixon dubs her voice. Tonight at the Oscars awards ceremony the Warner Bros. movie sweeps eight trophies including Best Picture, Actor (Rex Harrison, reprising his stage role) and Director (George Cukor). In a moment of sweet revenge, Andrews wins Best Actress for the title role in Walt Disney's *Mary Poppins*, her film debut. Hepburn, not even nominated, gamely attends and graciously applauds when Andrews wins.

"He played a nameless man, a silent, malevolent antihero cowboy who moved across the screen with a sinister but deadly grace."

—journalist Meriel McCooey

WAY OUT WEST

April 1968 was a good month for music from Big Sky Country, as the haunting title track from the spaghetti western *The Good, the Bad, and the Ugly* broke into the Top 40, and eventually reached #2. The Hugo Montenegro song, whose famous opening refrain was based on the howl of a coyote, also kept composer Ennio Morricone's soundtrack—his biggest hit ever—on the album charts for almost a year. The musical success mirrored the film's box office popularity. A hit with audiences, it also cemented the stardom of rugged actor Clint Eastwood, who had previously been best-known for his role on the TV series *Rawhide*, but who had been becoming popular in spaghetti westerns such as 1964's *A Fistful of Dollars*. Now the big screen's laconic gunslinger would be known as "the man with no name," well before he adopted the persona of iconoclastic city detective Dirty Harry.

APRIL 6

1960 "Runaway Bride" shout the headlines as nineteen-year-old Gamble Benedict, heiress to the Remington typewriter fortune, defies her family and once again runs away with the chauffeur, thirty-five-year-old Romanian Andrei Porumbeanu. Only five months earlier the couple had eloped on an oil freighter to Antwerp and then to Paris, but her stern maternal grandmother (her mother had committed suicide when she was a girl) had her dragged back and the marriage annulled since the groom was already married. Tonight, with his divorce granted, they wed at a hunting lodge in North Carolina's Blue Ridge Mountains. The marriage lasts four years, after which Gamble gets custody of their two sons. She later quietly remarries a New York State Police investigator.

APRIL 7

1963 Golf legend Arnold Palmer and his legions of fans in "Arnie's Army" eagerly look forward to another Masters title—after all, he's won the Augusta, Georgia, tourney three of the last five years. But today fast-rising star Jack Nicklaus, twenty-three, of Columbus, Ohio, upends "Champagne" Tony Lema and veteran Sam Sneed to become the youngest player ever to win the prestigious event. Palmer finishes well off the pace. Nicklaus "indicated throughout the power of his long game and an uncanny touch on the greens....[His] careful reading of the carpets has paid off richly," notes one sportswriter. The next year Palmer comes back to again take the Masters crown, but Nicklaus wins in '65 and '66, the first player ever to take back-to-back titles. To the winner goes the famed kelly green blazer.

APRIL 8

1963 Breaking Bob Hope's string of three years straight, Frank Sinatra hosts tonight's Academy Awards gala at the Santa Monica Civic Auditorium. Striking blue-eyed Peter O'Toole, up for Best Actor for his title role in *Lawrence of Arabia,* hopes the selection of Ol' Blue Eyes as host bodes well for his chances—but Gregory Peck wins for his portrayal of Atticus Finch in *To Kill a Mockingbird.* Still, *Lawrence of Arabia* wins seven awards including Best Picture, Director (David Lean), Music (Maurice Jarré), and Cinematography (Fred A. Young). Peck's role stands the test of time, named by the American Film Institute in 2003 as the top film hero of the last 100 years. An epic battle between grandes dames of the screen (see Oct. 26) also enlivens this ceremonial night.

APRIL
9

1962 A few hundred yards from the Pacific Ocean, one finds West Side glory as *West Side Story* dances away with ten Oscars, including Best Picture and Director (feuding co-winners Jerome Robbins and Robert Wise, who snub each other at the ceremony). The rousing musical just misses *Ben-Hur*'s record of eleven wins but does take matching trophies for Best Supporting Actors: Rita Moreno and George Chakiris. Based on the wildly successful Leonard Bern-stein/Stephen Sondheim play that opened on Broadway in 1957, the United Artists film features a virtual un-known (Richard Beymour) in the lead role of Tony, a part feverishly but unsuccessfully pursued by a raft of stars including Warren Beatty, Bobby Darin, Troy Donahue, Anthony Perkins, and Elvis Presley. Beatty's girlfriend Natalie Wood, who accompanied him and read at his audition as a favor, wowed the producers and won the lead role of Maria.

APRIL 10

1962

More than 2,500 people cram into five galleries linked by closed-circuit television at Sotheby's in London for an auction of masterly artworks owned by acclaimed gay writer M. Somerset Maugham (*Of Human Bondage, The Razor's Edge*). The much-anticipated event nets nearly $1.5 million, including the sale of Pablo Picasso's two-sided *The Death of Harlequin/Woman Seated in a Garden* for $224,000—a record for a painting by a living artist. Most critics believe *Harlequin*, finished in 1905, to be the superior work. Other notable paintings sold today include works by Gauguin, Matisse, Monet, and Renoir. Maugham notes that his decision to sell was prompted by the "irksome business" of providing security at his Riviera home.

APRIL 11

"Herrrrrrrrrrrrrre's Johnny!"
—Ed McMahon

1967

Sidekick Ed McMahon climbs off the couch at *The Tonight Show Starring Johnny Carson* to begin a day job hosting an NBC quiz show, *Snap Judgment*. Packaged by game-show kings Mark Goodson and Bill Todman (*The Price Is Right, I've Got a Secret*), today's premiere episode features daytime stalwarts Betsy Palmer and Gene Rayburn. The series runs for two seasons, attracting celebrity participants like Bob Hope and Ed's nighttime boss Johnny. Big, enthusiastic McMahon began his showbiz career as a bingo caller, carnival barker, and boardwalk pitchman for a vegetable slicer. He made his television debut in 1950 on CBS's circus series, *The Big Top,* playing a clown. But it's clowning around with pal Johnny that nets McMahon the big bucks and ongoing fame.

APRIL 12

1966 Smooth purveyors of Southern California's surf and car sounds, Jan & Dean delivered a slew of infectious, harmonic Top 10 hits like "Surf City," "The Little Old Lady (from Pasadena)," and "Dead Man's Curve." Today that last song is eerily realized when Jan Berry, pulling around a slow-moving car, plows his Corvette Stingray into a parked truck in Beverly Hills. He's in a coma for months, suffers serious brain damage, and finally awakens to partial paralysis and impaired speech. Television later retells the tale in a movie of the week, *Dead Man's Curve*. Berry undergoes years of physical therapy before eventually reuniting with Dean Torrence, who during Jan's recovery had turned to graphic arts and designed album covers for artists like Harry Nilsson, the Nitty Gritty Dirt Band, and Linda Ronstadt.

APRIL 13

1964 Tonight at the Oscars, no one can keep up with the Joneses—*Tom Jones*, that is. The bawdy British period piece runs off with four awards including Best Picture and Director (Tony Richardson). But Albert Finney, who played the title character with great gusto and guts, is a no-show—he's off partying in Hawaii. Which wasn't such a bad idea, since the Best Actor award goes to Sidney Poitier for *Lillies of the Field*, making him the first African American to win an Oscar in a leading category. (Hattie McDaniel had broken the color barrier in 1939 as Best Supporting Actress in *Gone With the Wind*). Poitier basks in the near-religious fervor of the audience's wild reception. In 1967 he becomes the first black actor to place his handprints at Grauman's Chinese Theater in Hollywood, the same year he stars in a troika of box-office hits: *To Sir, with Love*; *In the Heat of the Night*; and *Guess Who's Coming to Dinner*.

APRIL 14

1960 Save the last kiss for me: A hip-thrusting rock 'n' roller (think Elvis) is about to be inducted into the army, so his agent (Dick Van Dyke) comes up with a last-minute promotional stunt—bidding a typical teenage girl goodbye with an all-American kiss. Such is the good-natured, fun-loving premise of the musical *Bye Bye Birdie*, which opens tonight on Broadway. A huge hit, it goes on to win four Tony awards for Best Musical, Actor (Van Dyke), Direction, and Choreography (Gower Champion). Three years later Hollywood comes a-calling, with Columbia pairing young swoon-worthies Bobby Rydell and Ann-Margret. The role ignites the latter's career, and she takes full advantage. The red-headed beauty torches the '62 Oscars, delivering a show-stopping version of "Bachelor in Paradise." Soon Ann-Margret's dancing up a storm opposite the real Elvis in *Viva Las Vegas*.

SAND, SURF, AND THE OLDER SET

Jazzed by the surfing craze, in April 1965 teenagers flocked to see the latest beach escapades of ex-Mouseketeer Annette Funicello and all-American Frankie Avalon in *Beach Blanket Bingo*. The movie broke records across the country and continued a long string of sun 'n' fun hijinks amidst lots of groovy singing and dancing. But the scene wasn't just for teens—here are some of the aging stars who tried to catch a wave by appearing in a beach-party flick.

- Don Rickles (*Muscle Beach Party, Bikini Beach, Pajama Party, Beach Blanket Bingo*)

- Paul Lynde (*Beach Blanket Bingo*)

- Buster Keaton (*Pajama Party*)

- Vincent Price (*Beach Party, Dr. Goldfoot and the Bikini Machine*)

- Buddy Hackett (*Muscle Beach Party*)

- Mickey Rooney (*How to Stuff a Wild Bikini*)

- Boris Karloff (*Bikini Beach, The Ghost in the Invisible Bikini*)

- Basil Rathbone (*The Ghost in the Invisible Bikini*)

- Dorothy Lamour (*Pajama Party*)

- Elsa Lanchester (*Pajama Party*)

APRIL 15

1966 Though the decade still has several years to run, *Time* magazine declares the race is over. Citing the previous prominence of cities like Vienna, Paris, New York, and Rome, the cover story heralds London as the city of the '60s and praises its overwhelming international influence on music, art, fashion, film, theater, and more. "Everything new, uninhibited, and kinky," *Time* writes, "is blooming at the top of London life." The Beatles and the Stones, Carnaby Street with its mods and miniskirts, hairstylist extraordinaire Vidal Sassoon, echoes of suave super-spy James Bond, outrageous "out" playwright Joe Orton—the city's ablaze with trendsetters. "London has something that New York used to have—everybody wants to be there," says one art gallery owner. "There's no place else. Paris is calcified." Introducing the soon-to-be-ubiquitous catchphrase "Swinging London," the article propels an unlikely songwriter, American country singer Roger Miller, to one of his biggest hits: "England Swings." At year's end, Italian director Michelangelo Antonioni captures the swirling world with *Blowup*, in which a narcissistic photographer (David Hemmings) prowls the city capturing its fab feel and fresh fashions. The character is inspired by real-life photographer David Bailey, whose of-the-moment shots of the "beautiful people" make him as famous as them.

APRIL 16

1969 It's a familiar story: unknown rock band jumps from tiny, independent label to bigger company after the group achieves some success. Today, one of those sudden leaps ends in a heap when Elektra Records drops hard rockers MC5. Former folk-music specialists, Elektra Records had enjoyed huge success by expanding to include rock acts like the Doors and Love. In 1968, they signed the MC5, an underground, Detroit-based band that had generated considerable attention after opening for superstars like the Jimi Hendrix Experience and Cream. Elektra rushed out a well-received live album, *Kick Out the Jams*, but the band's notorious foul language enraged parents. The band blithely takes it a step further: they place an ad in an underground Detroit newspaper that uses the f-word to criticize a local record chain for not stocking their album. Although Elektra drops the MC5, it later retreads its steps by releasing the first album by controversial Detroit rock band the Stooges, led by one Iggy Pop.

APRIL
17

1964 Desperately seeking a sports car to energize its line of aging, lackluster sedans, Ford unveils its new "pony" car, the Mustang, at the World's Fair in New York (see April 22). The man behind the small, stylish car is Lee Iacocca, who'd inherited the top job at Ford from bean counter Robert McNamera (who had left to become JFK's Secretary of Defense). The media raves, pandemonium erupts, and customers pounce—snapping up 22,000 of the vehicles within twenty-four hours at a sticker price of $2,372. Ford's goal of selling 100,000 cars in the first year is eclipsed in four short months. The car's name comes from ad man John Conley, who later christens the Pinto, Bronco, and Maverick. Some of the Mustang's smart original exterior colors include Chantilly Beige, Silversmoke Grey, Pagoda Green, Poppy Red, Prairie Bronze, Phoenician Yellow, Wimbledon White, and Twilight Turquoise. Brash Steve McQueen cements the Mustang's iconic status forever when he subsequently tears through the streets of San Francisco in one in *Bullitt*.

> **"I've always found that the speed of the boss is the speed of the team."**
> **—Lee Iacocca**

APRIL 18

1966 Less than a month before, the US Supreme Court had lifted a Massachusetts ban on the sale of *Fanny Hill,* a 200-year-old sexually explicit book. But the court also upheld an obscenity conviction for Ralph Ginzberg, publisher of the magazine *Eros.* Today, a new book delivers a true shock to the system of a still prudish America. Published by Little, Brown & Company, Dr. William H. Masters and Virginia E. Johnson's *Human Sexual Response* evokes an immediate public response, both pro and con. Their purposely non-salacious work, meticulously researching nearly 700 men and women over eleven years, presents a candid study of intercourse and masturbation. Instantly controversial, it presages the sexual revolution soon to flower, along with drugs and rock 'n' roll, in next year's "Summer of Love."

APRIL 19

1969 Keith Moon and John Entwistle of the Who have each been credited with coining the term "lead zeppelin" to describe a gig gone bad. Regardless of its exact origin, the quartet led by Robert Plant and Jimmy Page drop the "a" and form the hard blues-rock combo Led Zeppelin. Signed by Atlantic Records at the recommendation of Dusty Springfield, the band had several months earlier been opening for acts like Vanilla Fudge and Iron Butterfly, but the latter refused to follow them on stage after seeing the wild audience reaction. Today Led Zeppelin tours the US as incendiary headliners while their debut single, "Good Times Bad Times," climbs the charts. Their biggest single ever, "Whole Lotta Love," quickly follows, though in their native England the band eschews singles for blazing, increasingly heavy metal albums (simply titled with Roman numerals I–IV) that add to their mystique. It's album "IV" that contains "Stairway to Heaven," one of rock's most enduring anthems.

APRIL
20

1968 Formed from musicians answering an ad in the British music magazine *Melody Maker*, Deep Purple makes its live debut tonight in Denmark. The heavy metal rockers quickly land record deals in both the UK and US, the latter on a tiny label co-owned by comedian Bill Cosby. Less than four months later they crack the Top 5 stateside with a remake of Billy Joe Royal's "Hush." Next the band taps material from another American songwriter when they release their rendition of Neil Diamond's "Kentucky Woman." Deep Purple later shifts to an edgier, eardrum-shattering sound and scores its last hit with "Smoke on the Water," an unlikely retelling of the night a Swiss nightclub burned down during a set by Frank Zappa.

APRIL
21

1969 Today iconoclastic Italian director Pier Paolo Pasolini releases his sexually charged film *Teorema* ("Theorem") in the United States, where his films have never edged beyond cult classics. Young, handsome Terrence Stamp stars as a mysterious visitor who turns a rich, materialistic family's world upside-down when he seduces, then sleeps with, every member: mother, father, daughter, and son, plus the maid for good measure. Always an acquired taste, Pasolini confounds the critics, whose mixed reviews range from "brillant or maddening" to "a magical world about the improbable." Such confusion reigns among the religious, too, when the movie wins a Roman Catholic film review award at the Venice Film Festival. The decision is attacked by the Vatican, and the Italian government tries Pasolini for obscenity, but loses.

APRIL
22

1962 In the twilight of his career, acclaimed director John Ford delivers yet another destined-to-be-classic western, *The Man Who Shot Liberty Valance*. It features John Wayne, his favorite actor, who appears in more than twenty of the director's films, alongside Jimmy Stewart and Lee Marvin. Opening today, the movie is widely panned but later lauded as "the *Citizen Kane* of Westerns." It has one of film's most remembered lines—"When the legend becomes fact, print the legend"—but, interestingly, it doesn't contain its well-remembered title track. "The Man Who Shot Liberty Valance," by powerful pop vocalist Gene Pitney, misses the final cut but goes on to become his first Top 10 hit. Pitney later mines another Western setting with the Burt Bacharach/Hal David love-gone-wrong classic, "Twenty Four Hours from Tulsa."

TOGETHER FOR THE FIRST TIME

JAMES STEWART · JOHN WAYNE

JOHN FORD'S PRODUCTION

The Man Who Shot Liberty Valance

VERA MILES · LEE MARVIN · EDMOND O'BRIEN · ANDY DEVINE · KEN MURRAY

MEANWHILE...

MEET ME AT THE PEPSI PAVILION

Who needs international governments when you have international corporations? On April 22, 1964, a futuristic, corporate-heavy World's Fair opened in Flushing Meadows, New York, on the same site as the 1939–40 fair. But without the sanctioning of the Paris-based group that oversaw international expositions—which didn't approve of the fair's timing or charging for exhibition space—most major foreign nations decided not to show. American industry, however, was more than happy to step up to play a prominent role. US Steel's Unisphere, a twelve-story, gleaming stainless steel model of the Earth, symbolized the fair's wordy theme: "Man's Achievement on a Shrinking Globe in an Expanding Universe." Lavish pavilions equipped with Disney animatronics from General Electric ("Carousel of Progress"), Ford ("The Magic Skyway"), and Pepsi Cola ("It's a Small World"), among many others, impressed the more than fifty-one million fair-goers. But even with so many attendees, the fair lost money, and almost had to declare bankruptcy in its second season.

APRIL 23

1961

Hospitalized and treated last year for hepatitis, the singer had also just suffered through a painful divorce. Still, gallant Judy Garland believes the show must go on. So, after a rejuvenating European tour late last year, including a break to film a supporting role in Stanley Kramer's *Judgment at Nuremberg,* she appears tonight at a packed Carnegie Hall. Garland mesmerizes the adoring, celebrity-laden crowd with a mix of standards, show tunes, and show stoppers—including "Rock-a-Bye Your Baby with a Dixie Melody," "Over the Rainbow," "Stormy Weather," and the final encore, "Chicago." The SRO crowd goes wild. At the end, Rock Hudson lifts her children Liza, Lorna, and Joe on stage for a bow with their mother. Within weeks Capitol rushes out a double album, *Judy Garland at Carnegie Hall,* which tops the charts for thirteen weeks and nets five Grammy awards including Best Female Vocal Performance and, for the first time for a woman, Album of the Year.

APRIL 24

1961

Barely two weeks before, an up-and-coming but still unknown folk-singer had played his first live New York City gig, opening for legendary bluesman John Lee Hooker at Gerde's Folk City in Greenwich Village. Today nineteen-year-old Bob Dylan makes his recording debut, playing harmonica on a Harry Belafonte album, *Midnight Special,* for which he earns a $50 paycheck. Dylan idolizes Belafonte, later writing that "I felt like I'd become anointed in some kind of way....Harry was that rare type of character that radiates greatness, and you hope that some of it rubs off on you." Six months later, Dylan records his self-titled debut album and makes a little-noticed Carnegie Hall debut (see Nov. 4).

THE NOT-SO-GREAT PRETENDERS

Eternally envious of Johnny Carson's unparalleled success, in the late '60s competing networks searched for hosts to challenge the king of late night.

- In April 1967, ABC trotted out Joey Bishop, a smooth, veteran standup, if one of the lesser lights in the Rat Pack (see Aug. 10). *The Joey Bishop Show* was a mirror image of Johnny's program, replete with celebrity guests, lots of light patter, and a personable second banana: Regis Philbin. Though Bishop had guest-hosted for Carson many times, there was no love lost between them. "I wish him great success," said fierce competitor Carson, "in the storm door business."

- In 1969, ABC would fire the struggling Bishop and replace him with Dick Cavett. A former standup comedian who'd also written for top names like Jerry Lewis, Groucho Marx, and Jack Paar, he brought a wry, sophisticated touch to late night with *The Dick Cavett Show*.

- Next up was Merv Griffin (right), a pre-tested industry veteran who'd also created several game shows (see March 30). The smooth and savvy former singer jumped from his Westinghouse syndicated talk show to a new CBS entry that replaced its late night movies in August 1969. To try and differentiate *The Merv Griffin Show*, CBS went for an edgier slant on topical issues, and presented Carson's stiffest challenge to date.

- After Griffin switched to CBS, Westinghouse signed up Englishman David Frost. *The David Frost Show* offered a wider range of guests and more in-depth interviews for the ex–*That Was the Week That Was* host, whom *Look* magazine dubbed "TV's International Man." But regardless of the high esteem, Frost was just another pretender who failed to dislodge the king's crown.

APRIL 25

1966 A revolution is brewing: Big conglomerates are delivering inferior coffee in cans—and Americans are lapping it up. This mystifies Alfred Peet, the son of a Dutch coffee merchant and an expert in the coffee and tea trade. Today the prickly pioneer opens his first retail shop in Berkeley, California, a few blocks from the university. Soon the rich aroma of his signature dark roast attracts a growing clientele of coffee connoisseurs. "He was the big bang," says Corby Kummer (*The Joy of Coffee*). "It all started with him." Peet's shop anchors a culinary corridor later dubbed the Gourmet Ghetto, which gains luster when chef Alice Water opens her famed eatery, Chez Panisse, nearby in 1971. That same year the founders of Starbucks, then in the coffee equipment business, come calling and are unselfishly trained by the "grandfather of specialty coffee."

1969 Gimme a head with hair: No show epitomized the peace-and-love '60s better than the theatrical/musical phenomenon *Hair*. After a buzz-building off-Broadway debut, the show burst onto the Great White Way in April 1968. Its boundary-breaking nudity, obscene language, treatment of the flag, and pointed anti–Vietnam War rhetoric ignited a firestorm of attention and lawsuits—and big box office. Today, the soundtrack heralding the dawning of the Age of Aquarius hits #1, where it hangs for a hair-raising thirteen weeks—yet it will take another decade before director Milos Forman's film adaptation comes to the big screen.

APRIL
27

1963 Discovered by a family friend while singing at her cousin's wedding, fifteen-year-old Margaret Battavio had always wanted to be a professional singer. Today her wish comes true as she becomes the youngest female singer ever to reach #1, with "I Will Follow Him." By then the diminutive young teen has been renamed Little Peggy March. Her song, preceded by a successful French language version the year before by multi-lingual Petula Clark (see Jan. 23), also tops the charts in Australia, Japan, and other countries. Stuck previously at #2 for five weeks, "I Will Follow Him" finally displaces the Chiffons "He's So Fine" at the top spot. But this week, like any other, little Peggy listens to the countdown on WABC after dinner while doing the dishes.

APRIL
28

1964 Tonight the New York Drama Critics give their top award to the rousing musical *Hello Dolly!*, presaging its record-shattering Tony award night the following month. Starring Carol Channing (in a role originally intended for Ethel Merman or Mary Martin), the show wows critics and audiences alike and sweeps ten Tony awards (a record that stands for thirty-seven years until *The Producers* wins twelve in 2001). The play's young lyricist, Jerry Herman, credits Channing with his breakthrough success. During a pre-Broadway tryout he woke the star to ask if she'd listen to a new song—"Before the Parade Passes By"—he'd just composed. And she did. "I can't think of too many stars," says Herman, "who would be so supportive of their composer-lyricist at three a.m." The show becomes a true multi-media sensation: Louis Armstrong's recording of the title song—which he later sings in the 1969 film version starring Barbra Streisand—gives him the only #1 hit of his career.

APRIL 29

1961

A young sports producer takes a flyer, jetting around the globe to sign options on everything from British golf to Russian track meets. The chances of these little-covered sports even making it on air are slim. The network can't even line up a sponsor until the eleventh hour, when tobacco giant R. J. Reynolds finally signs on—primarily to secure its presence in the college football lineup beginning that fall. So begins ABC's *Wide World of Sports*, the omnibus program that its young producer, Roone Arledge, quickly turns from a fill-in summer series into a blockbuster franchise. It not only launches Arledge's career but also gives Americans a national catchphrase: "The thrill of victory… and the agony of defeat."

APRIL 30

1966

Over the years, California has produced many talented vocalists, but it's safe to say that Elva Miller is not one of them. Nevertheless the fifty-nine-year-old singer, who goes by the proper moniker "Mrs. Miller," captivates television audiences with her off-pitch, off-tempo operatic style on shows like *The Tonight Show Starring Johnny Carson*, *The Ed Sullivan Show*, and *The Hollywood Palace*. Beating the odds, her single—featuring excruciating versions of Petula Clark's "Downtown" and the Toys' "A Lover's Concerto"—enters the charts today. With a straight face her label Capitol promotes her "new sound," and her debut album—slyly entitled "Mrs. Miller's Greatest Hits"—sells an astounding quarter million copies in less than a month. Mrs. Miller's novelty career quickly wanes, but not before she accompanies Bob Hope on a tour of Vietnam, where she sings to (at?) the soldiers.

MAY

MAY 1

1960 "Rock 'n' roll is fading," claims swinging singer but poor prognosticator Peggy Lee in an interview in today's *New York Daily News*. Then again, she has a vested interest in hoping for a return of the jazzier pop standards of the big band era. After making her name in the '40s as lead vocalist in Benny Goodman's swing band, she began a strong solo career with nightclub engagements, radio programs, and star billing on many TV variety shows. In 1958 Lee scored her only Top 10 hit, the sultry "Fever." As the '60s draw to a close, she'll win a Grammy for her last single to make the charts, the ennui-heavy "Is That All There Is?" arranged and conducted by Randy Newman.

MAY 2

1968 Prolific playwright and screenwriter Neil Simon rose to prominence in television's "golden years," writing for '50s classics like Sid Caesar's *Your Show of Shows*. He then made his mark on Broadway with *Barefoot in the Park* and *The Odd Couple,* the latter winning four Tony awards, including best author (Simon) and actor (Walter Matthau). Today Paramount premieres a movie version of *The Odd Couple* with Matthau reprising his messy but lovable sportswriter opposite fussy roommate Jack Lemmon (replacing stage actor Art Carney). The enduring popularity of their opposites-attract personae later begets yet another hit incarnation, a '70s ABC sitcom—returning to Simon's TV roots—starring Jack Klugman and Tony Randall.

1962 "I like to be in America, okay by me in America..."—especially when you're on top of the charts in America. Having recently won ten Oscars, *West Side Story* delivers a soundtrack that today takes center stage. It'll spend a phenomenal fifty-four weeks at #1, the longest stay ever at the top spot on the album charts. The music and lyrics by Leonard Bernstein and Stephen Sondheim, respectively, also inspire hits for other artists: Ferrante & Teicher's arrangement of "Tonight," Johnny Mathis's "Maria," and Len ("1-2-3") Barry's "Somewhere."

MAY
5

1961 In the race to space, the USSR scored first when cosmonaut Yuri Gagarin orbited the earth last month. The news dismayed the American public, which tunes in today in record numbers (thirty million) to watch and applaud the splashdown of astronaut Alan Shepard, the first American in space. Celebrated as a hero for his Mercury mission aboard the *Freedom 7*, Shepard soon headlines ticker-tape parades in New York, Washington, DC, and Los Angeles. A few weeks later, President Kennedy tells a special joint session of Congress, "I believe that this nation should commit itself to achieving the goal, before this decade is out, of landing a man on the moon and returning him safely to Earth." The Apollo 11 mission in July 1969, six and a half years after JFK's assassination, does just that—with astronaut Neil Armstrong uttering one of history's most famous lines as he touches the moon's surface: "That's one small step for man, one giant leap for mankind."

MAY
4

1968 At the ninety-fourth Kentucky Derby, Dancer's Image dances across the finish line, one-and-a-half lengths ahead of Forward Pass. It's not a record time, but three days later a record of sorts is set—a rather unenviable one. Dancer's Image is disqualified after traces of a pain killer, phenylbutazone, are discovered in a post-race urine sample. While the drug is legal at some racetracks, Churchill Downs isn't one of them—though it later allows it. The Kentucky Racing Commission eventually rules that the win and top prize money must go to Forward Pass, a decision that the *New York Times* calls the "most controversial decision in all of Triple Crown racing."

MAY
6

1960 Many had tried, some had died. All had failed. The legendary 26,795-foot Mt. Dhaulagiri—Sanskrit for "white mountain"—in the Himalayas remained as mountaineering's ultimate goal, the highest unclimbed mountain in the world. Until today, when a sixteen-member international team reaches the top. It's led by intrepid Swiss climber Max Eiselin, who ran a small retail mountaineering-supply business, and began his career selling IBM typewriters. To finance the expedition, he offered investors postcards to be mailed from Nepal with the signatures of all the team's members. It's the first expedition to include a plane to ferry in supplies, though it crashes and delays the team's ascent.

"The Alpine-trained Swiss topped the icy dome-like peak of the mountain after inching up sheer rock walls that look like the pillars of an ancient temple."

—**Associated Press**

MAY
7
1966

Until now there have been successful groups consisting of guys, of girls, of guys with one girl, and girls with one guy. Today the equal-opportunity harmonizers the Mamas & the Papas change all that as their smooth "Monday, Monday" tops the charts. Coming on the heels of their breakout hit, "California Dreamin'," the quartet (formed in New York, actually) enjoys an enchanting, easy-listening run. Several singles have autobiographical roots: "Creeque Alley" celebrates the group's time in the Virgin Islands, while "I Saw Her Again" recounts member Denny Doherty's affair with Michelle Phillips, wife of the band's erstwhile leader and prime composer, John Phillips. The fourth member, big Mama Cass Elliot, later enjoys a top-shelf solo career with nightclub and TV appearances and sweet singles like "Dream a Little Dream of Me" and "Make Your Own Kind of Music." She dies of a heart attack in London in 1974.

MAY 8

1962

Ancient Rome resurfaces in modern-day New York as *A Funny Thing Happened on the Way to the Forum* opens on Broadway to rave reviews. The bawdy, classical farce stars Zero Mostel as Pseudolus, the lead role previously offered to Phil Silvers and Milton Berle. Mostel's bravura turn nets him the Tony award for Best Actor (one of six for the show, including Best Musical, Director, and Producer), presaging similar honors for the leads in the next two Broadway revivals (Silvers in 1972, Nathan Lane in 2006). Stephen Sondheim provides the music, prompting one of his mentors, the legendary Oscar Hammerstein, to later comment, tongue in cheek: "Steve won't really be a member of the working theatre until he has a flop." A United Artists film version of *Forum*, also starring Mostel, opens four years later.

MEANWHILE...

WASTE NOT, WANT MORE

WWII veteran Newton Minow, who'd become an attorney and clerked for a Supreme Court justice, was a somewhat surprising choice by President Kennedy to become Chairman of the FCC. His place in history was assured on May 9, 1961, when he addressed the National Association of Broadcasters (NAB) confab. He lambasted the assembled TV execs in what would become known as the "vast wasteland" speech, decrying their offerings across the board from adult programming to shows for children. "You must provide a wider range of choices, more diversity, more alternatives," said Minow. "It is not enough to cater to the nation's whims—you must also serve the nation's needs." Many feel his words still ring true nearly a half-century later.

MAY 9

1960

In its attempts to get Enovid approved as an oral contraceptive, manufacturer G.D. Searle had run the most extensive drug trials in history. Despite finding virtually no major side effects, the FDA sat on the application due to moralistic, heavily religious opposition to birth control. Incensed by the delays and allegations that the drug could cause cancer, a devout Roman Catholic and eminent physician, seventy-year-old John Rock, confronted the FDA. "Young man," he said to an inexperienced administrator, "I don't know how much training you've had in treating women with cancer, but I have been treating patients my entire life, and you have no idea how wrong you are." Today the FDA approves the sale of the controversial drug, and in five years more than five million women are taking it. Enovid's acceptance and effectiveness are so great that it's now simply referred to as "the pill."

MAY
10

1969 The running joke around Washington, DC, is that President Nixon's eldest daughter, Tricia, must use vanishing cream. "When you don't read about me in the newspapers," she says, "you know I'm having a good time." Tonight the blonde twenty-three-year-old bucks her reputation for privacy by spreading her social-butterfly wings, hosting 400 select guests to a black-tie masked ball at the White House. The Turtles and the Temptations provide hip musical entertainment, and an urban legend quickly sprouts about the Turtles snorting cocaine off Abe Lincoln's desk.

MAY
11

1968 Short, catchy tunes rule the charts, with conventional wisdom suggesting that a seven-minute number could never become a hit. That thinking ends today as rugged Irish movie star Richard Harris (*Camelot, Mutiny on the Bounty*) releases Jimmy Webb's ode to lost love, "MacArthur Park." The song, in three distinct parts, captures the public's imagination, especially with its odd metaphor "someone left the cake out in the rain." Versatile songwriter Webb, known for tunes like "By the Time I Get to Phoenix" (Glen Campbell) and "Up, Up and Away" (The 5th Dimension), is irked by Harris's constant mispronunciation in adding an "s" to the end of "MacArthur"—but the song climbs to #2. Donna Summer not only gets the pronunciation right but also the #1 spot with her disco-fied 1978 version.

MAY 12

1963 Tonight TV's savviest showman snags the most talked-about singer/songwriter in the country, Bob Dylan. Most singers would kill for the chance to appear on *The Ed Sullivan Show*, but Bob's not most singers. After an afternoon dress rehearsal, network censors inform him he won't be allowed to play his protest song "Talkin' John Birch Paranoid Blues," despite the prior approval of both Ed and his producers. So Dylan walks. Ironically, the harmonizing Chad Mitchell Trio sang their version of the Dylan song the night before on ABC's *Hootenanny* with nary a complaint. Apparently their audience of college students at the University of Virginia is more open-minded than the CBS suits.

MAY 13

1967 The Supremes' tenth #1 hit, "The Happening," is notable for several reasons. It's the only Supremes recording featured in a motion picture, a lighthearted caper film of the same name, starring Anthony Quinn and Faye Dunaway (in her first leading role). It's the last of the group's chart-toppers written and produced by the powerhouse Motown team of Holland-Dozier-Holland. It's also the last Supremes song featuring original member Florence Ballard. And, finally, it's the last single credited to "The Supremes" during Diana Ross's tenure. From this point on, the group becomes known as "Diana Ross and the Supremes" until Miss Ross departs several years later for a solo career.

TELEPHONE

MAY 14

1965

Long before Joan Rivers started delivering her trademark phrase—"Can we talk?"—gals are doing just that on a dishy syndicated talk show, *Girl Talk,* which *Time* magazine calls "the brightest female panel discussion in television." Hosted by bouffant-haired Virginia Graham, a former reporter and soap opera writer, the show attracts a bevy of top talent, including tonight's guest, Joan Crawford, as well as previous guests Pearl Buck, Bette Davis, and Joan Fontaine. Exchanges can get downright catty, as when a society columnist says Zsa Zsa Gabor "has an age complex, and she has a right to one. Wasn't she Miss Chicken Paprika of 1910?" Watching her guests pacing before one show, Graham tells her producer, "They're smelling each other like three bitches at the Westminster dog show."

MAY 15

1965

Combining folk and rock with a jingle-jangle sound, the Byrds release their first single, a version of Bob Dylan's "Mr. Tambourine Man." The inventive tune soars to the top of the charts, the first #1 rock record for Columbia Records, a bit tardy to embrace the rock revolution. Produced by Terry Melcher, son of singer Doris Day, it features the vocals and twelve-string guitar work

of Jim (later Roger) McGuinn—but none of the other band members. Pressed for time, Melcher tapped some ace studio session players, including Leon Russell and Glen Campbell. Thereafter, the Byrds do play on all their hits, like the follow-up #1, "Turn! Turn! Turn!" Ever the artistic innovators, their future material includes "Eight Miles High" (mistakenly construed as a drug paean, but actually referring to their first flight to England) and the satirical "So You Want to Be a Rock 'N' Roll Star." Their nascent folk/rock sound later spawns supergroups like the Eagles and Crosby, Stills, and Nash.

THEY'RE PLAYING OUR SONG

Songwriter Burt Bacharach's best-known tunes to date had been about love gone wrong ("Walk on By," "Always Something There to Remind Me"). But on May 15, 1965, Burt married actress Angie Dickinson (whose legs, in a publicity stunt by Universal, were insured by Lloyds of London for $1 million). Here are some other notable celebrity marriages (some of them short-lived) in the '60s.

- Sandra Dee and Bobby Darin (1960)
- May Britt and Sammy Davis, Jr. (1960)
- Colleen Dewhurst and George C. Scott (1960)
- Joan Plowright and Laurence Olivier (1961)
- Lucille Ball and Gary Morton (1961)
- Lauren Bacall and Jason Robards, Jr. (1961)
- Joan Collins and Anthony Newley (1963)
- Judy Carne and Burt Reynolds (1963)
- Elizabeth Taylor and Richard Burton (1964)
- Britt Ekland and Peter Sellers (1964)
- Ethel Merman and Ernest Borgnine (1964)
- Suzanne Pleshette and Troy Donahue (1964)
- Mia Farrow and Frank Sinatra (1966)
- Liza Minnelli and Peter Allen (1967)
- Sharon Tate and Roman Polanski (right) (1968)
- Jill Ireland and Charles Bronson (1969)

MAY 16

1960 Unlike some inventors, he doesn't become a household name—but his discovery today produces extraordinarily profound effects on mankind. At the Hughes Research Laboratories in Malibu, California, physicist Theodore Maiman demonstrates the first light amplification by stimulated emission of radiation, i.e., the laser. Few at the time take notice or envision its vast potential. "A laser is a solution seeking a problem," says Maiman. Lasers go on to play crucial roles in communications, industry, medicine, and countless other fields. The amplified waves of atoms shoot out as narrow, intense beams of light, accomplishing countless tasks: reading CDs and bar codes, guiding missiles, removing ulcers, fabricating steel, and calibrating the distance from the earth to the moon, to name just a few of the many thousands of others.

MAY 17

1968 Savvy San Francisco impresario Bill Graham has a keen eye for talent, and the city's burgeoning psychedelic scene offers plenty. Tonight at the famed Avalon Ballroom he's blown away by the Santana Blues Band, whom he quickly signs on to manage. Soon they're regulars at his new club, the Fillmore West, a hall that matches his New York venue, the Fillmore East. Featuring a who's who of the era's top rockers, from the Allman Brothers to Neil Young, his eclectic bills also mix in blues, folk, jazz, and psychedelic acts. "The use and the abuse of power," says Graham, "that's what rock 'n' roll is—the use and the abuse of power!" A Holocaust survivor, he carves out a unique place in rock history before dying in a helicopter crash in 1991 after attending a Huey Lewis & the News concert.

MAY 18

1968 With his inimitable falsetto and unforgettable look, Tiny Tim hits the charts today with his version of a 1929 #1 hit, "Tip-Toe Thru the Tulips With Me." The unusual, gangly fellow had performed the song, complete with ukulele, on *Rowan & Martin's Laugh-In* earlier in the year. But contrary to popular belief, that wasn't his debut television appearance. Last year, Tiny acted and sang on the pilot episode of NBC's detective drama *Ironside,* starring Raymond Burr. Yet neither of these is his most famous television appearance. That comes on December 17, 1969, when he weds his young bride "Miss Vicki" on *The Tonight Show Starring Johnny Carson*, an episode that draws worldwide attention.

> **"I'd love to see Christ come back to crush the spirit of hate and make men put down their guns. I'd also like just one more hit single."**
>
> —Tiny Tim

MAY
19

1968 At the height of the Cold War, the world is enamored with the adventures of secret agents. The suave fictional creation of British author Ian Fleming, James Bond, debuted in *Casino Royale* (1953), followed by a string of successful, saucy novels. They sold en masse, with teenage boys especially enjoying the naughty 007 escapades. But when Sean Connery kicked off the movie franchise with *Dr. No* (1962), popularity soared. Hollywood capitalized with wry James Coburn as *Our Man Flynt* and tongue-in-cheek Dean Martin as Matt Helm (*The Silencers*). American television networks leapt in, too, turning out a spate of spy shows that tonight sweep many Emmys: Best Drama (*Mission: Impossible*) and Comedy (*Get Smart*); Lead Actor (Bill Cosby in *I Spy*) and Actress (Barbara Bain in *M:I*) in a Drama; and Lead Actor in a Comedy (Don Adams in *Get Smart*).

MAY 20

1967 The Young Rascals topped the charts last year with a remake of the Olympics' "Good Lovin'," but the blue-eyed soul singers were eager to flex their songwriting skills. Today they hit #1 again with the mellow "Groovin'," which dovetails nicely with the favorite hippie catchword, "groovy." The song's inspiration is a happy byproduct of co-writer/lead singer Felix Cavaliere's latest romance, which produces a fertile font of hits like "I've Been Lonely Too Long," "A Girl Like You," and "How Can I Be Sure." Soon thereafter the group realizes it's getting older and drops the adjective, becoming simply the Rascals. Deeply affected by the assassinations of Martin Luther King, Jr., and Robert Kennedy, Cavaliere co-writes their last #1, "People Got to Be Free."

MAY 21

1967 Cheeky, dashing English crime-fighter Simon Templar (a.k.a. *The Saint*) makes his NBC debut tonight. Created by author Leslie Charteris in the late 1920s, the character had enjoyed a long run in various British and American radio and television incarnations. This new version stars Roger Moore as a modern-day Robin Hood operating on both sides of the law, dispensing a unique brand of retribution against evildoers. Though Moore tires of the part and moves on to other TV and film projects, he later re-adopts a similar persona when assuming the showcase role of James Bond—much to the chagrin of Sean Connery purists—in *Live and Let Die* (1973), going on to star in seven 007 flicks.

> **❝I enjoy being a highly overpaid actor.❞**
> —Roger Moore

MAY 22

1964 Jamaican Millie Small, daughter of a poor sugar plantation worker, became a recording star on her native island in the early '60s. Budding music impresario Chris Blackwell, born in England but raised in Jamaica, believes its catchy ska sound will be the next rage. So he takes fifteen-year-old Millie back to England and records her bubbly, infectious "My Boy Lollipop." Released today, the chirpy hit zooms to #2 on the US charts. "There hasn't been a voice like it since Shirley Temple," exclaims the *Daily Express*. Unconfirmed reports speculate that a young Rod Stewart plays harmonica on the recording. Regardless, it opens the door for more lilting island sounds to come, most notably Johnny Nash's "Hold Me Tight" and Desmond Dekker and the Aces' no-holds-barred Jamaican-reggae "Israelites." Blackwell later discovers Bob Marley and introduces the reggae superstar and his matchless (yet pungent) music to the world.

MAY 23

1969 Runnin' wild in the streets, student strikes in Paris last year spread nationwide, triggering riots and a workers' strike that paralyzed France. The socio-political strife even forced the cancellation—championed by New Wave filmmakers François Truffaut and Jean-Luc Godard—of the famed Cannes Film Festival. Two months before the riots, iconoclastic director Lindsay Anderson started shooting *If…*, a provocative tale of a nonconformist schoolboy (Malcolm McDowell, in a mesmerizing performance three years before *A Clockwork Orange*) who leads a rebellion at a proper, private English boarding school. Tonight *If…* echoes the turbulence of the previous year by winning the French festival's coveted Palme d'Or, despite attempts by the British ambassador to France to have the film withdrawn as "an insult to the nation."

MAY 24

1969 It's not unusual to throw your underwear at someone—not after tonight, at least, as strapping Welsh sex symbol Tom Jones performs his Vegas-style show at NYC's Copacabana. A woman in the audience tosses her panties on stage and starts a trademark career ritual. Mass hysteria, it appears, extends beyond rock concerts and soccer matches. "My wife doesn't care about the women throwing underwear—as long as I come home," says Jones, a mainstay on the pop charts since his 1965 debut #1 UK single "It's Not Unusual." He continues to score on both sides of the Atlantic with hit records ("What's New Pussycat?," "Green, Green Grass of Home"), TV and nightclub appearances, and an expanding array of women's lingerie—plus, he adds, "at the end of the night, I always find a couple of pairs of Jockeys from the men."

MAY
25

1969 What a difference a role makes. After shooting to fame as a clean-cut boy toy in *The Graduate,* Dustin Hoffman takes his sweet time—almost two years—before veering 180° to portray scraggly, street-smart Enrico "Ratso" Rizzo in *Midnight Cowboy.* He cons and then befriends Jon Voight, the new stud in town and in the making. Together this odd couple negotiates the gritty streets of New York, or as Rizzo tells a reckless cabbie while crossing the street: "I'm *walkin'* here!" Released today, it becomes the first (and only) X-rated movie to win the Oscar— another sharp reversal since 1968's winner, *Oliver!,* was the only G-rated film to win that honor. Hoffman's savvy choice of roles makes him a leading man, a far cry from the days when he split his time between acting lessons and working at restaurants, a morgue, and Macy's.

MAY 26

1969

A degreed doctor from Harvard, Michael Crichton had written several previous works of fiction under pseudonyms. Today, he sees the publication of his medical techno-thriller *The Andromeda Strain*, about a fatal disease of extraterrestrial origin. The book becomes an instant bestseller. "Crichton's narrative line is so strong, and his resources for sustaining it are so abundant," writes a reviewer in the *New York Times*, "that *The Andromeda Strain* can't miss popular success." That quote aptly describes the writer's whole career. The book quickly spawns a feature film, and Crichton goes on to become a household name with books like *Jurassic Park* and *Rising Sun*, as well as screenplays and a little TV series that he creates and co-produces—called *ER*.

MAY 27

1961

Quick to recognize the power and influence of television, handsome movie star Ronald Reagan made a smart career move to the small screen in the early '50s. He became the host and sometime star of *General Electric Theater*, an early and long-running drama anthology series—and today he graces the cover of *TV Guide*. The show not only makes him wealthy but affords him extraordinary visibility. As General Electric's spokesman, Reagan visits more than 100 GE plants and addresses hundreds of thousands of employees. Repeating the company's slogan—"Progress is our most important product"—he hones his communications and speechwriting skills. They come in handy, for the Democrat-turned-Republican has larger ambitions. He slides smoothly from entertainment to politics, winning the governorship of California five years later. The White House looms.

TRENDSETTER

A DISPOSABLE WARDROBE

What was supposed to be a promotional gimmick turned into a bona fide trend when the Scott Paper Company introduced disposable paper dresses. The $1.25 sleeveless frocks—made from 93 percent paper-napkin stock and 7 percent nylon weave—were sold in grocery stores in spring 1966 to promote Scott's new colored tissues. But after a half a million were sold, other manufacturers joined the paper chase. Sponsors like Baby Ruth and Mastercharge (forerunner to Mastercard) emblazoned their logos on paper garb; Air India even made a paper sari. Silver foil dresses were manufactured to echo the popular space-age look of *Star Trek* and *Lost in Space*. Department stores like Abraham & Strauss and Stern Brothers opened boutiques featuring paper jackets, paper evening gowns (left), paper bell-bottomed jumpsuits—even paper swim trunks. So great was the frenzy that when "Yellow Pages" dresses for a dollar were advertised in a May 1968 issue of *Parade* magazine, 80,000 orders were received in one week. The fad faded the next year just as fast as it came, owing to a combination of increased environmental awareness and a sad realization: paper clothes really aren't that comfortable.

MAY 28

1963 Today Paul Newman solidifies his leading man status when *Hud*, one in a string of "H"-titled Newman movies (*The Hustler, Hombre, Harper*) is released. His portrayal of a loutish modern-day cowboy ("the man with the barbed-wire soul," screams the poster) wins him his third Oscar nomination for Best Actor, but the third time's not a charm either. Though the film wins three trophies, including Best Actress (Patricia Neal) and Supporting Actor (Melvyn Douglas), Newman doesn't take home an award. It'll take another four nominations and nearly a quarter century before he snags an Oscar for Martin Scorsese's *The Color of Money*, reprising the role of pool-hall shark "Fast Eddie" Felson that he initially played in *The Hustler*.

MAY 29

1966 Known for his bestselling novel *Native Son*, pioneering author Richard Wright wrote a book in 1954 entitled *Black Power*. But that influential term doesn't come into widespread use until today, when US Representative Adam Clayton Powell invokes it during a speech at Howard University. Coinciding with the rise of the civil rights movement, *black power* soon becomes a recognizable social and political slogan representing black pride and socioeconomic independence. "The only way we're going to stop them white men from whuppin' us is to take over," says civil rights proponent Stokely Carmichael at a protest rally next year. "What we're going to start saying now is 'Black Power!'"

MAY 30

"If everything seems under control, you're just not going fast enough."
— Mario Andretti

1969 One of America's most celebrated racecar drivers wins one of America's most celebrated races—the Indianapolis 500—for the first time. Mario Andretti, along with his twin brother, Aldo, had emigrated from Italy in 1955 and honed his driving skills while working in his uncle's garage. He sped to success early on, winning Rookie of the Year at his first Indy 500 in 1965 and winning the Daytona 500 two years later. After back-to-back second-place finishes at Indy, he takes top honors today with a course record 156.867 miles per hour in his STP Oil Treatment Special. Andretti drives on to achieve long-term success, becoming the only person to be named Driver of the Year in three successive decades: the '60s, '70s, and '80s.

MAY
31

1969 John Lennon and Yoko Ono have been in bed for almost a week when their war protest/performance art again captivates the world. For a follow-up to their well-received Holland honeymoon "bed-in" two months earlier, the couple chose Montreal, which was actually their *third* choice. John found the Bahamas too hot for a week in bed, and New York was nixed after US authorities refused entry because of his previous marijuana bust (see Oct. 19). So the happy-go-plucky couple flew north and checked into a corner suite at Montreal's Queen Elizabeth Hotel. Tonight they set the recorders going for an impromptu group performance of the anthem "Give Peace a Chance." The popular spoof that later emerges goes, "All we are saying, is pull down your pants."

1

1968 "And aah-way-ay we go!" Beginning as a summer replacement for *The Jackie Gleason Show*, the enigmatic *The Prisoner*, starring suave Patrick McGoohan, debuts on CBS. Part Kafka and part Lewis Carroll, the surrealistic series takes place in a pastoral British seaside resort, "The Village." Referred to only as "Number 6," the retired secret agent has secrets his shadowy captors want revealed. Why did he resign? Who are his fellow prisoners? Can he escape? Questions abound, but not answers. McGoohan also co-creates the series and writes and directs some episodes. An instant cult classic, *The Prisoner* is endlessly debated by hardcore fans, many of whom believe that the lead character is John Drake, his previous role in his earlier British spy series *Secret Agent*. McGoohan, characteristically elusive, denies any link.

JUNE 2

1964 America is shocked—shocked!—when *Look* magazine publishes today the first photo of designer Rudi Gernreich's topless swimsuit (shot tastefully from behind). The real furor erupts several weeks later when a nineteen-year-old model, sporting one on a Chicago beach, is promptly arrested. Her indecent exposure case makes national news, prompting a *Life* magazine story that includes a photograph of Gernreich's favorite model, Peggy Moffett, wearing the suit while strategically crisscrossing her arms. "This is a family magazine," says an employee, "and naked breasts are only allowed if the woman is an aborigine." The topless craze largely bypasses America but not Europe, where *Playboy* shoots a racy 1965 spread at the Riviera. It spotlights buxom gals who "take eye-filling advantage of a recent French court decision allowing topless beach attire."

JUNE 3

1968 Late on a quiet Monday afternoon, after browsing at Bloomingdale's, artist Andy Warhol arrives back at his Union Square headquarters ("the Factory"). Waiting outside is a slight ex-prostitute and extreme feminist named Valerie Solanas. A fringe player in Warhol's avant-garde world, she'd done a scene in one of his movies and was anxious for him to produce her own pornographic script. When they exit the elevator on his floor, she pulls out a .32 automatic and fires three times. Pouring blood, Warhol collapses. Solanas also wounds a visiting art critic before departing, as the Factory erupts in panic. Warhol is rushed to the hospital, where he is declared clinically dead. Doctors cut open his chest, massage his heart, and perform a five-hour operation that saves his life. For the rest of his life, Warhol suffers from his wounds and fears that Solanas will return. "I am a flower child," she says upon turning herself in later that day. "He had too much control over my life." Solanas receives a three-year sentence and later pens a screed called *The SCUM Manifesto*—the Society for Cutting Up Men, that is.

> **Before I was shot, I always thought that I was more half-there than all-there. I always suspected that I was watching TV instead of living life. Right when I was being shot and ever since, I knew that I was watching television.**
>
> —**Andy Warhol**

JUNE
4

1966 For Tommy James & the Shondells, it all begins with a little "Hanky Panky." Actually it began three years earlier when the band recorded the bubblegum tune for a small local label in Michigan. The tune didn't catch on, but two years later a Pittsburgh deejay discovered and started playing a copy. "Hanky Panky" gets its nationwide release today and later hits the coveted #1 spot. Its veteran writers Jeff Barry and Ellie Greenwich ("Leader of the Pack," "Chapel of Love"), who'd written it as a throwaway B tune, are floored. "I was kind of ashamed when it first came out," says Barry, "but then I found out what a big hit it was. Maybe it had something I just didn't see." Tommy quickly re-forms the Shondells (the original members had gotten on with their lives) and racks up a slew of hits like "I Think We're Alone Now," "Mony Mony," "Crimson and Clover," and "Crystal Blue Persuasion."

BRITISH INVASION IN REVERSE

While the Beatles-led British Invasion was catapulting the overseas careers of many UK acts, some Americans also quietly ventured to England. Paul Simon, who was having little commercial success stateside, played and recorded in London in 1965 until the hit "The Sounds of Silence" brought him home (see March 10). James Taylor, who had moved overseas to help kick a heroin addiction, recorded his first album for Apple in 1968. More established solo artists like Roy Orbison and Del Shannon embarked on major tours of England, too, as did many Motown acts in a 1965 group tour—but to little acclaim. "Because of the poor reception given to Tamla Motown artists in Leeds recently," wrote one newspaper, "we are forced to the following conclusion—that the English audiences are either stone deaf or cabbages in disguise." On June 4, 1967, by contrast, a crowd was alive and rockin' at London's Saville Theater for the headliner, guitar virtuoso Jimi Hendrix, who attracted an audience studded with leading British rockers like George Harrison and Paul McCartney. Hendrix opened with an audacious cover of their brand new "Sgt. Pepper's Lonely Hearts Club Band"—and brought down the house.

JUNE 5

1967 England, Sweden, Italy, and even the Soviet Union have professional organizations to promote film. Today the US belatedly enters the arena with the formation of the American Film Institute (AFI). "[It's] a fresh and brave attempt to bring distinction to what has long been taken for granted in this country, the movie," says reporter Bob Thomas of the private nonprofit corporation funded initially by the National Endowment for the Arts, the Motion Picture Association of America, and the Ford Foundation. Its inaugural director, George Stevens, Jr., takes the position only after receiving guarantees that the government won't intervene in its activities to train filmmakers and preserve America's vanishing film heritage. "The AFI," says Stevens, "is the result of an exploding and increasingly sophisticated audience demand for fine cinema, and the hard core of that audience is students."

JUNE

6

1960 Rockabilly artist Roy Orbison had been only marginally successful as a singer, with one minor hit, "Ooby Dooby," in 1956. As a songwriter, though, he'd gotten the Everly Brothers to record his "Claudette," named after his wife. When he brings the popular duo ("All I Have to Do Is Dream") his latest composition, Don and Phil Everly suggest he cut the song himself. Good advice: "Only the Lonely," released today, rockets to #2 in the US and #1 in England, instantly establishing "The Big O" as an international star. His phenomenal vocal range backbones a string of hits like "Running Scared," "Crying," and "Oh, Pretty Woman" that one writer dubs "three-minute operas." Wearing his soon-to-be-trademark sunglasses, Orbison tours England in 1963 with a fast-rising opening act that soon replaces him as the headliner: The Beatles.

JUNE 7

1963 Not only does President Kennedy have many high-profile friends in Hollywood, he now has a project there. Today he sells the TV rights to his Pulitzer Prize–winning book, *Profiles in Courage*, which NBC later turns into a 26-episode anthology series. JFK donates his royalties—estimated to run around $350,000—to charity. Later this month he gets some big screen exposure, too, as Warner Bros.' *PT 109* opens. The film, about his experiences as a torpedo boat commander in the South Pacific during World War II, features stalwart Cliff Robertson in the lead—a role he reportedly won with the president's approval. Yet JFK's administration is most often associated with *Camelot*, the musical retelling of the legend of King Arthur and the Knights of the Round Table. Before his inauguration, he and Jackie attended a performance of the lavish production featuring Richard Burton, Julie Andrews, and Robert Goulet. This last performer was making his Broadway debut with *Camelot*, delivering what will become his signature song: "If Ever I Would Leave You."

JUNE 8

1962 Something's got to give—and today it does, quite literally, when 20th Century Fox fires Marilyn Monroe from its troubled romantic comedy *Something's Got to Give.* Her erratic behavior had enraged director George Cukor, who was forced to work around her frequent no-shows by filming scenes with co-stars Dean Martin and Cyd Charisse. Last week Monroe had departed for a previously scheduled appearance at a Madison Square Garden birthday party for JFK, an absence that rankled the producers even more. They hire Lee Remick to replace her, but Deano, who has leading lady approval, insists: "No Marilyn, no picture." Begrudgingly, they rehire Monroe and fire Cukor at Marilyn's insistence. Her death two months later, however, marks the end of this misbegotten project.

JUNE 9

1969 The day after drug-addled, addicted Brian Jones quits the Rolling Stones, the band announces his replacement: little-known guitarist Mick Taylor from the John Mayall Group. "I no longer see eye-to-eye with the discs we are cutting," says Jones, a superb musician and founding creative force of the band. He was also a quintessential bad boy, living largely and recklessly. A raging controversy over his departure ends abruptly and sadly when he's found dead in his country estate's swimming pool on July 3. The coroner rules it an accidental drowning while under the influence of drugs and alcohol. Two days later the band dedicates a free concert to him before 250,000 fans at London's Hyde Park. Mick Jagger recites Shelley's *Adonais*, and 3,000 butterflies are released. "I hope he is finding peace," says Jagger.

JUNE 10

1966 Fashion designer Mary Quant is today awarded an OBE (Order of the British Empire) for putting England on the international fashion map. Whether or not she actually invented it is open to debate, but no designer is more associated with popularizing the mini-skirt ("the gymslip of permissive society"). From her Chelsea boutique, Bazaar, Mary becomes famous and synonymous with hip "Swinging London" (see April 15) fashions of the day. Quant uses simple shapes to make bold statements, later pioneering the micro-mini, paint-box makeup, shiny plastic raincoats, and—*ta-da*—hot pants! "Good taste is death," says Quant. "Vulgarity is life." For the award ceremony, she turns up in (what else?) a mini-skirt and cutaway gloves.

Twenty years ago, John Wayne netted his first Oscar nomination for *Sands of Iwo Jima* but lost to Broderick Crawford (*All the King's Men*). Today Paramount releases *True Grit*, with sixty-two-year-old Wayne portraying over-the-hill, one-eyed marshal Rooster Cogburn amidst a solid supporting cast, including Glen Campbell, Robert Duvall, and Dennis Hopper. One of the Duke's finest hours, *True Grit* finally delivers the gruff but beloved Hollywood star his only Oscar for Best Actor. "If I'd known this," he says in accepting the award, "I'd have put that eye-patch on forty years ago."

1968 What should be the happiest of times descends into a terrifying nightmare for a young expectant couple (Mia Farrow and John Cassavetes). Based on Ira Levin's bestselling novel, director Roman Polanski's *Rosemary's Baby* opens today, blurring fantasy and reality as Rosemary's pregnancy turns ambiguous, alienating—and much, much worse. Can the spawn of Satan be upon us? Lesser imitations of the film soon abound, but the original smokes like a witches' cauldron. Off-screen, Polanski must deal with his lead actress's fragile mental state as her marriage to Frank Sinatra is collapsing. Next year, the director's life acquires an even darker edge with the murder of his pregnant wife, Sharon Tate, by the crazed Manson family.

JUNE 13

1964 Following an elephant act named Bertha & Tina, the Rolling Stones—on their first American tour—make their national US television debut on the variety series *The Hollywood Palace*. Their taped performance of "I Just Want to Make Love to You" draws ridicule from guest host Dean Martin with inanities like "They're challenging the Beatles to a hair-pulling contest." The crooner's ill manners are matched by the producers' ignorance. During rehearsals, the stage manager sees the Stones' scruffy attire and assumes they can't afford the suits or tuxedos customarily worn by the show's performers. So he offers to provide free, sharp outfits—white cable-knit sweaters, white trousers, shoes and socks—that the boys can keep when the show's over! Their manager, Andrew Loog Oldham, refuses this kind, but clueless, offer.

JUNE 14

1967 Little Scottish singer Lulu has made quite the name for herself in the UK. Her cover of the Isley Brothers' "Shout" so impressed the Beatles that they mistook her for a black American singer. Now she tours England, co-stars in a BBC series, and becomes the first British female singer to perform behind the Iron Curtain when she plays in Poland with the Hollies. Her star finally ascends stateside today with the opening of *To Sir, With Love*, featuring Sidney Poitier as a neophyte teacher trying to control his cantankerous charges. Lulu not only sings the title track, which later jumps to #1,

but acts in a role that began quite small but grew larger after producer/director/co-writer James Clavell liked what he saw. So does Maurice Gibb of the Bee Gees, who marries Lulu two years later. Though the marriage doesn't last, her career does. She goes on to star in several TV series, record numerous songs—including the theme for Roger Moore's 007 adventure *The Man With the Golden Gun*—and co-write "I Don't Wanna Fight," a '90s Top 10 hit for Tina Turner.

JUNE 15

1960 Film director Billy Wilder delivers a withering attack on the Establishment today in the unlikely form of a mild-mannered insurance clerk (Jack Lemmon). Jack's just a minor cog in the business machine, but a major enabler of business "machinations"—since he's willing to lend higher-ups the keys to his apartment for their private romantic trysts. *The Apartment* co-stars Shirley MacLaine as his secret love interest, an elevator operator who's currently the paramour of his loathsome boss (Fred McMurray). A box-office and critical winner, the film takes five Oscars, including Best Picture, the last black-and-white film to win that honor. "It would only be proper," says Wilder at the Oscar gala, "to cut [the statue] in half and give it to the two most valuable players—Jack Lemmon and Shirley MacLaine."

JUNE 16

1960 After delivering glossy Technicolor hits like *Vertigo* and *North by Northwest*, Alfred Hitchcock reverts to stark black and white for a taut psychological thriller. Opening today, *Psycho* teems with a potent brew of lust and fear, secrets and deception, innocence and evil. Its brilliantly edited shower scene remains one of the most riveting sequences ever captured on film. While many films don't age well, *Psycho* remains an unrivaled original in a sea of lesser imitators. The Hitchcock chiller is also remembered for bravura performances by Janet Leigh and archetypal mama's boy Anthony Perkins. "Mother—" he says, "what is the phrase?—isn't quite herself today."

JUNE
17

1961 In a Cold War adventure seemingly ripped from the pages of novelist John le Carré, Rudolph Nureyev today dashes to freedom. Closely shadowed by KGB agents while on tour with the Kirov Ballet, the larger-than-life dancer nevertheless seeks political asylum at a French airport. In the West, his star ascends as he transforms the world of ballet forever and becomes the most celebrated male dancer since Nijinsky. His famous teaming with Margot Fonteyn transforms landmark ballets like *Swan Lake* and *Giselle*, and they become close friends. Offstage he's temperamental, impulsive, and promiscuous, with little regard for authority or convention. Nureyev leaps into a jet-set, celebrity lifestyle, but the gifted, openly gay star denies he has AIDS until his death from the disease in 1993 at age fifty-four.

JUNE
18

1962 Small town Mason City, Iowa, home of composer Meredith Willson, hosts the state's biggest parade ever—some 125,000 strong. It's a gala preview of the motion picture *The Music Man*, emceed by Arthur Godfrey and attended by stars Robert Preston, reprising his Tony award-winning Broadway role, and Shirley Jones. The tale of a charming con man features a rousing soundtrack that includes favorites like "76 Trombones," "Trouble," and "Till There Was You," the last being the only show tune ever recorded by the Beatles. One of the year's most successful films, it boosts the career of Preston (the producers originally wanted the more bankable Frank Sinatra in the role) and features comedian Buddy Hackett and a young Ronnie Howard, who goes on to future stardom with *Happy Days* and a notable directorial career. Willson's next musical, *The Unsinkable Molly Brown*, also enjoys a successful Broadway run that begets another popular movie version.

JUNE 19

1965 The British Invasion rolls on with a dynamic double bill, the stateside debut of both the Kinks and the Moody Blues at NYC's Academy of Music. Later this year, the Birmingham-based Moodies open for the Beatles on their final UK tour, and then return to New York for deejay Murray the K's Christmas Show with Peter and Gordon, the McCoys, and more. Led by mercurial Ray Davies, the Kinks score three straight Top 10 US hits—"You Really Got Me," "All Day and All of the Night," and "Tired of Waiting for You"—but this disastrous US tour is best summed up by the Moody Blues' debut US single: "Go Now!" The Kinks battle with promoters, cutting short or canceling gigs. Backstage at a Hollywood Bowl show, Ray gets into a fistfight with an official from the American Federation of Television and Radio Artists. As a result they're unofficially banned from the US for four years, as their applications for visas are routinely denied. When they do finally return in 1969, this book's co-author Solomon catches them at the Boston Tea Party, the famed underground club in the shadow of Fenway Park. Trust me, they rock—and "Lola" brings down the house.

JUNE 20

1967 Claiming that his Muslim faith precludes his entering the armed services, Muhammad Ali refuses to register for the draft. "I ain't got no quarrel with them Viet Cong," he says, instantly becoming a symbol of opposition to the Vietnam War that's beginning to divide the country. Though he'd always been a controversial figure, his stance ignites a firestorm. In quick order the World Boxing Association strips him of his title and the government confiscates his passport. Convicted today of draft evasion, Ali receives a $10,000 fine and five years probation. In 1971 the Supreme Court reverses the decision, paving the way for his world championship comeback with celebrated wins over George Foreman and Joe Frazier.

JUNE 21

1966 While entertainment has moved to color, John Wayne still sees the world in black and white. Today, while visiting US servicemen in Vietnam, a sniper's bullets hit the ground thirty-odd feet from where he's signing autographs. "Hell," says the Duke, "I didn't even know we were being fired at until I saw the marines running for cover." Though the Vietnam War is beginning to polarize the country, Wayne doesn't flinch. He directs and stars in *The Green Berets*, enlisting his son Michael to produce. Released on the fourth of July in 1968, it's an unabashedly anti-communist propaganda piece. The critics hate it, less for its flag-waving than for its recycled clichés and lack of authenticity. Most Hollywood studios avoid the subject altogether. "It's an unpopular war," says one anonymous executive, "and we don't want any part of it."

JUNE 22

1967 British blues rockers The Jeff Beck Group kick off their first US tour with a raucous, crowd-pleasing set at Bill Graham's Fillmore East in New York City. Many think they even outshine the headliners, the Grateful Dead. Robert Shelton of the *New York Times* praises "the interaction of Mr. Beck's wild and visionary guitar against the hoarse and insistent vocals of Rod Stewart, with gutsy backing on drums and bass." Later in the tour Stewart mischievously enjoys deceiving reporters who mistakenly call him "Mr. Beck." Despite the warm reception, their first US album, *Truth*, isn't released for another year, but soon gains a reputation as a seminal rock album.

JUNE 23

1966 After a brief four-week run, Ike and Tina Turner's "River Deep, Mountain High" disappears from the US charts after reaching only a disappointing #88. It's the first song by the duo produced by Phil Spector, who incorporates his legendary "wall of sound" that has backboned hits for the Crystals, the Ronettes, and many more. Spector's devastated by the poor response, though in England it reaches #3 and solidifies their status there as major stars. Still relegated to the R&B circuit in the US, Ike and Tina tour the UK that fall, opening for the Rolling Stones and the Yardbirds. Within a couple years they're opening for the Stones stateside as well, as white America finally discovers the magic of the inimitable Tina Turner.

JUNE 24

1965 Jane Fonda, daughter of legendary leading man Henry, begins to carve out her own Hollywood career by playing the wayward title character in the western comedy *Cat Ballou*. Assuming a role turned down by Ann-Margret, she earns strong reviews, but it's Lee Marvin in dual roles as a soused gunslinger and his arch-enemy who steals the film, later winning an Oscar for Best Actor. Smooth crooner Nat King Cole, who died several months before the film's debut, and Stubby Kaye appear as traveling minstrels. Two months later Fonda marries director Roger Vadim, and later assumes bombshell status as an adventurous adventuress in the sci-fi sex romp *Barbarella*. Later her vocal anti–Vietnam War stance and trip to North Vietnam will generate a far different kind of media attention.

JUNE 25

1967 Satellite television makes history today as an estimated 400 million people in twenty-six nations worldwide tune in to watch *Our World*. The live, 2½-hour black-and-white program, organized by the BBC, requires a Herculean behind-the-scenes effort by hundreds of technicians, cameramen, and producers. It opens with glimpses of newborn babies in Denmark, Japan, Mexico, and Canada, and moves to segments about food supplies, housing, and sports in many countries. But the unquestioned highlight is the Beatles performing a new song, "All You Need Is Love," a perfect embodiment of the Summer of Love and a counterpoint to the divisive Vietnam War. Their festive studio broadcast includes a sing-along with a host of friends, including various Rolling Stones, Marianne Faithfull, Eric Clapton, and Graham Nash.

JUNE 26

1963 Embarking on a goodwill tour of five European nations, President John F. Kennedy touched down first in Germany. He spoke to huge, wildly cheering crowds in Bonn, Cologne, and Frankfurt. Today he arrives in the divided city of Berlin, where 120,000 people began gathering before dawn in a plaza near the Berlin Wall (see Oct. 5). When he reaches the podium, shortly after having visited the notorious crossing point Checkpoint Charlie, the enormous crowd bursts into ecstatic applause lasting several minutes. JFK delivers a short speech assailing communism. "Freedom has many difficulties, and democracy is not perfect," he says, "but we have never had to put a wall up to keep our people in, to prevent them from leaving us." He closes with one of the most memorable lines of modern times: "All free men, wherever they may live, are citizens of Berlin, and therefore, as a free man, I take pride in the words, *Ich bin ein Berliner*." The crowd goes wild.

JUNE 27

1969 Late tonight, New York City police raid a gay bar, the Stonewall Inn, near Greenwich Village. But this very ordinary occurrence triggers an extraordinary response: fierce resistance. Tired of longtime harassment, surveillance, and entrapment—arrests, abuse, and worse—the patrons fight back. Details of who started what and when remain in question, but out of those chaotic, cacophonous streets is born the beginning of the gay rights movement. By the time the *New York Daily News* runs a story about the Stonewall riots on July 6, the *New York Times* has already run three. "The Stonewall was a street queen hangout in the heart of the ghetto," writes Vito Russo (*The Celluloid Closet*), "a place everyone loved to hate—seedy, loud, obvious, and heaven."

JUNE 28

1960

Eccentric, satirical, topical—and bursting with puns. *Rocky & His Friends* broke all the rules for cartoon shows when it premiered last fall on Thursday afternoons on ABC. Today its visionary and legendarily cantankerous creator, Jay Ward, gets the welcome news that General Mills is renewing its sponsorship. So dim Bullwinkle, perky Rocky, dastardly Boris & Natasha, inept but well-meaning Dudley Do-Right, and its other assorted memorable characters live on. After ABC cancels the show next year, NBC picks it up and debuts the renamed *The Bullwinkle Show* in a rare primetime slot, a testament to its ability to cross over and attract adult viewers. But NBC tires of Ward's frequent on-air jabs at its expense, and shifts the show back to an afternoon slot. "It is with great ennui and professional personal apathy that the National Broadcasting Company announces the renewal of *The Bullwinkle Show*," writes Ward in a mock press release, adding that despite its downgraded time slot, "Oh well, it's in color."

BULLWINKLE

SIXTIES SOAPS

Taking their name from their original sponsors like Procter & Gamble and Colgate-Palmolive, soap operas began as radio serials in the '30s. They quickly became a staple of television's early years when shows like *As the World Turns, The Guiding Light, Search for Tomorrow,* and *The Edge of Night* successfully transitioned to the new visual medium. In the '60s, these long-running melodramas were joined by a new generation of daytime soaps, including ABC's *General Hospital* in 1963, NBC's *Another World* in 1964, NBC's *Days of Our Lives* in 1965, and ABC's *One Life to Live* in 1968.

But it was in June of 1966 that ABC broke with the conventions of earlier "sudsers" by introducing the eerie, supernatural

Dark Shadows. The serial daytime drama became a fierce fan favorite, what with its ghosts and witches and werewolves—and even a vampire Barnabas Collins (Jonathan Frid). Exerting an effect on pop culture unlike any other soap opera, the cult show even spawned two theatrical films, and generated a Top 20 hit—a first for a soap opera—in "Quentin's Theme." Fans would lament the show's passing five years later, with one praising its scenes as "Rembrandts in motion." But an angel emerged from *Dark Shadows* after its cancellation: Kate Jackson, a show regular for a season, later achieved lasting fame as one of *Charlie's Angels.*

JUNE
29
1968

In the midst of a lengthy European tour that crisscrosses the English Channel many times, Pink Floyd headlines the first large-scale free rock concert in London's Hyde Park. "It was like a religious experience," says pioneering English deejay John Peel. "They just seemed to fill the whole sky and everything….I think it was the nicest concert I've ever been to." Flush with the success of last summer's trippy single "See Emily Play" and debut album *Piper at the Gates of Dawn*, Pink Floyd is preceded by two budding rock outfits also on the edge of breakout success: Jethro Tull, shortly to release their first album *This Was* but still a year away from leader Ian Anderson's first masterpiece, *Stand Up*; and Tyrannosaurus Rex, featuring charismatic lead singer Marc Bolan, who've just notched a minor hit with "Debora" but are several years away from banging their gong with their signature song, "Get It On."

JUNE
30
1966

Conferences come and go by the score, often with little to show. But today in Washington, DC, the attendees of one conference emerge with something that changes America forever: NOW, the National Organization for Women. Outraged by the refusal of the newly formed Equal Employment Opportunity Commission to end sexual discrimination in employment, a handful of pioneering women decide to take charge. Passionate, provocative author Betty Friedan (*The Feminine Mystique*) jots the acronym NOW on a napkin, and an organization is born. The group soon holds its first press conference, at which Friedan, its first president and most visible spokeswoman, declares: "We will take strong steps in the next election to see that candidates that do not take seriously the question of equal rights for women are defeated."

JULY

JULY 1

1963 Up until yesterday, all you had to do to mail a letter was write a name and address on an envelope and stick a stamp in the corner. That changes today as the US Post Office introduces the Zoning Improvement Plan, which assigns a five-digit code to every town and parts of every city. It instantly becomes known by its acronym, ZIP code. Television spots promoting its use (mandatory at first for bulk mailers only) feature a cartoon mailman, Mr. Zip, with a jingle to the tune of—what else?—"Zip-a-Dee-Doo-Dah," sung by none other than Ethel Merman. "We may now get our junk mail much sooner than before," opines the *New York Times*. "But will we get our first-class mail any more quickly? We can dream, can't we?"

JULY 2

1962 The outside world doesn't take much notice, but today retail history is written by ex-GI Sam Walton. The restless, relentless entrepreneur opens the doors of his first Wal-Mart Discount City in tiny Rogers, Arkansas. The town already has a Ben Franklin five-and-dime whose executives journey from Chicago, troop into the new store opening, and leave displeased by the competition. Walton, who pioneered locating discount stores in small towns instead of higher-cost urban areas, simultaneously becomes a famous price-chopper and an infamous killer of mom-and-pop stores. "Spirited competition," says the man who winds up heading the world's biggest retail chain, "is good for business."

JULY 3

1960 Like its famed older sibling the Folk Festival, the Newport Jazz Festival has grown in popularity. Perhaps a bit too much—it's shut down today after inebriated crowds riot in the streets of the tony New England oceanside resort. An eerie precursor to looming civil rights and anti-Vietnam War rallies, this decidedly non-political fracas makes headlines—even in the USSR, where the newspaper *Izvestia* rails about decadent Western youth. Pelted with bottles and cans, the police fire tear gas and high-pressure water hoses, eventually arresting nearly 200. Inside the festival, its producers ask the artists—including Ray Charles and Oscar Peterson (left)—to play longer so that the record-breaking audience of nearly 15,000 won't exit directly into the melee. The city council votes 4-3 to cancel the fest's remaining days, prompting one organizer to lament, "Instead of treating the sickness, they shot the patient. But the germs are still there."

JULY
4

1963   A smashing example of American independence, producer/director John Sturges's *The Great Escape* is born on the fourth of July. But before opening in theaters nationwide today, it had a private screening in Indiana at the Culver Military Academy, whose commander was a former prisoner of war. Doubtless few of the cadets in attendance realized they were witnessing what would become a film classic. With a dashing ensemble cast, including Charles Bronson, Steve McQueen, Donald Pleasance, James Coburn, and James Garner, the spirited war yarn features a script by James Clavell (*Shogun*) based upon a book by a former prisoner of war. With the Nazis in hot pursuit, motorcycling McQueen soars over a field's long barbed-wire fences. He even dons a uniform and doubles as one of the soldiers on cycles chasing him. (Only the last, spine-tingling leap is performed by a stuntman, Bud Ekins.) Bette Davis recalls asking McQueen, "Why do you ride those motorcycles like that and maybe kill yourself?" His response: "So I won't forget I'm a man and not just an actor."

JULY
5

1961 Leaving his mark on virtually every style of modern music—from jazz to soul to rock to country—Ray Charles has been riding high on the charts with hits like "What'd I Say." Today the virtuoso pianist/singer hits a New York studio, recording two tracks that'll solidify his status as the most popular R&B artist of his time. "Hit the Road Jack," penned by songwriter Percy Mayfield, has a call-and-response refrain similar to "What'd I Say," and revs its way to #1. He also records "Unchain My Heart," a follow-up Top 10 hit. Unlike most black artists, Charles's material and delivery cross over to white audiences seemingly effortlessly. "Ray Charles," says none other than consummate showman Frank Sinatra, "is the only genius in our business."

MEANWHILE...

FOR FREEDOM AND HONOR

On July 4, 1963, the Presidential Medal of Freedom was revived by President John F. Kennedy, who deemed it the nation's highest civilian honor. The first recipients were contralto Marian Anderson, cellist Pablo Casals, pianist Rudolf Serkin, photographer Edward Steichen, and author Thornton Wilder (along with twenty-six others), and later notable winners in the decade included Ellsworth Bunker (Ambassador to South Vietnam), Aaron Copland, Walt Disney, Helen Keller, Edward R. Murrow, Leontyne Price, Carl Sandburg, and John Steinbeck. Though JFK designated the award for those who've made "an especially meritorious contribution to the security or national interests of the United States, or to world peace, or to cultural or other significant public or private endeavors," the award was originally established by President Truman in 1945 for meritorious military service. One of its first recipients—rewarded for "heroism in the rescue of three men following the ramming and sinking of his motor boat"—was none other than Lieutenant John F. Kennedy.

JULY
6

1964 Sure, they can sing, but can they act? Beatlemania proves equally overpowering on film as on vinyl when the Fab Four's first motion picture, *A Hard Day's Night*, opens today. "The 'Citizen Kane' of juke box movies," gushes the *Village Voice*, and other critics and audiences respond with similar enthusiasm. Shot in black and white, the madcap film from director Richard Lester portrays the Beatles as themselves, spirited young lads on the go whilst pursued by ardent female fans. Its title song, not surprisingly, is an instant smash, as are several others from the soundtrack—the first Beatles album to feature Lennon/McCartney songs exclusively. George gets a bonus, too: on the first day of filming he meets a young actress and former model named Pattie Boyd. Instantly smitten, he's off meeting her mother and sisters by week's end, and marries her two years later. Director Lester, meanwhile, continues his exuberant ways with the band's follow-up, *Help!* (1965), and then *A Funny Thing Happened on the Way to the Forum* (1966).

JULY 7

1968 In these high days of the counterculture, hippies are going back to the land by founding communes. Even among the mainstream, a nascent environmental movement gains power. Today, into the mix comes a six-page mimeographed list touting tools and books and ideas that, this fall, will evolve into the first *Whole Earth Catalog*. Devised by iconoclastic Stewart Brand, the book sells millions of copies and becomes an unofficial handbook of the young and committed. Later, competing against works by Norman Mailer, Mike Royko, and Tom Wolfe, it becomes the first catalog ever to win a National Book Award. Jurists of the prize call it a "Space Age Walden."

JULY 8

1967 Imagine, if you can, a more unlikely double bill than Jimi Hendrix and Tiny Tim. That pairing actually happened a couple nights ago as a one-time event at a New York City club, the Scene. Okay, how about this one? "Pleasant Valley Sunday" meets "The Wind Cries Mary"? Yes, tonight countercultural icon Hendrix begins a twenty-nine-show national tour in Jacksonville, Florida, opening for...the Monkees?! This improbable combination quickly splits apart, as Hendrix's music and outrageous showmanship are entirely inappropriate for (and unappreciated by) the Monkees' bubbly teenybopper audience. Eight gigs later, including one at the Forest Hills Music Festival in New York, Jimi's a wild thing *gone*.

> **"The Monkees were very theatrical in my eyes and so was the Jimi Hendrix Experience. It would make the perfect union."**
>
> —Mickey Dolenz of The Monkees

JULY 9

1962 Soon to be a trademark fixture of the New York scene, rising pop artist Andy Warhol (born Warhola) has his first-ever art gallery opening today—in Los Angeles! Irving Blum, co-owner of the Ferus Gallery on La Cienega Blvd., had spotted Warhol's work while in New York and quickly convinced the little-known artist to stage a show. It features Warhol's small, soon-to-be-legendary series of thirty-two paintings of different Campbell's soup cans (at $100 apiece). The savvy owner of a nearby grocery store stacks actual cans in his window and posts a sign: "The real thing for only 29¢ a can." But Warhol still sells out the show. Later he turns to silk screening to create his memorable images of Marilyn Monroe, Chairman Mao, and Elvis that change the face of art forever.

JULY 10

1962 Cape Canaveral in Florida, the launch site of governmental space expeditions, today hosts its first privately sponsored launch. The Telstar 1 satellite rockets into orbit. It's one giant leap for communications, allowing instantaneous live transmission of television broadcasts and telephone calls between the US and Europe. Two weeks later, President Kennedy conducts the first live transatlantic press conference. Media interest peaks, inspiring one pioneering British music producer to greater heights. Joe Meek writes an otherworldly sounding instrumental, "Telstar," for a group called the Tornadoes. The tune shoots to #1 in England that October, and three months later repeats the feat stateside. The first #1 song by a British band in the US, it predates the Beatles' "I Want to Hold Your Hand" by thirteen months. In a sad postscript, an increasingly depressed and hit-less Meek commits suicide in 1967, eight years to the day after the death of his idol, Buddy Holly.

JULY 11

1966 With so much attention riveted on the Vietnam War, CBS preempts its popular daytime quiz show *Password* to cover a live press conference with Secretary of Defense Robert McNamara. But millions of uninterested viewers switch channels to ABC instead and watch the debut of *The Newlywed Game*. This unexpected bonanza provides a huge boost for the show, hosted by affable Bob Eubanks, which pits four recently married couples in a contest to answer revealing, often embarrassing, questions about their spouses. It does so well that it soon lands a primetime slot, as does *The Dating Game*, likewise created by manic producer Chuck Barris, who later claims to have been working simultaneously as a CIA assassin. Bet they never thought to ask the contestants *that* question.

JULY 12

1960

At the 1959 International Toy Fair in Nuremberg, Germany, the president of US toy company Ohio Art spotted an ingenious invention. *L'Ecran Magique* (Magic Writer), a grey screen enclosed in a red plastic frame, featured two knobs that, when twisted, scraped aluminum powder from the back of the glass to etch lines. At first the company decided to pass on the invention, by Frenchman Arthur Granjean, but later bought in. Today, Ohio Art introduces the Etch A Sketch with its first ever television campaign (the toy did resemble a TV set). Winning seals of approval from such prestigious magazines as *Good Housekeeping* and *Parents*, it quickly becomes the company's flagship product and ubiquitous in family homes nationwide. Sears alone sells ten million units through the decade.

JULY 13

1966

At a time when mass murder is almost unheard of in the US, the name Richard Speck conjures up unimaginable horror and revulsion. Early this morning he forces his way into a Chicago townhouse shared by nursing students and methodically rapes, strangles, and stabs eight nurses. A ninth, who survives by wriggling under a bed, emerges hours later to discover the bloodied corpses. "This is the man," she says nine months later, walking across a courtroom to within a foot of the seated defendant and pointing. With that identification and a fingerprint lifted from the scene, the jury takes less than an hour to return a death sentence verdict, later converted to life in prison. In 1996, five years after Speck died of a heart attack, a secret video shot in jail surfaces, showing him partying with fellow inmates. Asked on the tape about the murders, he shrugs and jokes, "It just wasn't their night."

SHORTLIST

HIP TOYS OF THE '60S

In the '60s, the Etch A Sketch wasn't the only cool new toy for kids across the US. Here are ten more must-have playthings that were released in the decade.

- Astro-Ray Gun
- Easy-Bake Oven
- Big-Play NFL Electric Football
- Twister
- Beatles bobble-head dolls
- G.I. Joe
- Hot Wheels
- Spirograph
- Addams Family "Thing" coin bank
- Frosty the Sno-Cone Maker

As the '60s draw to a close, that idealistic feeling of peace and love has evaporated in the wake of the assassinations of Martin Luther King, Jr., and Robert Kennedy and the escalating Vietnam War. Roaring onscreen today to the strains of Steppenwolf's "Born to be Wild" comes the downbeat but riveting *Easy Rider*. Co-starring Peter Fonda, Dennis Hopper, and a young Jack Nicholson—in a role originally slated for Rip Torn—this quintessential road movie-slash-'60s time capsule ("a trip worth taking" says critic Peter Travers) revs along on sex, drugs, rock 'n' roll, adrenaline, and casual violence. The low-budget indie becomes a smash hit: an enduring, iconic take on times that indeed were a-changin'.

JULY 15

1967

It's the summer of luv, baby, but budding folksinger Janis Ian has a decidedly different take. As a student she'd penned "Society's Child," a tale of doomed interracial romance eons apart from pop's conventional love songs. Nervous about its controversial subject manner, her label (Atlantic) quietly declined to release it, so the single appeared on Verve. Today it peaks at #14, fueled by her national television appearance on a CBS rock-music special hosted by Leonard Bernstein (featuring an eclectic mix that includes Frank Zappa, Herman's Hermits, and Canned Heat). Self-appointed guardians of public morality rage, and some radio stations ban it. Ian hits even bigger eight years later with "At Seventeen," a tale of teenage angst and cruelty. English progressive rockers Spooky Tooth redo "Society's Child" and their single causes a similar furor in the UK.

JULY 16

1961

An art theft today at a museum in St. Tropez, France, bags fifty-seven modern paintings worth an estimated $2 million. The robbery seems to trigger a rash of art thefts over the next month in Europe: a Picasso and a Miro later in July, a Cezanne and a Goya in August. All but one of the paintings from the original robbery are recovered in a barn fifty miles west of Paris in late 1962. Coincidentally or not, several heist films—a time-honored movie genre—soon surface. Producer/director Jules Dassin's smashing *Topkapi*, based on a novel by suspense master Eric Ambler, features Melina Mercouri and Peter Ustinov (in an Oscar-winning role). Peter Sellers plays Inspector Jacques Clouseau in *The Pink Panther*, then reprises the role six months later in *A Shot in the Dark*. Plus, in 1968, Faye Dunaway and Steve McQueen team in *The Thomas Crown Affair*, a cool, complicated caper.

JULY
17

1965 Poverty, prejudice, prison—James Brown had lived it all growing up. Making his name on the R&B circuit in the mid-'50s, "The King" and his backup group, the Fabulous Flames, started packing black clubs. The pioneering singer sold millions of records ("Please Please Please," "Try Me"), dominating the field with prize bookings at top dollar. His electrifying 1962 performance at Harlem's legendary showcase, the Apollo, remains a show-stopping classic. Yet Brown remained virtually unknown to whites, at least in America; in Britain, he had many white fans. Today "Papa's Got A Brand New Bag" enters the charts and soon leaps into the Top 10. The crossover starts happenin', baby, with Brown building a huge new white audience with "I Got You (I Feel Good)," "It's a Man's Man's Man's World," and half a dozen others. The Godfather of Soul has arrived.

> " The one thing that can solve most of our problems is dancing. "
> —James Brown

JULY
18

1969

Any hopes for the Kennedy family to recapture the White House in the near future expire early this morning on a desolate dirt road on Martha's Vineyard. After a late-night party on Chappaquiddick Island, an Oldsmobile driven by Senator Ted Kennedy spins out of control and overturns into a small pond. Sole passenger Mary Jo Kopechne, a secretary who'd worked for his late brother Robert, drowns. Though Kennedy claims to have tried to rescue her, he doesn't report the accident for ten hours. Front-page media coverage erupts, but her family quickly buries the body, so no autopsy is ever performed. Kennedy later pleads guilty to leaving the scene of an accident, but many questions remain unanswered—and claims of a cover-up endure.

JULY
19

1961

TWA was known for its high-flying firsts: the first airline to serve freshly brewed coffee, the first to introduce a non-smoking section. Today it sets up a Bell & Howell projector in the first-class cabin and inaugurates another novelty: the first regular in-flight movie service. The flight, en route from New York to Los Angeles, premieres *By Love Possessed*, an otherwise forgettable glossy soap opera co-starring Lana Turner, Efrem Zimbalist, Jr., and Jason Robards, Jr. As the popularity of television cuts into movie attendance, studios are eagerly eying new venues— and airplanes become a favored and popular destination.

JULY 25

1965 The peasants are revolting. The purists are enraged. Iconoclastic Bob Dylan never cared much for convention, and he shows it tonight after strapping on an electric guitar at the famed Newport Folk Festival. Some in the crowd boo when he and a makeshift band rip into "Maggie's Farm" and "Like A Rolling Stone," but he later placates them with solo acoustic versions of "It's All Over Now, Baby Blue" and "Mr. Tambourine Man." However, the die has been cast. The following month, on his new tour, Dylan introduces a fresh format: acoustic, intermission, electric. The crowds go wild, then and forever. "The young figurehead of the folk movement," says festival creator George Wein, "had remade himself into a rock star. The repercussions were huge."

JULY 26

1966 Advertised as a "Dance and Show," the Temptations open at Bill Graham's legendary Fillmore West (see May 17) in San Francisco. In the midst of an eight-week run atop the R&B chart with "Ain't Too Proud to Beg," the polished Motown quintet shows off their spirited vocals and intricate dance moves ("sharper than a serpent's tooth on stage," says rock critic Lillian Roxon). Over the next five years they'll become one of Motown's most dependable hitmakers, delivering a dozen Top 10 songs, including "Beauty Is Only Skin Deep," "Cloud Nine," and "I'm Gonna Make You Love Me." Soon, live and greatest hits albums appear just months apart, with more #1 songs like "I Can't Get Next to You" and "Just My Imagination (Running Away with Me)."

JULY
27

1963 Best known for popularizing the miniskirt, couturier André Courrèges dazzles with a Parisian show opening today. "He has an unerring sense of proportion," gushes one reporter. "He knows how to cut, and he has taste." Courrèges honed his cutting skills for eleven years for the legendary Cristobal Balenciaga before beginning his own house with his wife Coqueline in 1961. Bringing an unadorned menswear aesthetic to women's clothing, the former civil engineer delivers collections in which form follows function: modernist, sharp, spare styles. An early pioneer of the unisex look, he adds only one decoration: white daisies, often fashioned out of sequins or lace.

JULY
28

1968 Everybody may love Lucy, as a rule, but it's a different story when examined in detail. The top-rated show nationwide last fall, *The Lucy Show* drops when discrete demographic groups are examined. The top show in the Northeast, for instance, is *The Jackie Gleason Show*, while the South prefers *Gunsmoke*. Blue-collar families love good ole Andy Griffith best of all, while white-collar homes opt for smoothie Dean Martin. A new *TV Guide* story today details the research sampling studies undertaken "for the insistent demands of TV merchandising." Translation: advertisers are increasingly demanding detailed viewer information broken down by geography, age, economic status, education, and more. The story notes one anomaly: the goofy sitcom *Gomer Pyle, U.S.M.C.,* starring Jim Nabors, appeals only to children and to adults over fifty. "Certainly something to ponder," the story concludes.

JULY 29 1961

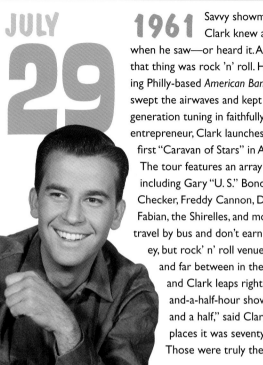

Savvy showman Dick Clark knew a good thing when he saw—or heard it. And for him that thing was rock 'n' roll. His pioneering Philly-based *American Bandstand* swept the airwaves and kept the younger generation tuning in faithfully. Ever the entrepreneur, Clark launches today his first "Caravan of Stars" in Atlantic City. The tour features an array of top acts, including Gary "U. S." Bonds, Chubby Checker, Freddy Cannon, Duane Eddy, Fabian, the Shirelles, and more. They travel by bus and don't earn much money, but rock' n' roll venues are few and far between in the early '60s, and Clark leaps right in. "A two-and-a-half-hour show for a buck and a half," said Clark. "In some places it was seventy-five cents. Those were truly the early days."

JULY 30 1966

Even the band thinks the lyrics are incredibly corny, but the Troggs decide to give "Wild Thing" a try. Today the Brit band's first US single tops the charts and becomes an anthem, recorded in years to come by artists from Jimi Hendrix to just about every garage/bar band in sight. "Wild Thing" also claims an unusual dual parentage. Due to conflicting record contracts, the record appears on two labels—Atco and Fontana—the only #1 ever to have a simultaneous release. The Troggs manage a couple more hits in a more melodic mode, like "With a Girl Like You," but it's this chart-topper than endures. A few months later, "Wild Thing" gets a second life when a satirical imitation of Senator Robert F. Kennedy reciting the lyrics becomes a Top 20 hit.

A CRASH...

On July 29, 1966—soon after releasing his scorching double album *Blonde on Blonde*—Bob Dylan crashed his Triumph 55 motorcycle on an interstate near his home in Woodstock, New York. It's never been fully revealed what happened, but it was reported that Dylan suffered serious injuries, and he dropped out of sight for more than a year. While his reclusion/recuperation provoked intense interest from the public, Dylan privately recorded hours of songs (both compositions by himself and others) with his friends from The Band, in their basement. He finally made his return to the stage with the group on January 20, 1968, at a Woody Guthrie memorial concert at Carnegie Hall. A portion of The Basement Tapes wouldn't be released until 1975.

...AND A SMASH HIT

Across the pond, also on July 29, 1966, supergroup Cream—Eric Clapton (ex-Yardbirds), Jack Bruce (ex–Manfred Mann), and Ginger Baker (ex–Graham Bond Organisation)—played their first gig in a Manchester club. Three months later, Baker collapsed from exhaustion after playing a twenty-minute drum solo at a nearby university. Within a year Cream had left its imprint on FM music with the dense, driving sounds of "Strange Brew" and "Sunshine of Your Love." Sold-out US tours would follow, but dissension reared up and the band called it quits after two standing-room-only shows at London's Royal Albert Hall in November 1968.

1969 The luster was off the King's crown. He hadn't performed a live concert in more than eight years. His last #1 hit was a distant seven years earlier, and pop music from the British Invasion to Motown to California folk-rock had left him seemingly out of touch. But today Elvis Presley rekindles the magic and re-hits his stride, opening a comeback engagement at the Intercontinental Hotel in Las Vegas. With a kickin' new live back-up band, the King wows 'em with both his early hits and new material like "In the Ghetto" and the soon-to-be-#1 "Suspicious Minds." His four-week, fifty-seven-date stay generates a wildly successful double album, *From Memphis to Vegas/From Vegas to Memphis.* Elvis begins touring again to adoring, sold-out crowds, and—at least for now—the King is back.

AUGUST

1

1960 Every queen has to start somewhere. For an eighteen-year-old gospel singer recording her first secular tracks, that somewhere is a New York studio. Today Aretha Franklin records her first songs, including "Over the Rainbow," for Columbia Records. For years to come, the label's orchestral arrangements of pop standards barely dent the charts. Finally, Atlantic Records pioneer Ahmet Ertegun lures Franklin away, betting that a return to a more rootsy R&B sound will end the drought. And does it ever. The Queen of Soul breaks through with "I Never Loved a Man (The Way That I Love You)," quickly followed by her first #1, a song written by Otis Redding and one that gives Aretha the "Respect" she deserves. Her hometown of Detroit later declares "Aretha Franklin Day," and Martin Luther King, Jr., presents her with the Southern Christian Leadership Award at Cobo Hall.

AUGUST

AUGUST 2

1967 Racial tensions still run so deep in America that the producers shot *In the Heat of the Night* in Illinois rather than in its actual small-town setting in Mississippi. Today the murder melodrama explodes onscreen, featuring a racist police chief (Rod Steiger) who grudgingly investigates a homicide alongside an arrogant black detective (Sidney Poitier) from "back east." The film seethes and sizzles, delivering one of cinema's most famous lines when Poitier pointedly replies to a question, "They call me *Mister* Tibbs." *In the Heat of the Night* goes on to win five Oscars, including Best Picture (over the favored *Bonnie and Clyde* and *The Graduate*), Actor (Steiger), Screenplay, Editing, and Sound.

AUGUST 3

1966 Two utterly unique personalities—one famous, the other infamous—ODed young in LA's summer heat. The first was thirty-six-year-old film legend Marilyn Monroe, who died of an overdose of sleeping pills on August 5, 1962. Today, four years later, controversial stand-up comic Lenny Bruce (see Dec. 19) dies of a morphine overdose in his home on Hollywood Boulevard. "Finally, one last four-letter word concerning Lenny Bruce—dead," says old friend Dick Schapp. "At forty. *That's* obscene." Bruce's obscenity-laced tirades against the system had made him a bull's-eye for police, and at the end almost no US clubs would book him for fear of an obscenity charge. In 2004, Comedy Central rates him the #3 comedian ever, trailing only George Carlin and Richard Pryor, each of whom cited Bruce as an influence.

AUGUST
4

1960 Possessing a short fuse and a long record of on-field fisticuffs, fiery Cincinnati second baseman Billy Martin takes exception to a brushback pitch by Chicago Cubs pitcher Jim Brewer during the second inning of a game at Wrigley Field. After the two exchange words, Martin throws an unexpected punch that breaks the hurler's cheekbone. "He threw at my head," says Martin, "and nobody is gonna do that." Martin is suspended, and Brewer's eye becomes infected and requires additional surgery. Eventually Martin pays a $10,000 fine and later goes on to a memorable career as manager of the New York Yankees, whom he leads to a World Series title in 1977.

AUGUST
5

1967 It quickly becomes America's favorite parlor game question: just what in the heck did Billie Joe McAllister throw off the Tallahatchee Bridge? Released today as a B side, "Ode to Billie Joe" immediately generates airplay and controversy. Running a then-lengthy (for AM radio) four minutes, the Southern gothic song paints a haunting picture of a farming family trying to cope with a local lad's suicide. Three weeks later it leaps to #1, making singer/songwriter Bobbie Gentry (named after the sudsy 1952 drama *Ruby Gentry*) an overnight sensation. She wins three Grammy awards, sings duets with Glen Campbell, becomes a headliner in Las Vegas, and lands television shows on both CBS and the BBC. Her signature song inspires a 1976 movie starring Robbie Benson that implies that Billie Joe committed suicide because he was tormented by his possible homosexuality.

AUGUST
6

1962 On this hot summer afternoon, teenage girls in pink tights and net skirts dance ballet on the White House lawn to the music of a 103-member youth orchestra. Waiters ferry trays of lemonade and cookies to the thirsty young crowd, gathered for the concert sponsored by First Lady Jackie Kennedy. "Last year more Americans went to symphonies than baseball games," says a smiling JFK, a longtime Red Sox fan. "Some may think this an alarming statistic, but I think that both baseball and the country will endure." His extemporaneous remarks are incorrect, but had he referenced all concerts, not just symphonies, he would have been right. Nonetheless, the president lauds the hard work and discipline necessary for success in the arts, and praises the young orchestra's focus on international composers.

AUGUST
7

1965 Their lightweight sound and scrubbed good looks make Hermit's Hermits a teenybopper's dream British Invasion band. The group makes a lot bigger splash stateside than in their native England with syrupy sweet songs like "Can't You Hear My Heartbeat" and "Mrs. Brown, You've Got a Lovely Daughter." Today they top the US charts again with "I'm Henry VIII, I Am," based on an authentic turn-of-the-century music-hall song that's deemed too square for British audiences. Despite critical disclaim—one calls lead singer Peter Noone "the Paul Anka of the Beatle era"—Herman's Hermits attract a rabid young crowd and score more than a dozen Top 10 hits in the US. They also go the film route, appearing alongside Liberace and Louis Armstrong in Connie Francis's campy *When the Boys Meet the Girls*. And they star in their own vehicle, a dud called *Hold On!* that critics wryly note is best described by the title of one of their hits: "A Must to Avoid."

MURDER MOST FOUL

Headlines screamed the news on August 8, 1969: Pregnant actress and friends savagely butchered. As the LA police investigated, the celebrity-obsessed world hung on every detail of the grisly deaths of Sharon Tate—wife of director Roman Polanski, who was in London working on a film—and four others. The infamous crime scene at a house in the Hollywood Hills included words like "pig" and "helter skelter" scrawled in blood. A week later, police arrested mesmerizing, crazed ex-con Charles Manson and his "family" of followers on auto theft charges, and soon figured out that he'd ordered them to do the killings. Since Manson was obsessed with the Beatles' lyrics, lawyers threatened to subpoena John Lennon and Paul McCartney. Though the stars never ended up having to appear, the prosecuting district attorney later titled his book *Helter Skelter: The True Story of the Manson Murders.*

LA5)LOS ANGELES, Dec.2--CULT LEADER?--Charles Manson, above, 34, was described today by the Los Angeles Times and attorney Richard Caballero as the leader of a quasireligious cult of hippies, three of whom have been arrested on murder warrant issued in the slayings of actress Sharon Tate and four other at her home. Manson is in jail

> ❝ **I am what you have made me, and the mad dog devil killer fiend leper is a reflection of your society.** ❞
>
> —Charles Manson

AUGUST 8

1960 With his heavily pomaded hairdo in heartthrob Fabian style, young Brian Hyland doesn't look much like a beach boy. But today the Queens native leaves the city streets and heads to the beach, hitting #1 with his perky "Itsy Bitsy Teenie Weenie Yellow Polka Dot Bikini." An instant summertime classic, the song was inspired by its co-writer's two-year-old daughter frolicking on the beach in said bikini. The song jumpstarts Hyland's career, and he continues to deliver popular songs like "Sealed With a Kiss"—with a similarly summery feel—until the Beatles-led British Invasion swamps the clean-cut crooner sound. Traveling with Dick Clark's "Caravan of Stars," along with Bobby Vee, Little Eva, and the Ronettes, Hyland is in Dallas on November 22, 1963. He watches the motorcade of President Kennedy pass by moments before the President is assassinated.

AUGUST
9

1967

Scandalous! Salacious! Shocking! Whatever the sensational adjective, Joe Orton fits the bill. The playwright delights in flouting conventional mores, and his smash West End black comedies like *Entertaining Mr. Sloane*, *Loot*, and *What the Butler Saw* never fail to elicit critical praise or outrage. One critic calls *Loot* a "snappy, brilliantly outrageous take on death, greed, and morality." Suggested to the Beatles as a possible screenwriter for their third film, Orton dashes off an anarchic farce in which the Beatles are portrayed as adulterers and murderers—not exactly the image their management wants. The project quickly dies and, sadly, so too does Orton, bludgeoned to death today by his jealous, older lover Kenneth Halliwell, who then commits suicide. At Orton's funeral, they play the Beatles' "A Day in the Life."

DO YOU HAVE THAT IN BLUE?

In August of 1963, on the heels of hits "Roses Are Red (My Love)," and "Blue on Blue," crooner Bobby Vinton released his latest color-themed tune, "Blue on Blue," which eventually rose to #1 and became a romantic classic for the ages. But Vinton didn't have a lock on the blues (or pinks or yellows) in the '60s. Here's a rainbow of songs from the decade:

- "Blue Christmas" (Elvis Presley)
- "Crystal Blue Persuasion" (Tommy James & the Shondells)
- "Pink Panther Theme" (Henry Mancini)
- "Red Roses for a Blue Lady" (Wayne Newton)
- "Red Rubber Ball" (The Cyrkle)
- "White Room" (Cream)
- "A Whiter Shade of Pale" (Procol Harum)
- "Green Green" (The New Christy Minstrels)
- "Green Tambourine" (The Lemon Pipers)
- "Deep Purple" (Nino Tempo & April Stevens)
- "Purple Haze" (Jimi Hendrix)
- "Mellow Yellow" (Donovan)
- "Yellow Submarine" (The Beatles)
- "Paint It, Black" (The Rolling Stones)
- "Black Is Black" (Los Bravos)
- "Brown Eyed Girl" (Van Morrison)
- "Orange Blossom Special" (Johnny Cash)

1960 Synonymous with the high-living, high-rolling lifestyle of Las Vegas, the incomparable Rat Pack debuts today in the film *Ocean's Eleven*. Frank Sinatra, Dean Martin, Sammy Davis Jr., Joey Bishop, and Peter Lawford, plus assorted hangers-on like Angie Dickinson, co-star in the film that plots a grand rip-off of five casinos on New Year's Eve. It's shot, naturally enough, on location while the boys do their live acts at the Sands and other nightclub venues. Sold-out audiences delight to their polished musical, dancing, and comedic routines that feature lots of joshing, ad-libbing, smoking, and drinking. The swingin'-est cats on the block, the Pack commands attention from one and all—even JFK. Sinatra had reportedly introduced the prez to mob moll and future mistress Judith Campbell during their high-flying Vegas stay the previous February.

AUGUST 11

1966 Arriving for their latest US tour, the Beatles land in Chicago to a clamoring mob of reporters and cameras. But the focus isn't music. A *London Evening Standard* profile of John Lennon five months earlier had barely raised a stir, but recently a US teen mag, *Datebook,* took a quote— "We're more popular than Jesus right now"—out of context and triggered a firestorm. Some radio stations, especially in the Bible Belt, ban the Beatles and hold bonfires of their records. Hate mail pours in. "I wasn't saying whatever they're saying I was saying—I'm sorry I said it, really," says an unusually contrite Lennon at today's live press conference at the Astor Towers Hotel. "I never meant it to be a lousy anti-religious thing. I apologize, if that will make you happy." The band still plays to huge crowds, but the mood has darkened. It will be the Beatles' last US tour.

AUGUST 12

1965 In the eerie light of dawn, much of South Central Los Angeles looks like a war zone—acres of broken glass and debris, burned-out cars, looted businesses. Last night, white cops stopped a black motorist for suspected drunk driving. A crowd gathered and things quickly escalated, with hurriedly called reinforcements battling angry mobs. And it's about to get worse, much worse. The tinderbox explodes, fueled by escalating racial tension and lingering hostility over rampant joblessness, poor housing, bad schools, and other inner-city ills. A blistering heat wave doesn't help either. By the time the Watts riots end five days later, at least thirty-four people have died. More than a thousand are injured, and total property damage runs to at least $200 million. The sides grow even further apart, with black radicals applauding the grim spectacle and conservative whites viewing the uprising as the cost of recently enacted civil rights legislation.

AUGUST 13

1967 Mixing fairytale farce with brutal violence, director Arthur Penn's *Bonnie and Clyde* explodes onscreen in a hail of critical fire. Based on the true story of a murderin', thievin', white trash couple that terrorized the south in the early '30s, the film makes stars out of young Warren Beatty and Faye Dunaway (producer Beatty's fourth choice after being turned down by Tuesday Weld, Jane Fonda, and Sue Lyon). "They're young, they're in love, and they kill people," declare its ads. The film nets ten Oscar nominations, eventually winning two, for Best Supporting Actress (Estelle Parsons) and Best Cinematography. It also has major pop-cultural influence, triggering a revival of '30s music, hairdos, and clothing. "In combining slapstick and gravity," wrote *Rolling Stone* critic Peter Travers decides later, "Penn brought a French New Wave energy to the movie that is still being imitated."

AUGUST 14

1965 "They say we're young and we don't know..." In this case, "they" would be Atlantic Records, convinced that "It's Gonna Rain" is the hit side of a just-recorded 45 by the novice duo Sonny and Cher. Musical jack-of-all-trades Sonny Bono had met sixteen-year-old Cherilyn LaPierre at a local Hollywood coffee shop, and they'd both sung background on Phil Spector–produced smashes like "Da Doo Ron Ron" and "Be My Baby." Sonny feels so strongly that the hit is on the flipside that he gives radio station KHJ an exclusive, and the station plays the song every hour. Today his instincts pay off as "I Got You Babe" rockets to #1, the pair's only chart-topper despite Top 10 hits like "The Beat Goes On" and "Baby Don't Go." Savvy Sonny also engineers Cher's solo career, which produces a slew of #1's like "Gypsys, Tramps, & Thieves," "Half-Breed," and "Dark Lady." Soon the husband-and-wife team head up a CBS variety hour, putting an acceptable face (with outrageous clothing) on hippie culture for all America to see.

AUGUST
15

1969 The long-haired hippie/freak crowd that descends upon Max Yasgur's farm in Bethel, New York, earns a spot in history today as the most famous rock event of all time begins: the Woodstock Music and Art Festival. Hoping to attract 200,000 attendees at $18 apiece, the promoters get a bit more than they anticipated—more than half a million (mostly nonpaying) guests. The revelers imbibe, inhale, and enjoy four days of major acts, beginning with Richie Havens and ending with Jimi Hendrix. Joni Mitchell, forever identified with the milestone event through her anthemic "Woodstock" ("We are stardust, we are golden…and we've got to get ourselves back to the garden") never actually makes it to the festival herself. She cancels after her agent insists that she keep her slot on *The Dick Cavett Show*.

BEYOND WOODSTOCK

Though Woodstock is the most revered rock event of the '60s (and perhaps of all time), there were plenty other musical milestones making news. Here are some of the most famous (or infamous) concerts of the decade.

- The Rat Pack, emceed by Johnny Carson, performed at the Kiel Opera House in St. Louis (June 20, 1965)

- Bob Dylan went electric at the Newport Folk Festival (July 28, 1965)

- The Beatles' performed their first stadium show, at Shea Stadium (August 15, 1965)

- A "Be-In" outdoor extravaganza was held at Golden Gate Park (January 14, 1967)

- The Byrds and the Jefferson Airplane flew high during the Monterey International Pop Festival (June 16–18, 1967)

- The Rolling Stones saluted the late Brian Jones in Hyde Park, London (July 5, 1969)

- Elvis Presley had his comeback concert at the International Hotel, Las Vegas (July 31, 1969)

- The Isle of Wight Festival featured Bob Dylan and the Band and the Who (August 30–31, 1969)

- A free concert headlined by the Rolling Stones at the Altamont Speedway in California made headlines after four fans were killed (December 6, 1969)

AUGUST 16

1969 These eyes are crying—tears of joy, most likely, as the Guess Who's first RCA single, "These Eyes," goes gold (selling 500,000 copies) today. Through the year this harmonious rock band enjoys a run of four Top 10 singles, including "Laughing" and "No Time" and culminating in their only #1, "American Woman." Interestingly, they actually hail from Winnipeg, Canada, and chafe at having to endure long waits before receiving the visas needed to tour the US. One proposed solution is to renounce their citizenship, to which one band member replies, "I wouldn't let someone take my Canadian citizenship from me for anything." Lead guitarist and main-mover Randy Bachman later departs to form Bachman-Turner Overdrive, which tops the charts in 1974 with the hard-driving but grammatically challenged "You Ain't Seen Nothing Yet."

AUGUST 17

1960 America has egg, and a lot worse, on its face today as the trial of Air Force pilot Francis Gary Powers begins in Moscow. After the USSR shot down his U2 spy plane last May, 1,200 miles inside its border, the US government claimed it was simply a weather plane. That lie embarrassingly collapses when the Soviets produce not only the plane but also its pilot. Russian leader Nikita Khrushchev demands an apology from President Eisenhower, but none is forthcoming. Pleading guilty, but claiming he was just following orders, Powers is asked if he thinks his actions could have provoked a military conflict. "The people who sent me," he says, "should think of these things." Convicted and sentenced to ten years, he serves two before being released in a prisoner swap for a Russian colonel. Alternately praised and reviled at home, Powers is exonerated for losing the plane but blackballed by the military. After he dies in a helicopter crash in 1977, his family lobbies successfully and he's awarded the Distinguished Flying Cross and several Department of Defense medals—honors denied during his lifetime.

AUGUST 18

1960 Though never mistaken for a great actor, handsome and charismatic Elvis Presley does translate nicely to film. His 1956 debut in *Love Me Tender* set the standard: public acclaim, critical disdain. But the camera loves him, and so do his legions of ardent female fans. Today, their two-year wait while he was in the Army ends as Presley opens alongside Juliet Prowse in *G.I. Blues*. Lines wrap around blocks nationwide for the King's latest, which features him singing an early hit, "Blue Suede Shoes." The producers had begun filming in Germany, but to avoid any speculation about favorable treatment didn't shoot Presley until after his discharge. They shot his scenes in Hollywood, but not everyone was especially enthralled. The Hollywood Women's Press Club votes him "Least Cooperative Actor of 1960."

AUGUST 19

1968 Down the highways and byways of America rolled an unlikely vehicle with an unlikely crew: a colorfully decorated Day-Glo 1939 school bus, piloted by author Ken Kesey along with his Merry Pranksters. Fueled by his earnings from *One Flew Over the Cuckoo's Nest* and *Sometimes a Great Notion*, Kesey and his ragtag fellow travelers embarked on their grand California-to-New York psychedelic adventure in 1964. Nicknamed "Further" (originally misspelled Furthur), the bus was often driven—often maniacally— by Neal Cassady, of Jack Kerouac's *On the Road* fame. All along the way, its madcap passengers conducted LSD-laden "acid trips." Today a kaleidoscopic retelling appears with the publication of Tom Wolfe's *The Electric Kool-Aid Acid Test*, a countercultural canon that recaptures life in the eye of the subversive storm.

TRENDSETTER

IN THE PRESENCE OF PERSONAGES

The '60s produced many countercultural outlaws besides Ken Kesey and his merry travelers, but five stand out as iconoclasts who articulated the decade's rebellious spirit. They are: avant-garde novelist and Beat Generation savant William Burroughs (*Naked Lunch*); nonconformist, non-materialist Beat poet Allen Ginsberg (see Oct. 18); confrontational, commercially successful novelist Norman Mailer, also a vocal anti–Vietnam War activist and erstwhile political candidate; complex, socially conscious Tom Robbins (*Another Roadside Attraction, Even Cowgirls Get the Blues*); and passionate, pioneering Hunter Thompson (*Fear and Loathing in Las Vegas*).

AUGUST
20

1966 Many radio stars never made the transition to television. But loveable Red Skelton, son of a circus clown, became one of the new medium's biggest players. Today he graces the cover of *TV Guide*, a feat he'll repeat five times while hosting one of television's longest-running weekly comedy/variety shows. The affable funnyman delights with an assortment of endearing characters like Freddy the Freeloader, The Mean Widdle Kid ("I dood it!"), and Clem Kadiddlehopper. Frequent collaborator Marcel Marceau later writes, "Red Skelton brought joy, happiness, and poetry to millions of children and grown-ups. In his field he had no peer." Skelton memorably closes every show with a sincere "God bless."

AUGUST
21

1965 Often heard in coffee shops but rarely on the radio, protest songs begin taking on new prominence with the rise of Bob Dylan and stirrings of dissent over the Vietnam War. The times are indeed a-changin', and ex-folkie Barry McGuire (of the New Christy Minstrels) answers the call. Today he releases "Eve of Destruction," which in three-plus minutes encapsulates the younger generation's fears and frustrations over the Cold War and the "hot" war in Vietnam, the civil rights struggles, and the nuclear arms race. Voices rise on both sides, but even banning the controversial song on some stations can't stop its charge to the top of the charts in late September. A conservative rejoinder, "The Dawn of Correction," by a hastily concocted band called the Spokesmen, cracks the Top 40, but doesn't have the same resonance as the original.

AUGUST
22

1964 Ex-boxer and sometime songwriter Berry Gordy had a dream—to create America's penultimate soul sound. So the hard-driving Detroit entrepreneur borrowed $800 from his family and opened Hitsville USA, a.k.a. Motown, in 1959. Gordy combined an astute ability for discovering raw talent, of both the singing and songwriting varieties, with a keen ear and production sense. Today one of his biggest acts, the Supremes, tops the charts with "Where Did Our Love Go," the first of an unprecedented, incredible run of five consecutive #1 releases. The others? "Baby Love," "Come See About Me," "Stop! In the Name of Love," and "Back in My Arms Again." The driven Gordy just keeps on coming. "You can go broke with hits," he says, "if someone else is producing the records."

1969 Released a day after the funeral of Brian Jones (see June 9), the Rolling Stones' "Honky Tonk Woman" hits #1 today and stays atop the charts for a month. Still, it's been a long, hard summer for the band. Jones left the group by mutual agreement in June and drowned in his swimming pool a month later. Bassist Bill Wyman divorced in early July. Last week, filming the troubled movie *Ned Kelly* in Australia, Mick Jagger accidentally shot himself in the hand. Arriving in the US this coming October, they're stung by criticism of exorbitant ticket prices. "Can the Rolling Stones really need all that money?" asks respected critic Ralph Gleason. "It says they despise their audience." In response, the band opts to give a free concert at the end of its upcoming tour, which turns out to be a wicked bad idea (see Dec. 6 sidebar).

AUGUST 24

1966 What's it all about? For early birds in line at two NYC movie theaters, it's tea and crumpets. That's what they're served while waiting to see the debut of *Alfie*, a British play-turned-film that turns Michael Caine into an international star. But he almost didn't get to play the philandering title role since the producers preferred Terrence Stamp, who'd acted the role on Broadway. Stamp declines, and his good friend Caine inherits the breakout role that ensures he won't fall victim to typecasting after playing a steely-eyed agent in the Cold War thriller *The Ipcress File*. Jane Asher, currently engaged to Paul McCartney, plays one of his many conquests. Dionne Warwick sings the Burt Bacharach/Hal David title song in the US release, while in Britain native songbird Cilla Black does the honors. Unlike Alfie, Caine finds true love: when he spies Miss Guyana 1967 in a TV commercial, he contacts her—smitten—and in storybook fashion they later wed.

AUGUST 25

1963 His stunning film version of Eugene O'Neill's *Long Day's Journey into Night* had made director Sidney Lumet one of Hollywood's hottest properties. Today, though, he also appears to be one its more troubled, as police report he took an overdose of sleeping pills—apparently in reaction to his divorce from society grand dame Gloria Vanderbilt. Lumet dismissively chalks it up to "seven vodkas, a Miltown [tranquilizer], and idiocy." In any event, he quickly rallies and delivers two of next year's most intense films: Cold War chiller *Fail-Safe* and *The Pawnbroker*, the latter featuring a bravura turn by Rod Steiger as a haunted Holocaust survivor. By year's end, Lumet also rebounds personally, marrying Gail Jones, the daughter of Lena Horne.

AUGUST 26

1968 On the day the Democratic National Convention opens in Chicago, the mood is ugly. Rocks and tear gas fly as police beat and bloody protesters in the streets. Mayor Richard Daley's iron-fisted response attracts massive media attention, rocking the nation and overshadowing the convention itself. Mass arrests culminate in a later circus-like trial for the Chicago Eight, which includes Tom Hayden, co-founder of Students for a Democratic Society (SDS), and Yippie cohorts Abbie Hoffman and Jerry Rubin. Already reeling from the assassination of Robert Kennedy in June, the Dems reject the anti-war candidacies of Eugene McCarthy and George McGovern for establishment favorite Vice President Hubert Humphrey. But the street spectacle, and the war-bound legacy of the Johnson administration, take their toll. On Election Day Humphrey loses to Richard Nixon.

AUGUST
27

1964   As parents antici-
pate, and kids dread,
the approaching back-to-school
time, Disney eases the moment with
its much-anticipated *Mary Poppins*.
Co-stars Julie Andrews and Dick Van
Dyke attend today's premiere at
Grauman's Chinese Theater in Hollywood—Disney's first gala opening
there since *Snow White* in 1937.
Walt Disney's twenty-year pursuit
to secure the film rights from the
book's author, PL Travers, pays off
magnificently. In a flash, all kids want
a nanny like Mary, with her magic
umbrellas. If you're a grade-schooler
who doesn't know the words to
songs like "Chim Chim Cher-ee,"
you may as well stay in at recess.
There's plenty in *Mary Poppins* for
parents, too: groundbreaking special
effects that mix animated dancing
with that of Andrews (who wins the
Oscar—see April 5) and Van Dyke,
which can only be described as...
supercalifragilisticexpialidocious!
Wholesome Andrews soon returns
to the singing governess spotlight
in the blockbuster *The Sound of
Music*, putting her in the year's two
highest-grossing movies.

KING-SIZED DREAMS

On August 28, 1963, some 200,000 people gathered on the Mall in Washington, DC. Fearing that a major march on the nation's capitol would jeopardize civil rights legislation and tarnish America's image abroad, President Kennedy had tried to convince civil rights leaders to cancel the March on Washington for Jobs and Freedom. They refused, and instead gathered to hear singers like Joan Baez, Bob Dylan, and Peter, Paul and Mary, and speakers like labor leader Walter Reuther and civil rights activists John Lewis, Bayard Rustin, and Roy Wilkins. But the event would forever belong to Martin Luther King, Jr., whose eloquent "I Have a Dream" speech from the steps of the Lincoln Memorial signaled a watershed moment for the civil rights movement.

> **"I have a dream that one day this nation will rise up and live out the true meaning of its creed: We hold these truths to be self-evident, that all men are created equal."**
>
> —**Martin Luther King, Jr.**

AUGUST 28

1964 Having dinner in their Delmonico Hotel suite in Manhattan after a concert at Forest Hills Tennis Stadium, the Beatles receive an unexpected, iconic visitor: Bob Dylan. After some awkward chitchat he asks if they want to get high, mistakenly believing the refrain in "I Wanna Hold Your Hand" to be "I get high" instead of "I can't hide." Bob rolls a joint. With a squad of police on security detail in the hall outside, the band (led by Ringo) and manager Brian Epstein retreat to a back room sealed with rolled towels under the doors. Soon they're puffing away on joint after joint, their first group-wide indulgence, though several had sampled pot during the early years playing in Hamburg. Dylan amuses himself by answering their phone, "This is Beatlemania here."

AUGUST 29

1967 On this hot summer night, the running finally stops. It's the series finale of *The Fugitive*, a show inspired by the real-life sensationalistic murder case of Dr. Sam Sheppard (see Nov. 16). High atop an amusement park tower, Dr. Richard Kimble (David Janssen) finally corners his wife's murderer, the infamous one-armed man. As they tussle, Kimble's relentless pursuer, cop Philip Gerard (Barry Morse), watches. Realizing he's been wrong about Kimble, he shoots the one-armed man, who tumbles to his death. With his alibi gone, Kimble seems doomed until a witness steps forward and he's finally exonerated. More than 25.7 million people tune in for Kimble's swan song. The largest audience for a TV episode ever, the record won't be broken until the "Who Shot J.R.?" episode of *Dallas* thirteen years later.

AUGUST 30

1960 Today, after packed congressional hearings, the House outlaws both payola and game-show rigging, ending years of dirty little secrets that made big headlines. In the late '50s, TV and music had one shameful thing in common: corruption. Rigged television quiz shows led to the exposure of erudite professor Charles Van Doren, who after strenuously denying charges finally admitted to receiving answers in advance on *Twenty-One*. "I was involved, deeply involved, in a deception," says Van Doren. "I have deceived my friends, and I had millions of them." Radio investigations close in on Dick Clark and Allen Freed, the deejay who coined the term rock 'n' roll, charging them with accepting payola from record companies in exchange for playing certain records. The practice had been common for years, prompting some to suggest that it was all a trumped-up attempt to halt the rise of rock. Clark cooperates and is exonerated; Freed gets a suspended sentence, a $500 fine, and a ruined career.

AUGUST 31

1969 After galloping out of the old west in *Butch Cassidy and the Sundance Kid,* one of the year's biggest crowd and critic pleasers, Robert Redford, plunks down some of his earnings today to buy a small ski resort in Utah called Timphaven. The film also provides him with an appropriate new moniker for the site: Sundance. Rejecting ideas from hungry investors intent on building a luxury hotel/condo complex, Redford follows his strong environmental leanings. He begins to fashion an ecologically and artistically friendly site and, within a couple years, combines it with an existing Utah film festival (no, he didn't quite start the Sundance Film Festival). Thanks to the generous financial and creative support of Redford and friends, the Sundance Institute grows to become one of the world's most celebrated, successful places to nurture and grow independent film talent.

SEPTEMBER

SEPTEMBER 1

1964

Often imitated, never duplicated, *Mad* magazine held a special spot in the staid '50s and into the permissive '60s—an anarchic, satiric spot. Beloved by kids, targeted by feds, it was the brainchild of iconoclastic publisher William Gaines. No target was taboo for the illustrated mag, which used irreverent parodies and spin to tackle topical issues like drug abuse, gun control, hippies, pollution, psychoanalysis, the sexual revolution, and lots more. "Gaines never put out more than eight issues a year, and he never broke a sweat," wrote John Robert Tebbel. Today, however, Universal Pictures threatens to sue over its spoof cover illustration of a Boris Karloff–inspired *Frankenstein*. Gaines's response: What, me worry?

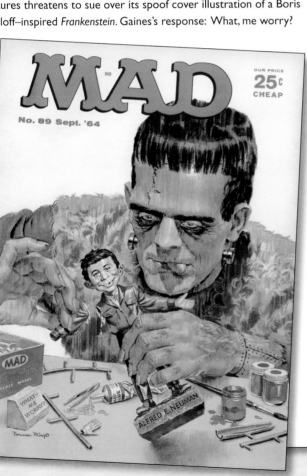

MAD #89 © 1964 E.C. Publications, Inc. All Rights Reserved. Used with Permission.

SEPTEMBER 2

1962

Marine biologist and nature writer Rachel Carson, fifty-five, had investigated the harmful effects of pesticides like DDT for years. Today Houghton Mifflin triggers a firestorm when it publishes her environmental clarion call, *Silent Spring*. One chemical company spokesman predicts doomsday, claiming "If man were to follow the teachings of Miss Carson, we would return to the Dark Ages, and the insects and diseases and vermin would again inherit the earth." Eventually, their profit-conscious fears are drowned out by a newly empowered environmental movement. All the while, Carson secretly hides her cancer that her powerful enemies could have used against her. Carson dies less than two years later, but her seminal book changes the world forever. In 1980, she receives a posthumous Presidential Medal of Freedom.

MEANWHILE...

WHO DO YOU TRUST?

On September 2, 1963, CBS doubled the length of its evening newscast to thirty minutes, and within a week NBC followed suit. CBS dominated broadcast news, thanks largely to Walter Cronkite, who'd assumed the *CBS Evening News* anchor desk from Douglas Edwards the year before. A former radio and wire service reporter, Cronkite was recruited by renowned correspondent Edward R. Murrow. The anchor's previous on-air coverage of political conventions had led to strong audience acceptance and a moniker: "the most trusted man in America." When Cronkite called the Vietnam War a "stalemate," President Lyndon Johnson famously said, "If I've lost Cronkite, I've lost America." Competing primarily against NBC's Chet Huntley and David Brinkley, Cronkite anchored for nineteen years, ending each broadcast with his trademark, "and that's the way it is," followed by the date.

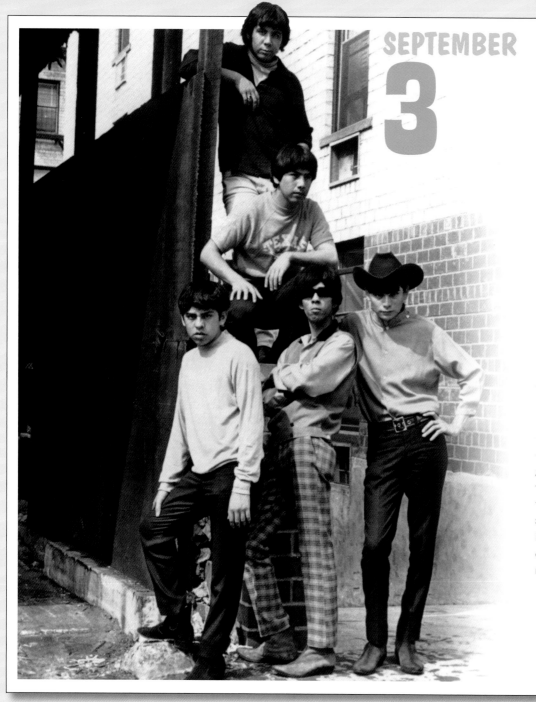

SEPTEMBER 3

1966

The dream of every local garage band in America —a #1 hit!—is about to come true for an unknown Michigan quintet. Today Cameo Records releases "96 Tears" by ? & the Mysterians. Though his identity is a purposely-kept secret, the lead singer behind the dark sunglasses is Rudy Martinez, born in Mexico but now a Michigan resident. The primitive, pre-punk single climbs next month to #1, presaging the punk rock movement that catches fire in the '70s with artists like Patti Smith and the Sex Pistols. On their *96 Tears* album is a song called "8-Teen," later to be a hit for Alice Cooper as "Eighteen." Though "Question Mark" and the lads quickly fade away, it's not quite correct to term them a garage rock band: "96 Tears" was actually recorded in their manager's living room, along with its flip side, "In the Midnight Hour"—another quintessential garage (or living room?) band favorite.

SEPTEMBER 4

1967 Just sit right back and you'll hear a tale… of a show that just got cancelled. Today marks the end of a three-season tour for the kitschy *Gilligan's Island* on CBS. It's been an eventful, extended sojourn on the uncharted desert isle for the S.S. *Minnow*'s skipper (Alan Hale, Jr.) and first mate (Bob Denver), the millionaire and his wife, the movie star, the professor, and gal pal Mary Ann.

Excoriated by the critics, the campy sitcom provided the ultimate in light escapist fare. It attracted a strong fan base, especially among the younger set—so much so that two weekend-morning cartoon series based on the series later run on both ABC and CBS. Even the inevitable reunion special in 1978 scores big ratings, while the original becomes a longtime hit in reruns.

SEPTEMBER 5

1964

Talk about good timing. Last night the Animals made their American debut at Brooklyn's Paramount Theater alongside Jan & Dean, Chuck Berry, and Del Shannon. Today their version of the old blues/folk standard "The House of the Rising Sun" tops the US charts, just as it's done in their native England. Knocked off in only thirteen minutes in a recording studio two months ago, the instant pop classic is powered by Eric Burdon's smoky vocals and Alan Price's blistering organ. Over the next few years, the band adds a dozen hit singles, including "Don't Let Me Be Misunderstood," a bluesy cover of a Nina Simone song. Her version doesn't even chart, and she's reportedly piqued by their (far more successful) interpretation.

SEPTEMBER 6

1969

Fresh off the stage at Woodstock, where he got more than a little help from thousands of his friends, Joe Cocker makes his first-ever cover of *Rolling Stone* magazine. Looking typically rough 'n' rowdy, the raspy rocker has recently become a master at converting others' compositions into his own, from Leon Russell's "Delta Lady" (written about Rita Coolidge) to Dave Mason's "Feelin' Alright." "With a Little Help from My Friends" isn't the only Beatles song Joe puts a new coat of paint on: shortly after the release of *Abbey Road* next month, he redoes "She Came in Through the Bathroom Window," his first Top 40 hit in America. Soon he's hitting his stride with his *Mad Dogs and Englishmen* tour, though his increasing abuse of drugs and alcohol leads to a self-imposed, extended period of recuperation.

SEPTEMBER 7

1968

Burn those bras! And girdles, hair curlers, false eyelashes, spike heels—whatever smacks of "degrading, mindless boob-girlies," as one protestor's sign reads. Around a hundred feminists picket tonight's live Miss America pageant in Atlantic City, providing vociferous visibility to the budding women's liberation movement (or as *All in the Family*'s Archie Bunker famously misidentified it, the women's lubrication movement). Their giant Miss America puppet has chains dangling from its red, white, and blue bathing suit, but the crowd watching beyond the police barricade is largely unsympathetic. A tiny, three-person counter-demonstration begins, led by a former Miss America runner-up wearing a hand-painted sign—"The Only Thing Wrong With Miss America Is That She's Beautiful"—pinned to her dress alongside a "Nixon for President" pin.

1966 A phenomenon later on, *Star Trek* is anything but when it debuts tonight on NBC. In its first season it ranks a mediocre #52 and is regularly beaten by competitors like *Bewitched* and *My Three Sons*. In successive years NBC shifts its date and timeslot, but audience interest falls even further. The show is finally axed at the end of its third season.

However, diehard trekkies keep the flame alive. Paramount tries an animated series for a couple years until it releases its first feature film in 1979, and the overwhelming response triggers a steady stream of movies and syndicated series ever since. "Gallivanting around the cosmos," says William Shatner (a.k.a. Captain Kirk), "is a game for the young."

8

MAKE FIGHTING AFIELD

In a monumental David-versus-Goliath battle, the downtrodden rose up and changed America forever. On September 8, 1965, migrant farm workers went on strike against their overseers, the all-powerful grape growers, in Delano, California. Experienced at breaking strikes, the owners soon met their match when the strikers merged with another nascent group and formed the United Farm Workers of America (UFW). Ardent activist Caesar Chavez tied the plight of poor Filipino and Mexican immigrants to the larger civil rights movement, reaching out to church groups and student activists for support. "We are men and women who have suffered and endured much," he said, "and not only because of our abject poverty, but because we have been kept poor." Committed to nonviolence, the movement engaged in walkouts, community organizing, marches, and, perhaps most effectively, consumer boycotts. Millions of Americans joined in by refusing to buy non-union grapes, eventually forcing the growers to sign historic labor contracts in 1969. Immediate gains included better wages, protection from widely used pesticides, a medical plan, and provisions of fresh water and toilets in the fields. The battle had just begun, however, as lettuce growers in Salinas later brought in the Teamsters to prevent a similar situation. More strikes, disturbances, arrests, and several deaths ensued, until a new California law gave workers the right to secret-ballot elections. The UFW overwhelmingly won.

SEPTEMBER 9 1966

Question: What do you do if you're the #3-rated television network with the #1 campy superhero? Answer: introduce another campy superhero. With Adam West's *Batman* a ratings smash (*KAPOW!*), the show's producers hope lightning will strike twice with tonight's premiere of *The Green Hornet*, starring the dashing Van Williams and whip-fast, charismatic kung fu master Bruce Lee as his partner Kato. The formula is virtually identical—a superhero (with a souped-up car, the Black Beauty) and his buddy fighting evildoers—but the result isn't. Eventually, as a ploy to attract viewers, the duo does two crossover episodes with Batman and Robin, but it's not enough to save *The Green Hornet* from cancellation after a lone season. Williams' career quickly fades, while Lee ascends to iconic status as a pioneering kung fu star who, on the side, trains folks like Steve Mc-Queen and UCLA's Lew Alcindor. He dies, mysteriously, at the height of his popularity in 1973.

SEPTEMBER
10

1963 Long envious of the lavish annual blowouts at Venice and Cannes, New York City tonight unspools its own film festival. Yet the New York Film Festival at Lincoln Center isn't a showy industry competition but a straightforward exhibition. The twenty-one feature films are heavy on foreign entries like Luis Bunuel's *The Exterminating Angel* (Mexico), Roman Polanski's *Knife in the Water* (Poland), and Harold Pinter's *The Servant* (England). Audiences react in spectacular fashion, as the ten-day event draws 50,000 people and sells out most screenings. Attendees range from long-haired beatniks in sandals to elegantly turned-out patrons more likely to be seen at the opera, all demonstrating what one critic calls "panting enthusiasm for what has suddenly become the early fall season's biggest and most sensational cultural event."

SEPTEMBER
11

1967 While the variety show format is fading, one versatile vagabond gathers together an ensemble cast and strikes gold. Premiering tonight, *The Carol Burnett Show* showcases the clowning, singing, dancing actress/comedienne, alongside friends Tim Conway, Harvey Korman, Vicki Lawrence, and Lyle Waggoner. Hardly a "straight man" in the bunch, they often have trouble keeping a straight face in their sketches—but that's half the fun. Their chemistry shines in spoofs like the soap opera "As the Stomach Turns" and the Civil War drama "Went With the Wind." Burnett and a guest star open each show by taking questions from the audience, and she ends each with a little tug on the ear—originally a secret signal to the grandmother who raised her.

SEPTEMBER 12

1964

Riding an incredible opening burst, the Dave Clark Five have pounded out three Top 10 singles in under six months. Today they move to a softer ballad, "Because," which soon becomes their biggest yet—up to #3. In the heyday of the British Invasion, this clean-cut band of moptops draws comparisons to the Beatles. Though not quite in the Fab Four's league, the DC5 does have an upbeat, thumping sound and a cute Beatle-like lead singer in Mike Smith (Dave Clark plays the drums). They star in their own movie, *Having a Wild Weekend*, and make twelve appearances on *The Ed Sullivan Show*, a record for any UK group. Clark's also an entrepreneur whose portfolio in later years includes not only the group's music but also a savvy pickup on TV, the seminal British rock 'n' roll series *Ready, Steady, Go!*

SEPTEMBER 13

1969

Amidst a multitude of superstars at Woodstock the month before, the relatively unknown Santana electrified the crowd and generated extraordinary buzz. Led by virtuoso guitarist and vocalist Carlos Santana, their self-titled first album (recorded live at Woodstock) debuts today on the charts en route to a two-year stay and two-plus million in sales. Soon they're in demand, touring nationwide but still managing to squeeze in an appearance on *The Ed Sullivan Show* the next month. Their follow-up album, *Abraxas*, cements their reputation as pre-eminent, percussion-heavy Latin rockers with Top 10 singles "Evil Ways" and "Black Magic Woman." "For pure spirituality and emotion," says Eric Clapton, "Carlos Santana is number one." The band's fee for playing Woodstock? $500.

SEPTEMBER 14

1962 Tired of the usual drive-in fare? Hungry for something other than traditional Hollywood entertainment like *The Music Man* or *That Touch of Mink*? Then today's your day to catch the debauched debut of *Mondo Cane*, an Italian documentary that trolls the world in search of the bizarre and macabre. All the rage at last spring's Cannes Film Festival, its travelogue vignettes of strange cultures and practices combine to create a new genre: the "shockumentary." More follow soon, like the *Faces of Death* series and *Shocking Asia*. "The season's most argued-about film," writes *Life* magazine of *Mondo Cane*. Its theme song, "More," becomes an international hit, and new versions, by jazz musician Kai Winding and singer Vic Dana, respectively, later chart in the US. An eclectic group of artists will also record the song, from Ed Ames to Doris Day to Marvin Gaye.

SEPTEMBER 15

1962 When recording artists hit #1 with their first song, many think they're an overnight success. But the various members of the Four Seasons had actually paid their dues for a decade, in other bands and/or singing backup. Today the unmistakable, piercing falsetto of Frankie Valli shoots "Sherry" to the top of the charts, and they're off. Two more #1's—"Big Girls Don't Cry" and "Walk Like a Man"—quickly follow, and the boys from Jersey will rack up forty more chart hits before the decade ends. Since their label Vee-Jay also (temporarily) owns the rights to a handful of Beatles songs, Frankie Valli and company even appear on a double album entitled *The Beatles vs. The Four Seasons*, with hyped-up cover copy proclaiming "The International Battle of the Century...You Be the Judge and Jury."

SEX AND THE SMALL TOWN

Based on the notorious bestselling novel by Grace Metalious, *Peyton Place* burst into primetime on September 15, 1964, in the form of a steamy ABC soap opera (below). Set in a small New England town teeming with scandalous secrets and romantic entanglements, the potboiler ran for five seasons. Two major stars emerged from its large and ever-changing cast: Mia Farrow, who left after two seasons, and Ryan O'Neal. The series followed on the heels of a successful feature film starring Lana Turner, also based on the original source: Metalious's 1956 novel, which sold a phenomenal 60,000 copies—at $3.95 apiece—in only ten days.

SEPTEMBER 16

1964 With rock 'n' roll sweeping the country, ABC gets the jump on its rivals by debuting a musical showcase called *Shindig*. Hoping to duplicate the success of British programs like *Ready, Steady, Go!*, it opens with Sam Cooke, the Everly Brothers, and the Righteous Brothers, plus smiling host Jimmy O'Neill and those oh-so-fine Shindig Dancers. A few months later, NBC joins the party with *Hullabaloo*, featuring more fab dancers and hosts like Paul Anka and Jerry Lewis (with his rock star son Gary). Performers include the Supremes, the Ronettes, Sonny and Cher, and lots more. *Hullabaloo* also goes the extra mile—many miles actually—by featuring a segment taped in London during its first three months. Impresario Brian Epstein hosts, introducing top British acts like Gerry and the Pacemakers, Marianne Faithfull, and the Moody Blues. But he never delivers his main attraction, the Beatles, who appear on the show only after Epstein's segment ends.

SEPTEMBER 17

1967 The reputation of bad boy Jim Morrison, lead singer of the Doors, precedes him. So when the band's booked tonight to appear on *The Ed Sullivan Show*, the host makes Jim promise to amend the line "Girl, we couldn't get much higher" from their smash hit "Light My Fire." Ed feared it would be construed as—gasp!—a *drug* reference. (Last January he'd successfully prevailed on the Rolling Stones to change "Let's spend the night together" to "Let's spend some time together.") But where Mick kowtowed, Jim doesn't. He sings the song as usual, and since the show's live, out to the world it goes. Out, too, go the Doors. An incensed Ed refuses to shake their hands, and a producer tells them backstage that they'll never be invited back. "So what?" chortles Jim. "We just *did* the Sullivan show."

SEPTEMBER
18

1964

You rang? Halloween comes a bit early to primetime tonight as ABC premieres the creepy, kooky *The Addams Family*. The live-action versions of the characters created by cartoonist Charles Addams for the *New Yorker* magazine become instant fan favorites: somber mother Morticia (Carolyn Jones), googly-eyed father Gomez (John Astin), and especially seven-foot-tall Franken-butler Lurch (Ted Cassidy), who even starts a brief dance craze. Next week more monsters—make that *Munsters*—invade living rooms as CBS opens a frighteningly similar sitcom about a ghoulish family inhabiting a musty gothic mansion. This one features Fred Gwynne as Herman Munster, Yvonne DeCarlo as his wife Lily, and Al Lewis as Grandpa. Both series last two seasons, but survive beyond the grave in animated and live-action syndicated reincarnations.

SEPTEMBER
19

1962

If movie-theater westerns can run for an hour and a half, why can't their television counterparts? Apparently they can, as NBC tonight debuts *The Virginian*, the small screen's first ninety-minute weekly series. Set in 1890s Wyoming on the Shiloh Ranch, the show stars James Drury as the laconic title character, alongside Lee J. Cobb and Doug McClure. Though westerns are somewhat on the wane after peaking in the late '50s, they still maintain a strong primetime presence with shows like *Bonanza*, *Rawhide*, and *Wagon Train*. Most are shot on film by Hollywood studios, foreshadowing the end of the live, theater-inspired programming that emanates from New York. *The Virginian* enjoys a nine-season run and serves as a springboard for young series regulars like David Hartman, Lee Majors, and Tim Matheson.

SEPTEMBER 20

1967

Tens of thousands gather to watch Her Majesty the Queen launch the *Queen Elizabeth II* (QE2), Cunard's latest luxury liner. "May God bless her and all who sail in her," pronounces Queen Elizabeth, with Prince Philip and Princess Margaret by her side, before pressing a button that shatters a bottle of champagne across the bow of the 58,000-ton, 963-foot ship. With nearly a thousand cabins and luxury appointments that include crockery designed by the Marquess of Queensberry, the vessel becomes Cunard's flagship. Over the years, the QE2 carries more than two-and-a-half million passengers and crosses the Atlantic more than 800 times. Upon her retirement in 2008, the ship is acquired by the government of Dubai, which plans to refurbish her into a luxury floating hotel, retail, and entertainment destination.

SEPTEMBER 21

1969

Growing up in Hell's Kitchen in Manhattan, Mario Puzo tried to follow his mother's advice to avoid the mean streets. After serving in World War II, he published his first novel in 1955, to little acclaim. Then he toiled in pulp fiction, to middling financial success, until he decided to draw upon stories he'd heard growing up. Today, *The Godfather* shoots to the top of the *New York Times* bestseller chart and catapults its author to legendary literary status. "[It's] an epic of crime, sung in the plain idiom of the streets," writes Geoffrey Wolff in the *Washington Post*. "A world of cunning and treachery, where power is a function of a leader's ability to seem to say one thing while he intends to perform the opposite." When Puzo's landmark novel generates a $410,000 fee for paperback rights, he telephones his mother to share the good news. She misunderstands, thinking he's saying $40,000. When she finally grasps that it's a six-figure deal, she warns him: "Don't tell nobody." This time he doesn't follow mama's advice, and soon he's translating his work to the big screen. With Puzo's extraordinary storytelling ability, director Francis Ford Coppola fashions a trilogy of *Godfather* films in the '70s that surpasses even its literary roots.

SEPTEMBER 22

1962

Is there a doctor on the set? Actually, yes, there are a couple of 'em—handsome, earnest young men who'll cure what ails you. For many, that's a bad case of "Casey-itis," as described in today's *TV Guide*. The story focuses on Vince Edwards, the brooding title star of ABC's *Ben Casey*, but strangely ignores his counterpart, handsome Richard Chamberlain (*Dr. Kildare*), whose NBC medical drama draws higher ratings. The story notes, punningly, that we're experiencing "if not an epidemic, at least a slight rash of medical shows." Laymen and practitioners alike tune in, as student nurses at New York's St. Vincent's Hospital are allowed to stay up past curfew on Monday nights to catch *Ben Casey*, a "masterfully contrived medicine cabinet of torn emotions and mended nerves."

SEPTEMBER 23

1961 From television's earliest days, the upstart medium and Hollywood had a rough relationship. Alarmed by falling theater attendance and fast-rising television numbers (of sets, viewers, and programs), film studios tried to hinder that growth by informally agreeing not to license their movies. In 1955, RKO broke ranks and began selling pre-1948 movies, and soon 20th Century Fox, Columbia, MGM, and Warner Bros. followed suit. But, today, a seismic shift occurs when a new deal allows NBC to premiere Marilyn Monroe's *How to Marry a Millionaire*—kicking off *Saturday Night at the Movies*. "Now that NBC has cast its electronic dice, will electrifying results come to pass?" asks the *New York Times*. The network's "nickelodeon night" succeeds, and soon color and post-1948 feature films begin filling the airwaves.

SEPTEMBER 24

1968 CBS's *60 Minutes*, television's first newsmagazine, debuts at a time when documentary-style news programs are known to bring prestige but little profit. *60 Minutes* changes all that, becoming a Sunday-night institution that attracts record viewers and advertisers. It also spawns a host of imitators but still leads the pack four decades later. Mike Wallace and Harry Reasoner are its first correspondents. When Reasoner departs for ABC, Morley Safer replaces him, and the two are later joined by now-familiar names like Dan Rather, Andy Rooney, Ed Bradley, and Diane Sawyer. The show's "you-are-there" approach thrives despite the personnel changes. "What we were able to do," says Wallace, "is bring the technique of live reportage to the documentary."

LOTS OF SPOTS: FAVORITE TV COMMERCIALS OF THE '60S

Though *60 Minutes* may have been the most famous TV show to ever utilize a ticking clock, in the '60s, the gimmick was more synonymous with newsman-turned-spokesman John Cameron Swayze, who intoned, "It takes a licking and keeps on ticking," in Timex watch commercials. Here are more famous TV ads from the decade.

- **President Johnson's reelection.** A little girl idly plucks petals from a daisy as an ominous voice-over counts down. At zero, an image of an exploding mushroom cloud appears. (1964)

- **Noxzema Shave Cream.** The unmistakably bawdy refrain of David Rose and His Orchestra's "The Stripper" plays as former Miss Sweden, blonde Gunilla Knutson, urges men to "take it off—take it all off." (1966)

- **Marlboro cigarettes.** Cowboys awake on a foggy morning to fresh-brewing coffee over an open fire—and their first cigarette of the day—as an announcer says, "Come to where the flavor is. Come to Marlboro country." (1967)

- **AMC Rebel (car).** A harried driving-school instructor teaches a succession of hapless drivers. "Look out for that truck," he warns one Barbie-like young woman. "What truck?" she asks, clueless. "Behind the bus." "What bus?" she asks again as tires squeal. (1968)

- **American Tourister luggage.** Having been tossed a suitcase, a caged gorilla proceeds to throw it around and jump on it, grunting and howling, as an announcer intones, "Dear clumsy bell-boys... careless doormen... butter-fingered luggage handlers..." (1969)

- **Alka-Seltzer antacid.** A commercial within a commercial features a man ready to burst after fifty-nine takes of eating spaghetti and meatballs. He finally manages to deliver his line flaw-lessly: "Mama mia! That's a spicy meatball!" Then the oven door falls open, and he must do it again... luckily he has some Alka-Seltzer. (1969)

- **Volkswagen.** A funeral procession of big, fancy cars passes as the dearly departed's voice-over announces stingy bequests to his spendthrift wife, sons, and friends. He ends by leaving his $100 billion fortune to his thrifty nephew Harold, who brings up the rear of the procession in a black VW Beetle. (1969)

SEPTEMBER 25

1960 Recently released from prison for stealing 300 tires from a local car dealer, a heavyset, sixteen-year-old Los Angeles lad today joins a local R&B quintet called The Upfronts. The band, however, goes nowhere. Four years later, the young man arranges "Harlem Shuffle," an R&B hit for Bob & Earl, and later serves as a drummer/road manager. This versatile, still-oversized fellow is Barry White. Later he'll assemble a sexy female trio, Love Unlimited, and write them a million-seller. Then he'll unleash his own rich baritone, steamy lyrics, and forty-piece orchestra to deliver a torrent of lush '70s crossover hits, such as "Never, Never Gonna Give Ya Up" and "Can't Get Enough of Your Love, Babe." Despite tipping the scales at 300 pounds, Barry's partial to the appellation "Prophet of Love."

1960 "Some women, it is said, like to cook—this book is not for them." And so begins the culinary adventures of irreverent Peg Bracken, who's *I Hate to Cook Book* is published today. An advertising copywriter by day, she connects with millions of housewives eager to prepare fast, not fancy, meals. Her recipes rely heavily on common canned, frozen, and packaged ingredients, in strong contrast to celebrated gourmet chefs of the day, like James Beard. With titles like Skid Road Stroganoff, Old-Fashioned Farm Fry, and Stayabed Stew, the cookbook sells millions of copies (at $3.75 apiece) and propels Bracken's new career. She soon expands her range to include housekeeping and etiquette (*I Try to Behave Myself*), makes many television and radio appearances, and becomes a spokeswoman for Birds Eye frozen foods.

SEPTEMBER
26

1960 Television makes a grand entrance into presidential politics tonight in the first of four televised debates between the two nominees, Vice President Richard Nixon and Senator John F. Kennedy. Nixon's camp had decided to accept the challenger's offer of four televised debates, remembering how their man's 1952 "Checkers" speech had effectively defused a potentially damaging incident of accepting illegal contributions. But handsome, photogenic JFK impresses, while a sweaty, five-o'clock-shadowed Nixon—wearied from a recent knee injury—doesn't. A subsequent poll of radio listeners rates the debate a tie, but among seventy million television viewers, JFK is the clear winner. "Image wasn't the only thing that carried the day for Kennedy," writes reporter Beverly Carter. "His aggressive style eclipsed Nixon's more conciliatory posture. To many, Kennedy appeared more presidential."

SEPTEMBER 28

1961 The epic-within-an-epic drama that is *Cleopatra*, starring Elizabeth Taylor, starts shooting—again—in Rome, with a new director and two new stars: Richard Burton and Rex Harrison, replacing Stephen Boyd and Peter Finch. Extensive and expensive shooting earlier in London, where Taylor underwent an emergency tracheotomy, is scrapped. Soon the off-screen romance between Burton and Taylor heats up, prompting moral outrage that adds to the woes of the troubled, intensely scrutinized production. The film, made for 20th Century Fox, soldiers on as costs skyrocket from $2 million to $44 million, making it by far the most expensive motion picture to date. Taylor snags an unheard-of $1 million salary, which later tops $5 million after escalation clauses and lawsuits kick in. Critics and historians savage the beleaguered four-hour film upon its release in June 1963, and it nearly bankrupts the studio—though it does manage to win four Oscars, including Best Cinematography and Costume Design.

SEPTEMBER 29

1962 George Bernard Shaw's drama *Pygmalion* opened in Vienna in 1913. Adapting it into a musical proved a long and arduous task, but eventually the resulting *My Fair Lady* opened on Broadway in 1956. Starring Rex Harrison and newcomer Julie Andrews, it was an immediate smash that swept six Tony awards, including Best Musical, Actor (Harrison), and Direction (Moss Hart). Tonight, *My Fair Lady* closes after 2,717 performances—making it Broadway's longest running musical to date—and a tough act to follow. "*My Fair Lady* was the perfect musical play," says composer Andre Previn. "But it was so perfect that, afterwards, what else could you do? Alan [Lerner]'s adaptation was the last word as far as that kind of musical was concerned."

SEPTEMBER 30

1960

"Wilmaaaaaaaaaaaah!" echoes round the world as primetime's first animated sitcom, *The Flintstones*, debuts on ABC. Essentially a prehistoric cartoon version of *The Honeymooners*, it stars conniving "Everycaveman" Fred Flintstone, his patient wife Wilma, and their next-door neighbors, Barney and Betty Rubble. The producers, cartoon titans Bill Hanna and Joe Barbera (*The Yogi Bear Show*, *The Jetsons*) create the nighttime show after surveys reveal that adults comprise 65 percent of the audiences for their Saturday-morning kiddie fare like *Quick Draw McGraw*. Though *The Flintstones* (original title: *The Flagstones*) live in prehistoric times, they still enjoy "creature" comforts: a baby wooly mammoth serves (with its trunk) as the house's vacuum cleaner, while a long-beaked pterodactyl acts as the record player. Do viewers respond positively? According to the Nielsens, they yabba-dabba-do!

OCTOBER

OCTOBER
1

1962 An emotional Jack Paar departed as host of The *Tonight Show* last March, but a contractual dispute with ABC delayed the arrival of his chosen successor, Johnny Carson, until now. Over the summer, a bevy of guest hosts from Joey Bishop to Arlene Francis to Soupy Sales filled in. Tonight the mischievous Groucho Marx introduces new full-time host Carson and his affable sidekick, Ed McMahon. NBC packs the guest lineup with stars: Tony Bennett, Mel Brooks, Joan Crawford, and Rudy Vallee. So begins the thirty-year late-night reign of the understated, unflappable Carson, inimitably introduced by McMahon with his booming, "He-e-e-e-re's Johnny!"

MACABRE MATINEE

With no rating system for movies yet in place, kids in Pittsburgh attending their usual Saturday matinees on October 1, 1968, were in for a shock. Sure they'd seen horror movies before, but nothing like this—a gory, ghoulish black-and-white chiller called *Night of the Living Dead*. "The film opens," said neophyte writer/director George Romero, "with a situation that has already disintegrated to a point of little hope, and it moves progressively toward absolute despair and ultimate tragedy." And just like that, Romero's decidedly non-family fare shot and slashed its way into movie history. Bored with making industrial films and TV commercials, Romero had maximized his shoestring budget ($114,000) with thrifty solutions like using chocolate syrup for blood and morticians' wax for zombie makeup. While the movie's flesh-eating zombies spelled doom for their human victims, they brought their creator newfound prominence as an innovative cinematic talent.

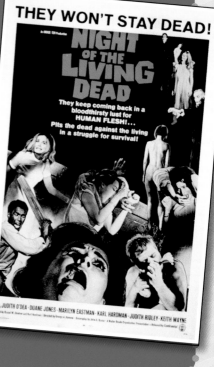

OCTOBER
2

1965 Of the many college football games played this Saturday afternoon, the Florida Gators/Louisiana State Tigers match-up goes down in history. But it's what happens *off* the field that really matters. In the unseasonable 102-degree heat, Florida introduces a secret weapon: a sports drink that rehydrates its athletes by replenishing their carbohydrates and electrolytes. Invented by nephrologist J. Robert Cade, the drink has a quasi-palatable flavor thanks to his wife's suggestion to add lemon juice. After some more tinkering, the end result—Gatorade—revolutionizes the world of sports, as millions upon millions of athletes start chugging it down. Kansas City Chiefs coach Hank Stram attributes his team's win in the '69 Super Bowl to the sports drink, and soon coaches everywhere feel the chilling effects of a new end-of-game ritual, the Gatorade shower. Back on the field this day, quarterback Steve Spurrier leads the Gators to a 14-7 win as their Gatorade-deprived opponents wilt in the second half.

OCTOBER
3

1968 Movie critics don't get any more influential—or feared—than Bosley Crowther of the *New York Times*. A forty-year veteran of the paper, he started on the city beat, became its first nightclub reporter, and later moved on to theater and film reviews. Twenty-seven years of his scholarly movie critiques come to an end today, due largely to his repeated, strident panning of Arthur Penn's *Bonnie and Clyde*. Though the controversial film garnered mixed reviews initially, it's later recognized as a landmark of American cinema. Fellow critic Andrew Sarris of the *Village Voice* denounced Crowther's "personal vendetta against a director and actor [Warren Beatty] he doesn't like." Crowther's editors worried that he had grown out of touch with the moviegoing public, and a bit bizarre besides (he'd praised, for example, the disastrous *Cleopatra*), and quietly encouraged his departure.

OCTOBER
4

1961 That brilliant flash emanating from the Lyceum on Broadway tonight signals the arrival of a major new force in theater. British playwright Harold Pinter's *The Caretaker* opens, unveiling a modern-day parable that starts as a comedy but ends in scorn and sorrow. Donald Pleasance crackles as the title character, a tattered tramp who invades the disordered lives of two demented brothers (Alan Bates and Donald Shaw). Plumbing the depths of the current social malaise, the multi-layered drama "teases and clings to the mind," showing that Pinter "has left many of today's serious playwrights behind," according to critic Howard Taubman. A film version with the same trio of players debuts several years later, by which time Pinter's well on his way to a long, distinguished career, capped in 2005 by the Nobel Prize for literature. "In his plays," the Academy writes, "[Pinter] uncovers the precipice under everyday prattle and forces entry into oppression's closed rooms."

OCTOBER 6 · 1966

Today California (and in two years, the entire country) outlaws LSD, the psychedelic compound discovered by Swiss chemist Albert Hoffman in the late '30s. The drug's unexpected hallucinatory properties led to a surge in recreational use in the mid-'60s, fueled by author Aldous Huxley's *The Doors of Perception* (from which the Doors took their name); Ken Kesey and his Merry Pranksters (see Aug. 19); and oft-arrested, ex-Harvard psychology professor Timothy Leary ("the most dangerous man in America," said President Nixon). Never mind that the CIA had secretly dosed unknowing subjects with LSD in the '50s, testing its ability as a truth serum.

Tripping becomes a favorite illicit pastime enjoyed by many and openly celebrated by the Beatles (though John Lennon always claimed that a drawing by his toddler son Sean inspired "Lucy in the Sky with Diamonds"). In 1967, when opening camera equipment shipped back from the Monterey International Pop Festival, they find a slight (and unnoticed by customs) addition: clear, custom-blended liquid acid by the Bay Area's LSD chemist of choice. Known simply as "Owsley," the ex–air force man turned Berkeley art student manufactures millions of doses of the psychedelic from his secret lab in the hills. Brian Epstein immediately throws an LSD bash at this country estate with celebrity guests Mick Jagger and girlfriend Marianne Faithfull, Lionel Bart, Klaus Voormann, Lulu, Robert Stigwood, and more.

> **"Everything in the room spun around, and the familiar objects and pieces of furniture assumed grotesque, threatening forms."**
>
> —chemist Albert Hoffman, on his first LSD trip

OCTOBER 5 · 1964

Barbed-wire fences sprang up overnight in August of 1961, splitting the city of Berlin into East and West. Later an imposing concrete barrier topped with barbed wire arose, becoming the most heated and hated symbol of the Cold War. Many East Germans succeeded at daring escapes before the wall was fully constructed, but many more were cut down by guards ordered to shoot to kill. Today, the West celebrates the largest mass escape—twenty-three men, thirty-one women, and three children—since the wall went up. Passing through a narrow, painstakingly dug 400-foot tunnel, the fifty-seven escapees also show perfect symbolic timing. Tomorrow, Soviet Secretary Leonid I. Brezhnev arrives for festivities celebrating the fifteenth anniversary of the founding of East Germany.

OCTOBER 7

1963 Inverate inventor Bill Lear continues his career of engineering firsts as his Learjet 23 makes a successful maiden voyage. The plane becomes an immediately recognized symbol, the gold standard for small corporate aircraft. With more than 150 patents to his name, Lear had previously invented the car radio, which he sold to Motorola, and the automatic pilot for airplanes. Energetic and exuberant, he shuns retirement and constantly keeps busy with both work and play. A hearty partier, Lear has a soft spot for beautiful women (marrying four times), craps, and fine scotch. "Before anyone ever flew supersonically, Bill was living that way," recalls one friend. Several years later he creates another electronic first, for which he is often not so fondly remembered: the 8-track stereo.

OCTOBER 8

1968 Students who wearily struggle to decipher the arcane language of William Shakespeare nonetheless flock to theaters for Franco Zeffirelli's sumptuous *Romeo and Juliet,* opening today. Unlike all previous versions, in which the actors were far older, the masterful Italian director insists on authenticity—the title roles are played by two previously unknown teens, Leonard Whiting (seventeen) and Olivia Hussey (fifteen), both delivering stunning performances. Critics rave: Roger Ebert calls it "the most exciting film of Shakespeare ever made [with] the passion, the sweat, the violence, the poetry, the love, and the tragedy in the most immediate terms." Bonuses include the uncredited narration of Laurence Olivier, Oscar-winning cinematography and costume design, and a haunting musical score. Henry Mancini's instrumental theme, based on the film, later tops the charts.

MPAA'S "RX" FOR DECENCY

A growing number of films, like *Who's Afraid of Virginia Woolf?*, *Alfie*, and *Blowup*, pushed the envelope in regards to sex, nudity, and language on the big screen. For years, Hollywood heard and deflected the criticism, but on October 8, 1968, Jack Valenti, President of the Motion Picture Association of America, announced the industry's first film ratings. The groundbreaking, voluntary classification system—G (general), M (mature), R (restricted under 16) and X (17 or older)—had to be enforced by theater owners beginning on November 1. Since producers must pay to have films rated, Valenti helpfully noted that fees would range from $3,000 to $25, the latter for "poverty-stricken producers." The next year an X-rated picture, *Midnight Cowboy*, won three Oscars, including Best Picture—for the first and only time. The designations change over the years, with the addition of PG and NC-17, but the ratings remain.

OCTOBER 9 1961

He'd tried out for the lead in *West Side Story*, but didn't get the part. Today, eight days before that film opens, Warren Beatty makes his film debut in director Elia Kazan's *Splendor in the Grass*. A Romeo and Juliet–like tale transplanted to the Midwest, the sudsy, steamy melodrama co-stars Natalie Wood. With Hollywood's first onscreen French kiss, the film heats up—offscreen as well. The Beatty/Wood pairing leads his fiancée, Joan Collins, to announce their breakup. (She then takes up with Robert Wagner, Wood's estranged husband.) *Splendor in the Grass* wins an Oscar for writer William Inge, who'd first mentioned his idea to Kazan while they were producing his play, *The Dark at the Top of the Stairs*.

OCTOBER 9 1967

In Sweden, its far more permissive country of origin, the X-rated *I Am Curious (Yellow)* premieres today to huge crowds and critical acclaim. The buzz builds internationally, and by the time it opens in America, two years later, the authorities are waiting. Erotic? Prurient? Obscene? The word "controversial" barely describes the frenzy that ensues. Many states ban the film and seize copies, generating unprecedented coverage of its unprecedented frontal nudity and sexual activity. Other than its notorious naughty bits, the film is termed rather boring by most critics, who nevertheless salute writer/director/co-star Vilgot Sjoman's adventuresome advance. "The message of the movie," says Charles Champlin of the *Los Angeles Times*, "is that there is evidently nothing the movies cannot show and tell an adult audience."

OCTOBER 11 1965

Awed by the angelic appearance of a winsome seventeen-year-old at a party, Rolling Stones manager Andrew Loog Oldham decides to make her a star. Starting with "As Tears Go By"—which won't be a hit for the Stones for another year—and "Come and Stay with Me," the alluring Marianne Faithfull develops a solid career…and quite the reputation as a party girl. Today, while she's recording "Yesterday" in a London studio, the songwriter himself—Paul McCartney—stops by. But Marianne's name soon becomes hitched to another famous rocker when she leaves her husband and baby to become Mick Jagger's constant companion. When Mick's later busted at Keith Richards' house, the tabloids trumpet the news that Marianne was discovered clothed only in an oversized shag fur rug. In court a prosecutor emphasizes the tawdry, naked lady twist, prompting Richards' famous retort: "We are not old men. We are not worried about petty morals."

OCTOBER 12 1968

What a voice! On this day, Texas-born Janis Joplin leads Big Brother & the Holding Company to the top of the charts with the seminal album *Cheap Thrills* (the label nixed their original title choice, *Dope, Sex, and Cheap Thrills*). One of the finest white singers of the blues, Joplin brings it like few others ever have—witness her torrid, achy "Summertime" and grinding, soulful "Piece of My Heart." Factor in that outsized, outrageous personality, and she soon goes solo. "On stage I make love to 25,000 people," she says. "Then I go home alone." But her persona also has a self-destructive side, fueled by massive consumption of alcohol and drugs. In LA two years later to record the album *Pearl*, she ODs in a Hollywood motel—and later scores her only #1 hit, "Me And Bobby McGee," posthumously.

OCTOBER 13

1962 The play sends "shockwaves through Times Square," reports one theater writer as Edward Albee's *Who's Afraid of Virginia Woolf?* ignites, and incites, Broadway. Legendary actress/acting coach Uta Hagen and Arthur Hill co-star in the stage production that one newspaper calls "a protracted bout of public marital warfare, savagely and hilariously sarcastic and pitifully true in its cyclic ebb and flow." Albee's masterpiece sweeps five Tony awards, including Best Play, Actor (Hill), and Actress (Hagen), and paves the way for a film version four years later that takes five Academy Awards. Elizabeth Taylor wins her second Oscar (her first was for *Butterfield 8*) after packing on thirty pounds to play the frumpy lead, Martha. Her co-star/hubby Richard Burton is also nominated, but loses the best actor trophy to Paul Scofield (*A Man for All Seasons*). Nominated seven times, Burton never wins an Oscar.

OCTOBER 14

1967 A beautiful beginning, a tragic ending: to exploit Marvin Gaye's image as a sex symbol, Motown pairs the smooth crooner with several of its popular female artists, including Mary Wells and Kim Weston. The duos produce several well-received songs, but the third connection is the charm. Beautiful Tammi Terrell matches Gaye note for note, and their sexy, playful personas make for a perfect pairing. "Ain't No Mountain High Enough" and "Your Precious Love," penned by Nicholas Ashford and Valerie Simpson, catch fire. Performing tonight at a homecoming concert at Hampden-Sydney College in rural Virginia, Terrell collapses after the second song. Gaye and a band member help her offstage, and he finishes the concert alone. Diagnosed with a brain tumor, Terrell never performs live again. She battles valiantly but passes away on March 16, 1970. Tammi Terrell was twenty-four.

OCTOBER 15

1966 Awakened by the clarion call of Rachel Carson's *Silent Spring* (see Sept. 2), the fledgling environmental movement takes a step forward today with the passage of the Endangered Species Preservation Act. Prompted in large part by the plight of the majestic whooping crane, the only crane species found exclusively in North America, the bill does little more than authorize the creation of an official list of endangered species. But it's a solid start, and within a year the secretary of the interior compiles a list of seventy-seven birds, fish, mammals, and reptiles. From the American alligator to the Texas blind salamander, many species begin to creep into the nation's consciousness after years of neglect and destruction. Future legislation and rulings increase protection, most notably in 1978 when the Supreme Court torpedoes Tennessee's nearly complete Tellico Dam by ruling in favor of the tiny snail darter. Though the delay proves only temporary, environmental activism has taken on new prominence.

OCTOBER

16

1962

In television's early days, Hollywood resisted and reviled the upstart medium. But when the studios realized that it was here to stay, they began licensing their older films for airplay. Today a milestone turnabout occurs—the debut of a feature film based on a TV teleplay. Rod Serling's *Requiem for a Heavyweight*, a searing story about an over-the-hill fighter, had premiered six years earlier on CBS to huge acclaim and five Emmys. Ralph Nelson again directs the theatrical release with a different but equally star-laden lineup: Anthony Quinn, Jackie Gleason, and Mickey Rooney, plus Cassius Clay as an early ring opponent of Quinn. Serling, meanwhile, goes on to create the landmark TV sci-fi anthology *The Twilight Zone*. But still he hammers the medium. "It is difficult to produce a television documentary that is both incisive and probing," he says, "when every twelve minutes one is interrupted by twelve dancing rabbits singing about toilet paper."

OCTOBER 17

1966 A game show's premiere on daytime television gives the phrase "star-crossed" an entirely new meaning. *The Hollywood Squares*, in which nine celebrities—including Wally Cox, Charley Weaver, Rose Marie, and Paul Lynde—form a human tic-tac-toe board, opens with high style and high-wattage banter that's far more important than the results of the two-player game itself. For example, genial host Peter Marshall asks: "Eddie Fisher recently said, 'I'm sorry, I'm sorry for them both.' Who was he referring to?" To which Lynde replies: "His fans." Stars pile in over the years, from semi-regulars Zsa Zsa Gabor and Ernest Borgnine to unlikely participants such as George C. Scott, Betty Grable, and Big Bird.

> **"I don't understand why people don't remember my name."**
>
> —Paul Lynde

OCTOBER 18

1965 Anti–Vietnam War rallies the weekend before in four major cities, including New York and Berkeley, stirred major attention. In Berkeley, police repulsed protesters' repeated attempts to march from the campus to the Oakland Army Base. At one confrontation, the Hell's Angels moved in, tearing down banners and cursing: "Go back to Russia, you f--king communists." (One speaker likened this behavior to "Hitler's Storm Troopers.") A Republican assemblyman demanded an investigation of the Berkeley campus as "once again the spawning grounds of these unlawful activities." Of more concern to the protesters are the Angels, who've threatened to disrupt their next march. So today Ken Kesey and his Merry Pranksters, and underground poet Allen Ginsberg, visit the home of the Angels' president, Sonny Barger. Stories circulate of a friendly powwow enlivened by LSD, and a truce emerges. It's Ginsberg who coins the term "flower power," becoming an iconic underground figure in anti-war circles, and later in the gay liberation, anti-nuclear, and environmental movements.

OCTOBER 1968
19

In a London courtroom stand John Lennon and Yoko Ono, busted yesterday for possession of pot. They'd been staying at Ringo's flat when detective John Pilcher of Scotland Yard arrived with constables and a dog. He'd earned quite the reputation as an anti-drug zealot who'd previously gone after Mick Jagger and Keith Richards (see Oct. 11). The case is adjourned to late November, and the couple emerges out on bail to a frenzied horde of reporters. Ono later miscarries, and Lennon pleads guilty to possession of cannabis resin in exchange for dropping the charges against her. He's fined 150 pounds, a conviction that later haunts him when the Nixon administration uses it to try to get him deported. The link between pot smoking and rock musicians surprises few people. At the Apple headquarters, writes Philip Norman (*Shout*), "Joints, as numerous as teacups, circulated democratically between bosses and office boys." Still, Lennon always maintains he was framed by Pilcher, who's later fired.

OCTOBER 20

1962

While performing one night in Los Angeles with a vocal group, aspiring actor Bobby Pickett breaks into a monologue between verses. He impersonates one of his movie idols, Boris Karloff. When another group member suggests they invent a song featuring the "monster vocals," Bobby passes—then changes his mind. In one take they record "Monster Mash," released under the name Bobby "Boris" Pickett and the Crypt-Kickers. Their producer shops it all around LA, but the major labels turn him down. Undeterred, he drops off copies at stations around California, and they start playing it—and playing it. Today it's definitely more treat than trick as "Monster Mash" climbs all the way to #1, enduring through years to become *the* most recognized Halloween standard.

LAND OF 1,000 DANCES

"Monster Mash" hit the same year as "The Twist" (see Jan. 13), the success of which spawned a dizzying variety of new dances, many with their own songs. Here's a sampling:

- The kids doing the Bristol Stomp in the township of Bristol, Pennsylvania, were "sharp as a pistol," say the Dovells (1961), who also returned the next year with the "Hully Gully."

- The Peppermint Twist was a twist with a twist, from the house band at New York's popular Peppermint Lounge: Joey Dee & the Starliters (1961).

- Chubby Checker raised the bar for dance hits by lowering it for dancers with "The Limbo Rock" (1962).

- Dee Dee Sharp turned a spud into the latest, greatest dance craze with "The Mashed Potato" (1962).

- The Watusi was "a dance made for romance" say the Orlons in "The Wah Watusi" (1962).

- Little Eva definitely gave us the notion with "The Loco-motion" (1962).

- Both Chubby Checker and Marvin Gaye gave the Hitch Hike a "thumbs up" (1962).

- With the Monkey, kids got Darwinian with Major Lance ("The Monkey Time") and the Miracles ("Mickey's Monkey"), three years before the invention of The Monkees (1963).

- Bobby Freeman still wanted to dance in his Sly Stone–produced hit, "C'mon and Swim" (1964).

- When the Larks took "The Jerk" into the Top 10, it no longer seemed that stupid (1964).

- British invaders Freddie & the Dreamers score with the wacky "Do the Freddie" (1965).

- The Frug never had its own hit record, but parodist Allen Sherman did complain about his kids doing it in his spoof of Petula Clark's "Downtown" (1965).

- Wicked Wilson Pickett's hit "The Funky Broadway" includes easy-to-follow instructions (1967).

OCTOBER
21

1968 Johnny Cash does some of his best work in front of (literally) captive audiences. Tonight *Johnny Cash at Folsom Prison* wins Best Album at the annual Country Music Awards, and "the Man in Black" follows it up early next year with *Johnny Cash at San Quentin*. Moving easily among country, folk, and rockabilly, Cash has had his share of hard knocks: many arrests (though he never serves more than a single night in jail), amphetamine addiction, divorce. "Ring of Fire" perhaps best epitomizes his romantic outlaw image, though his biggest crossover hit will be a novelty song, "A Boy Named Sue," penned by Shel Silverstein. "Success," says Cash, "is having to worry about every damn thing in the world except money."

OCTOBER 22

1961 Catch as catch can. Today, former bomber pilot Joseph Heller releases his first book, *Catch-22*. Blurring the line between sanity and insanity, the book captures the maddening, existential absurdity of war. There's no easy way out for protagonist John Yossarian, a WWII bomber pilot whose increasingly desperate plans to avoid flying missions are continually thwarted by higher powers. The absurdist, bitter novel catapults Heller to fame and turns its title into an international catchphrase. "Heller can fill one page with yammering, visceral horror, [and] can make the next prance with fleecy hilarity," writes *Time* magazine. A film adaptation appears in 1970 but is overshadowed by another anti-war black comedy: Robert Altman's *M*A*S*H*. Meanwhile, another WWII vet, Kurt Vonnegut, propels his prolific writing career with the sci-fi-infused masterpiece *Slaughterhouse-Five*.

OCTOBER 24

1962 At the height of the Cuban missile crisis, director John Frankenheimer today delivers his chilling *The Manchurian Candidate*. Based on Richard Condon's bestseller, the paranoid political thriller focuses on a troubled Korean War veteran (Frank Sinatra) who unravels a plot to brainwash an ex-GI (Laurence Harvey) into becoming an assassin. Angela Lansbury (only three years older than Harvey in real life) sparkles as the soldier's mother, a Machiavellian manipulator on behalf of her Joe McCarthy–like senatorial husband. This "enemy within" drama stirs intense controversy but only a so-so box office, though a 1987 re-release enhances its reputation as a Cold War classic.

OCTOBER 23

1969 Once-jolly TV host Art Linkletter, distraught over his twenty-year-old daughter Diane's recent suicide, takes up the mantle of anti-drug crusader. At the invitation of close friend Richard Nixon, he visits the White House and delivers a blistering attack on drugs and rock 'n' roll (no mention of sex). "Almost every time a Top 40 record is played on the radio," he intones, "it is an ad for acid, marijuana, and trips." Art and Diane's spoken-word and response recordings ("We Love You, Call Collect" by Art, "Dear Mom and Dad" by Diane), made before the suicide, wins a Grammy next year. An autopsy later reveals no presence of hallucinogens in Diane's system when she fell to her death from a West Hollywood apartment building. Speculation follows that depression, not drugs, led to her death.

OCTOBER 25

1964 Over twenty NFL seasons Jim Marshall will play in 282 consecutive games—an all-time record. The fearsome 6'4", 250-pound defensive end will also be voted to the Pro Bowl twice, and recover thirty fumbles. As it happens today, he'd gladly give one of those back. Marshall, a Minnesota Viking, scoops up a fumble by wide receiver Billy Kilmer of the San Francisco 49ers and rumbles sixty-two yards into the end zone—the wrong way. On the sidelines Vikings quarterback Fran Tarkenton follows, screaming for him to stop, but Marshall thinks he wants him to run faster. Entering the end zone, he flips the ball out of bounds, resulting in a safety. The Vikings still win the game, 27-22, and afterwards Marshall receives a phone call from former UC star Roy Riegels, who had run the wrong way for a safety in the 1929 Rose Bowl, when his team lost 8-7.

OCTOBER 26

1962 Grand gothic horror hits the widescreen today with the much-anticipated debut of the Bette Davis/Joan Crawford chiller, *What Ever Happened to Baby Jane?* In the first and only pairing of the real-life rivals, the black comedy delivers a campy take on the bitter, bizarre lives of an alcoholic, demented former child star (Davis) slowly torturing her crippled, ex-movie starlet sister (Crawford) in their gloomy, decaying mansion. Nominated for an Oscar for Best Actress, Davis seethes at the ceremony when a delighted Crawford accepts the trophy on behalf of the absent winner, Anne Bancroft (*The Miracle Worker*). "The best time I ever had with Joan Crawford," Davis says later, "was when I pushed her down the stairs in *What Ever Happened to Baby Jane?*"

OCTOBER 27

1960 After stints with several groups, most notably the Drifters, vocalist Ben E. King goes solo. The lead singer of "There Goes My Baby" and "Save the Last Dance for Me" heads into the studio today and records four songs, two of which will become his biggest hits: "Spanish Harlem" and "Stand By Me." Both crack the Top 10 next year, but soon the king's pinnacle has passed. Yet, twenty-five years later, his soulful classic is introduced to a new generation, when *Stand by Me* becomes the title of a coming-of-age movie. Director Rob Reiner's *Stand By Me*, based on a novella by Stephen King, co-stars brat-packish boys Wil Wheaton, Jerry O'Connell, and River Phoenix.

OCTOBER 28

1964 Stretching over two evenings at a packed Santa Monica Civic Auditorium, *The T.A.M.I. Show*—an extraordinary rock spectacular—gets underway tonight. From British Invasion to soul to surf, the acts cut across the spectrum of pop music: dapper Marvin Gaye in a white tux singing "Can I Get a Witness"; the Beach Boys in striped shirts doing their surfer hits; lacquer-haired Lesley Gore belting out "You Don't Own Me"; and the Barbarians doing their sole hit, "Are You a Boy or Are You a Girl." Plus the Miracles, the Supremes, Gerry & the Pacemakers, Martha & the Vandellas, and lots more, with closing sets by an electrifying James Brown and the Rolling Stones. Go-go dancers include then-unknowns Toni Basil and Teri Garr, while guitarist Glen Campbell plays in the house band.

MEANWHILE...

GIGANTIC GEM GETAWAY

On October 30, 1964, an audacious robbery took place at New York's venerable Museum of Natural History. The robbers netted twenty-four jewels, including the 563.35-carat Star of India blue sapphire and the 100-carat DeLong Star ruby, and the value of the stolen gems was virtually incalculable. The next day, a crush of reporters waited impatiently until the afternoon for the museum's director (who was having a tooth extracted that morning), who informs them that the window through which the burglars entered was unlocked, and the alarm systems had been disconnected due to budgetary constraints. Within two days, though, the police had sussed out the perpetrators and arrested three suspects, including Robert Jack Murphy, a.k.a. Murph the Surf. The Star of India and other jewels were recovered from a Miami bus station locker the following January.

OCTOBER 29

1969 Grandiose British rock band King Crimson blasts off today on a twenty-date US tour, begining at Goddard College in Plainfield, Vermont. Within a week, their self-produced debut album, *In the Court of the Crimson King*, explodes. A cornerstone album of progressive rock, it features guitarist Robert Fripp, who weaves jazz and classical influences into songs that are years ahead of their time. They're way too heavy, man, for pop AM radio but are tailor-made for freeform FM. "21st Century Schizoid Man" stands as a precursor to the '90s grunge movement, while the nine-minute title track delivers a bombardment of bombast. The tour concludes at the fabled Fillmore West in San Francisco (see May 17) two weeks before Christmas. The band breaks up shortly thereafter, with singer and bass guitarist Greg Lake forming Emerson, Lake, and Palmer, and flute and sax player Ian McDonald joining Foreigner.

OCTOBER 30   1968

The potent pairing of Peter O'Toole and Katharine Hepburn in *The Lion in Winter* proves a box-office winner. "I *worship* that bloody woman," says O'Toole. "I've never enjoyed working with anyone so much in my whole life, not even Burton." Opening today, the film nets Hepburn an Oscar to match the one she won last year for *Guess Who's Coming to Dinner*—though this year, in an Academy first, she'll share the honor with Barbra Streisand (who received the same number of votes for *Funny Girl*). Once again the feisty, independent Miss Hepburn declines to attend the ceremony, but continues to choose her parts well. More than a decade later, she'll set a record with her fourth Oscar for *On Golden Pond*, an extraordinary forty-eight years after receiving her first for *Morning Glory*.

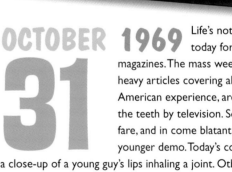

OCTOBER 31   1969

Life's not looking good today for *Life* and *Look* magazines. The mass weeklies, with photo-heavy articles covering all aspects of the American experience, are getting kicked in the teeth by television. So out goes family fare, and in come blatant appeals to the younger demo. Today's cover of *Life* shows a close-up of a young guy's lips inhaling a joint. Other recent youth-oriented covers include Woodstock, op artist Peter Max (whose vivid Day-Glo art epitomizes Flower Power), and shapely silhouettes by caricaturist Gerald Scarfe for "Sex in the Lively Arts: How Far Is Enough?" Heavier reporting weighs in, too, with cover stories on communes and strife on campus. Next week it's Paul McCartney, with his wife Linda and family, refuting the pesky "Paul is dead" rumors. Alas, the weekly versions of *Life* and *Look* are pronounced dead in 1972.

NOVEMBER

NOVEMBER 1960

With Election Day less than a week away, Senator John F. Kennedy and Vice President Richard Nixon barnstorm the country in the heat of the most closely contested presidential race in recent times. In San Francisco, Kennedy proposes a "peace corps" of young volunteers, men and women, to further the cause of peace around the globe. Nixon quickly attacks the plan as a haven for draft dodgers. Sworn in two months later, Kennedy reiterates his belief with his famed quote: "Ask not what your country can do for you—ask what you can do for your country." Young Americans respond enthusiastically, and the following August the Peace Corps, headed by his brother-in law Sargent Shriver, sends off its first group of volunteers to missions in Ghana and Tanzania.

A TIME FOR GREATNESS

U. S. SENAT JOHN F. KENNE FOR PRESIDEN

A NEW LEADER FOR THE 60's

KENNEDY FOR PRESIDEN

FACTS FOR NEW YORK VOTERS:

KENNEDY FOR PRESIDENT JOHNSON FOR VICE PRESIDENT
N. Y. Democratic State Campaign Committee
Biltmore Hotel, N. Y. 17, N. Y.

NOVEMBER 2

1966 Television comedy writer and stand-up comic Woody Allen makes his directorial debut with the zany *What's Up, Tiger Lily?* Dismantling a Japanese spy flick, Allen reconfigures, overdubs, and adds dialogue to produce a madcap secret-agent spoof about the search for a stolen egg salad recipe (!). Much to his dismay, the producers insist upon inserting the Lovin' Spoonful (fresh off their #1 "Summer in the City"), who appear inexplicably to sing "Rain On the Roof." The *New York Times* describes the uneven farce as an "innovation of sorts," but Allen's quickly off to his next project, writing and co-starring in *Casino Royale*, a Bond send-up that features buxom beauty Ursula Andress, with whom Woody had acted previously in *What's New, Pussycat?* Then he directs the mockumentary *Take the Money and Run*, leading into his prime '70s run of *Bananas, Sleeper, Annie Hall*, and lots more. The Spoonful, however, fall on hard times after two members are busted for pot. After ratting on their dealer, their popularity plummets. "In San Francisco in 1967 their name was mud," writes rock journalist Lillian Roxon. "Their albums were used as doormats, groupies were urged not to ball them."

NOVEMBER 3

1962 "Little symphonies for the kids" is how producer Phil Spector described his "Wall of Sound." His obsessive layering of instrumental tracks made him the greatest and most-imitated producer of the decade. Today his wall hits the ceiling as "He's a Rebel," credited misleadingly to the Crystals, makes #1. New York native Spector had bolted to LA to start his own record label, and found himself with a hot song (written by pal Gene Pitney) but a band back in New York. So he tapped the Blossoms to make the actual recording. The real Crystals score next with "Da Do Ron Ron (Then He Walked Me Home)" and "Then He Kissed Me." Then Phil's on to his squeeze Ronnie Spector and making Ronettes hits like "Be My Baby" and "Baby I Love You." He even finds time for the lead singer of the Blossoms, the lovely-named Darlene Love (born Wright), to shape "(Today I Met) The Boy I'm Gonna Marry." And the little symphonies just keep comin'.

NOVEMBER 4

1961 At New York's celebrated Carnegie Hall, a fresh-faced folksinger makes his concert hall debut in its 250-seat Chapter Hall Theater. While his shows at smaller clubs around the city have drawn rave reviews, tonight's performance attracts only 53 people at an admission price of $2. He jokes and interacts with the small crowd and sings his heart out. Two weeks later he records his first album for Columbia, including several songs played this evening, like "Fixin' to Die" and "Pretty Peggy-O." The artist's name? Bob Dylan. On this same day two years later, a much larger and more glittery crowd gathers across the Atlantic. It includes the Queen Mother and Princess Margaret, attending a Royal Command Performance at London's Prince of Wales Theater. Appearing seventh are the obvious headliners, the Beatles, who are instantly elevated to royal status. Other acts include a trio of zither players, barnyard animal puppets, and Marlene Dietrich. The Beatles perform four tunes, and John Lennon's cheeky intro to the last number, "Twist and Shout," makes worldwide headlines: "Will the people in the cheaper seats clap your hands? And the rest, if you'll just rattle your jewelry."

NOVEMBER 5

1966 Almost single-handedly inventing the teenybopper craze, here come the Monkees. Assembled by Hollywood movers and shakers, and waggishly dubbed "The PreFab Four," the band tops the charts today with their debut single, "Last Train to Clarksville." Starring in their new NBC sitcom *The Monkees*, the fresh-faced lads—Davy Jones, Mickey Dolenz, Peter Tork, and Mike Nesmith—sing the song, but session musicians including Glen Campbell and Leon Russell handle all instruments. Purists sneer, but teenyboppers—a much more coveted demographic—swoon. They snap up Monkees records, trading cards, even Monkees boots at neighborhood Thom McAn stores. The members demand to play their own instruments on subsequent records, but their popularity tumbles. Before exiting, though, they shoot an anarchic little movie called *Head* that's co-written by a young and already devilish Jack Nicholson.

COLLECT ALL 44 CARDS
28A/© 1967 RAYBERT PROD INC. TM. OF SCREEN GEMS, INC

COLLECT ALL 44 CARDS
22A/© 1967 RAYBERT PROD INC. TM. OF SCREEN GEMS, INC

COLLECT ALL 44 CARDS
38A/© 1967 RAYBERT PROD INC. TM OF SCREEN GEMS, INC

COLLECT ALL 44 CARDS
36A/© 1967 RAYBERT PROD INC. TM. OF SCREEN GEMS, INC

NOVEMBER 6

1967

No chatty host, fluffy talk, or segments on cooking and exercise. What kind of afternoon talk show is this? It's *The Phil Donahue Show*, which premieres today on a lone TV station in Dayton, Ohio, with guest Madelyn Murray O'Hare, the country's most prominent atheist. This debut typifies the show's more serious-minded, less celebrity-driven approach. With ample audience questions and call-ins, the host draws in the mothers and homemakers that stations covet most. Phil's show builds, especially in the Midwest, and relocates to Chicago. It continues to focus on current events, sometimes pitting opponents like anti-feminist Phyllis Schlafly and NOW president Eleanor Smeal. Ratings climb so high, amidst a host of imitators, that the show's name is shortened to simply *Donahue*—mirroring the success of single-named stars like Cher. But by the time Phil wears a skirt on a program devoted to men who dress like women, his popularity has already been eclipsed by another celebrity known by a single name: Oprah.

NOVEMBER 7

1963

Combining the words "cinema" and "panorama," the widescreen format Cinerama began wowing audiences in the early '50s with films like *This is Cinerama*. "People sat back in spellbound wonder as the scenic program flowed across the screen," wrote the *New York Times*. "The effect of Cinerama in this, its initial display, is frankly and exclusively 'sensational,' in the literal sense of that word." Today the franchise extends to a revolutionary movie house, the geodesic Cinerama Dome at the famed corner of Sunset and Vine in Hollywood. Based on a design by R. Buckminster Fuller, the landmark theater opens with a gala premiere of the madcap ensemble comedy *It's a Mad, Mad, Mad, Mad World*, featuring a who's who of Hollywood, from Milton Berle to Jonathan Winters—all more "sensational" than ever.

TRENDSETTER

A PUBLIC BIRTH

"While we work every day to produce new goods and to create new wealth, we want most of all to enrich man's spirit. That is the purpose of this act." With this rhetorical flourish and the stroke of a pen, President Lyndon Baines Johnson reshaped the television landscape forever on November 7, 1967, when he signed the Public Broadcasting Act of 1967. Though educational television had been around for many years, its funding and reach had been quite limited. In November, the nonprofit Corporation for Public Broadcasting formed, and two years later established its programming arm, PBS. In 1970, PBS launched and soon expanded to broadcast a diverse mix of fine arts, drama, science, public affairs, and children's programming.

NOVEMBER 8 **1969**

"Champagne soul" is how one music critic describes the smooth pop/R&B vocalizing of the 5th Dimension. With its knack for bridging the generation gap, the group soars to #1 today with "Wedding Bell Blues"—their second chart-topper of the year, following the *Hair* medley "Aquarius/Let the Sunshine In." The band feasts once again on the talents of singer/songwriter Laura Nyro, who wrote today's #1 plus previous hits "Stoned Soul Picnic" and "Sweet Blindness." Nineteen-year-old Nyro records sophisticated jazz- and folk-influenced albums herself that connect with critics but not with AM radio. Nevertheless, today she's got three compositions in the Top 40: "Wedding Bell Blues" along with Blood, Sweat & Tears' "And When I Die" and Three Dog Night's "Eli's Coming."

NOVEMBER
9

1961

Strikingly out of place (and out of his element) in a conservative pinstriped suit, upper-crusty music store manager Brian Samuel Epstein, twenty-seven, strolls from his shop to the dark, dank Cavern Club. Amidst a raucous lunchtime concert audience of young, working-class fans, he's mesmerized by the hard-edged sounds of the unruly rock band on stage. He's equally smitten with its four slim, leather-clad, sweat-drenched members—especially the most aggressive, who he later learns is named John Lennon. Proper but definitely not prim, the closeted Epstein makes a split-second decision that changes the course of history. Determined to get the Beatles into his life, he soon convinces them to sign him as their manager. Epstein succumbs to an accidental drug overdose six dizzying years later.

ROLL THE JOINTS ... I MEAN PRESSES

In 1966, twin pioneers of rock journalism, Greg Shaw and Paul Williams, began publishing mimeographed rock "zines." On the East Coast, Swarthmore student Williams founded *Crawdaddy!*, named after England's legendary Crawdaddy Club, where bands like the Rolling Stones and the Yardbirds played early gigs. Out West, Shaw—with his pageboy blond locks that gave him more than a passing resemblance to the Stones' Brian Jones—started a zine that evolved into the landmark *Who Put the Bomp* (later affectionately known as just *Bomp*), which covered the budding rock scene from bases in San Francisco and, later, Los Angeles. *Crawdaddy!* and *Bomp* each attracted strong contributors like Jon Landau, Greil Marcus, Richard Meltzer, and Lester Bangs, who sowed the seeds of rock writing in America.

Bangs would later become editor of *Creem*, which began kicking out the jams in the Motor City in 1969. Proudly (and preposterously) dubbing itself "America's Only Rock 'n' Roll Magazine," took a rowdy approach that matched its reckless hometown bands like the Amboy Dukes, MC5, Grand Funk Railroad, and the Stooges. By this time, *Eye*, the Hearst Corporation's often laughable attempt to cover youth culture, had come and gone in just fifteen issues.

But there was one magazine that bridged the gap between the mainstream and counterculture, and has stood the test of time: twenty-one-year-old Jann Wenner's and journalist Ralph Gleason's *Rolling Stone*, which premiered on November 9, 1967, with a shot of John Lennon (above, from his new movie, *How I Won the War*) on the cover. Based in San Francisco, the entrepreneurial duo assembled a group that included barb-penned, iconoclastic writers like Bangs and Hunter S. Thompson along with budding photographer Annie Liebovitz. The debut issue also included a free roach clip, firmly entrenching the mag as a countercultural arbiter of the highest order.

NOVEMBER
10

1969 In a wasteland of commercial dross for children, a young New York producer envisions a quality show that will help youngsters learn. Joan Ganz Cooney works tirelessly to attract funds and the advice of educators, and in 1968 forms the Children's Television Workshop. Today *Sesame Street* debuts, with Jim Henson's Muppets contributing to fun, fast-paced segments that cleverly present math and English education in an entertaining format that's never preachy or boring. Astutely hiring a stellar staff to work in front of and behind the cameras, Cooney delivers a deserving hit and creates a television milestone that's made a difference in the lives of millions of viewers, young and old.

NOVEMBER
11

1967 Pop music marches to the beat of a "Different Drum" today with a release that introduces the crystalline vocals of twenty-one-year-old Linda Ronstadt (with lyrics by the Monkees' Mike Nesmith). Lead singer of a West Coast folk-rock outfit called the Stone Ponys, Ronstadt soon goes solo and forms a backing band that eventually morphs into the Eagles. But her career doesn't shift into overdrive 'til the early '70s, when she meets her Svengali, producer Peter Asher. Once half of the British Invasion duo Peter and Gordon ("A World Without Love"), Asher turns her sound into an unqualified commercial success with hits like "You're No Good" and "When Will I Be Loved" and much-praised albums like *Don't Cry Now* and *Heart Like A Wheel*. Whatever the style—country, folk, pop standards, R&B, rock, a touch of light opera—Ronstadt scores big with an appreciative public. Later she even dabbles with a stage career, taking a role in Gilbert and Sullivan's *Pirates of Penzance*.

1969 As the Vietnam War inflames and divides the nation, six prominent actors call for an unusual boycott: of their own films. Paul Newman, Peter Fonda, Dennis Hopper, Alan Arkin, Arlo Guthrie, and Jon Voight ask moviegoers to stay away from today's screenings of *Midnight Cowboy, Butch Cassidy and the Sundance Kid, Alice's Restaurant,* and *Easy Rider.* "For a great many Americans, this war has created no pain," says Newman. "How can it stop if so many people slide through? We're sorry it will affect other people." He's referring to the owners of the nation's 13,000 theaters, whose trade organization chairman quickly blasts the actors' stand as "selfish." But today's a Wednesday, and all sides hope that business booms this weekend.

NOVEMBER 13

1960 Segregated America buzzes over the wedding between entertainer Sammy Davis, Jr., and blonde Swedish actress May Britt. Interracial marriage remains illegal in thirty-one states as the couple ties the knot today in his house in the Hollywood hills. The bride wears a sheath champagne dress with a short veil, and Frank Sinatra is the best man. Photographers plead for a kiss. "There are enough haters in the world already who are waiting for that shot," demurs Sammy, though he later gives her a peck on the cheek. The carousing rat-packer had similarly titillated America with an earlier affair with blonde actress Kim Novak, fresh off her starring role in Alfred Hitchcock's *Vertigo.* Enraged studio mogul Harry Cohn, grooming Novak as Columbia's answer to Marilyn Monroe, put out a mob contract on Davis. Instead Sammy married a black chorus girl named Loray White, with Harry Belafonte serving as best man. The couple divorced a few months later, paving the way for today's gala event with a starry reception at the Beverly Hilton.

NOVEMBER 14 **1960** Born in Georgia but raised in Florida, Ray Charles has had his native state on his mind for a while. He's heard the Hoagy Carmichael classic "Georgia on My Mind" sung so often by his driver while on the road that he decides to record it himself. Today the tune gives him his first #1 song. A dozen years before, Charles had left the South for Seattle and, in 1952, recorded his first session for the new Atlantic label. His classic blend of blues, jazz, country, and soul has brought steady R&B success—and now a mainstream breakout. "Georgia on My Mind" wins two Grammy awards, kicking off a run that'll include future #1s "Hit the Road, Jack" and "I Can't Stop Loving You." Yet it's "Georgia" that stays on the mind of the National Academy of Recording Arts & Sciences, which presents him with a Lifetime Achievement Award a quarter-century later.

NOVEMBER 15

1966

A five-time Most Valuable Player and twelve-time All-Star, basketball great Bill Russell has broken a lot of records on the parquet floor of the Boston Garden. Today he goes where no black man has gone before—to becoming an NBA coach—when he's named player/coach of the Boston Celtics upon the retirement of legendary coach Red Auerbach. One of the league's premiere defensive players, the 6'9" Russell backboned the Celtics dynasty that won eleven NBA championships during his thirteen seasons. An agile rebounder and shot-blocker extraordinaire, he demonstrates a quiet, steely determination both on and off the court. "The idea," Russell once said, "is not to block every shot. The idea is to make your opponent believe that you might block every shot."

NOVEMBER 16

1966

Guilty until proven innocent—that's the way it's been for Cleveland osteopath Sam Sheppard since his first wife, Marilyn, was found murdered on July 4, 1954. He claims a "bushy haired" intruder knocked him out and killed her, but few believe him. (The sensational case later inspires the TV series *The Fugitive*—see Aug. 29.) "Why Isn't Sam Sheppard in Jail? Quit Stalling, Bring Him In," yells one newspaper headline. "Somebody Is Getting Away with Murder," opines another. At a pretrial hearing, the presiding judge confides to a columnist, "It's an open and shut case…he's guilty as hell." Circumstantial evidence convicts Sheppard, who never stops fighting to prove his innocence. After his mother commits suicide shortly after his conviction and he serves ten years in jail, the US Supreme Court orders a new trial, condemning the bias and circus-like atmosphere of the previous one. Today, defended by noted attorney F. Lee Bailey, Sheppard is acquitted. As reporters pepper the freed physician with questions, he blurts out, "Are you going to bring my mother back?" DNA tests in 1997, seven years after Sheppard's death, prove that a third person was present at the time of the murder.

END OF AN ERA

As actor George Sanders put it in *The Picture of Dorian Gray*: "Isn't that monstrous the way people go about saying things behind people's backs that are absolutely and entirely true?" In her heyday, gossip columnist Louella Parsons lived by one motto: tell it to Louella first. She broke scoops while trading barbs with arch-rival Hedda Hopper, a former actress whom Parsons had once recommended for a writing job. Often vicious, always entertaining, Parsons blended fact and fiction to tell a darn good yarn. At her peak, some thirty million newspaper readers and radio listeners thrilled vicariously to her tales of Hollywood romance and intrigue. On November 17, 1965, Parsons retired. And perhaps it was time: some miffed stars like Frank Sinatra and Doris Day were refusing to grant her interviews, and worse still, a new generation of even less compliant stars had appeared.

"Nobody likes sweetness and light."

—Louella Parsons

NOVEMBER 17 1968

The Swiss are known for time-pieces, but today a little Swiss miss causes a most untimely occurrence. With sixty-five seconds remaining in an NFL game, the New York Jets kick a field goal to take a three-point lead over the Oakland Raiders.

As the clock approaches 7:00 pm, NBC cuts away after a commercial break to start its regularly scheduled movie, *Heidi*. "It literally blew out the switchboard," says former NBC executive Chet Simmons of the fans' protest calls. The Raiders wind up scoring two touchdowns in nine seconds to win 43-32, and NBC exacerbates their decision by running a crawl with the news at the bottom of the screen during *Heidi*. It was "a forgivable error committed by humans who were concerned about children expecting to see *Heidi*," says NBC president Julius Goodman in a statement released later that night, "I missed the end of the game as much as anyone else."

NOVEMBER 18 — 1963

Push button automatic car transmissions and stoves have flopped, but today AT&T bravely goes where no phone has gone before. Today it's goodbye rotary dial, hellooo Touch-Tone phone for residents of the towns of Greensburg and Carnegie, Pennsylvania. For a $5 installation charge and an additional $1.50 monthly fee, subscribers can make a seven-number call in an estimated two to five seconds (versus the ten seconds it takes to dial a standard rotary phone). "It was known as the touch tone," recalls one telephone design firm engineer, "but everyone called it the push button." At next year's World's Fair in New York, AT&T promotes the phone relentlessly—and its speed and convenience quickly establish it as the telephonic communications device of choice.

NOVEMBER 19 — 1964

When he turned fourteen, young Gary Lewis got a drum set from Dad—a.k.a. popular comedian Jerry Lewis, now riding high with *The Nutty Professor*. Today, at eighteen, Gary Lewis & the Playboys record "This Diamond Ring," a song penned by Al Kooper. It'll hit #1 early next year, and an avalanche follows: bubbly songs ("Count Me In," "Everybody Loves A Clown") and appearances on *The Ed Sullivan Show*, the CBS special *It's What's Happening, Baby*, and UK programs *Ready Steady Go!* and *Top of the Pops*. Though Gary's moment is short-lived, it's all the more impressive coming at the height of the chart-chomping British Invasion. Next year, as Gary and the boys shine, seven British acts top the US charts with twelve #1 songs, representing half of the year's total.

NOVEMBER 20 — 1966

Disorder outside, decadence and debauchery within—and the band plays on. Welcome to prewar Berlin's seedy Kit Kat Klub, the setting for impresario Harold Prince's latest Broadway musical, *Cabaret*. Joel Grey charms as the seductive emcee who "bursts from the darkness like a tracer bullet," according to Walter Kerr in the *New York Times*. As the Weimar Republic crumbles, the club's wanton air becomes that much more desperate. The show, which opened today, will shine brightly in a slinky sweep of eight Tony awards including Best Musical, Director, Composer and Lyricist, and Scenic and Costume Design. The 1972 film adaptation from director Bob Fosse, starring Liza Minnelli, later matches that total with eight Oscars.

NOVEMBER 21

1960

The success of the Shirelles has ushered in a new era of girl-group sounds. Not since the post-WWII "sister acts" (the McGuire, Fontane, and Lennon Sisters) has female harmony been so prevalent on the radio, with the Chantels, the Crystals, the Cookies, and Motown's Marvelettes trying to catch up with Shirley Owens and her three New Jersey schoolmates. "Will You Love Me Tomorrow?" enters the charts today en route to becoming the first #1 song from a female R&B group—and the first hit for entrepreneur/manager Florence Greenberg and Scepter Records. Even more significantly, it's the first #1 for songwriters Gerry Goffin and Carole King, who'll write dozens more, including "Take Good Care of My Baby," "The Loco-motion," and "Go Away Little Girl." The Shirelles have a couple of good years left, too, with "Soldier Boy" and "Baby It's You" still to come—the latter tapped by the Beatles for Vee-Jay's 1963 release *Introducing the Beatles*.

BREAKING UP IS HARD TO DO

The Beatles' sole output in 1968 had been four songs on two singles, led by "Lady Madonna" and "Hey Jude." But the foursome certainly compensated on November 22, 1968, when they released a double album simply titled *The Beatles*, but known ever after as "The White Album." Enduring a decaying relationship, each member made strong individual contributions to the album that presaged their future solo careers. Paul rocks harder than ever on "Helter Skelter," which became the blueprint for many metal bands to come—but got the boys in trouble when Charlie Manson's murderous minions scrawled the words in blood (see Aug. 8).

With help from the incomparable Eric Clapton, George delivers "While My Guitar Gently Weeps," widely regarded as a rock classic. John's reworking of "Revolution" established him as the iconoclast of the bunch, and Ringo closes the album with "Goodnight," the beautiful simplicity of which will serve him well during his later string of solo hits.

NOVEMBER
22

1963 Virtually everyone old enough to remember this day remembers where he or she was when first hearing the unfathomable news that President Kennedy had been shot in Dallas. For many Americans, the first word comes from Walter Cronkite, interrupting *As the World Turns* at 1:40 p.m. eastern time. Five minutes later, veteran announcer Don Pardo reads NBC's first bulletin. Instantaneously, the overwhelmed news departments of the three commercial networks begin round-the-clock live coverage, entailing a few images and lots of telephone interviews and studio talking heads. At 2:38 p.m. EST, Cronkite delivers the shocking news: "From Dallas, Texas, a flash, apparently official. President Kennedy died at one p.m., Central Standard Time." The clearest footage to emerge will be a twenty-six-second film from a top-of-the-line Bell & Howell 8mm camera operated by women's clothing manufacturer Abraham Zapruder. Two days later, millions of NBC viewers watch live and in disbelief as Jack Ruby guns down suspected assassin Lee Harvey Oswald (see Nov. 24).

NOVEMBER
23

1968 Thunderous, magnificent voices have rung through NYC's acclaimed Metropolitan Opera for the past eighty-five years. Tonight a promising European tenor makes his bow here in *La Bohème*—and a star is born. Luciano Pavarotti, son of a baker and a tobacco factory worker, grew up in the north-central town of Modena, Italy. Dreaming of a career as a singer, he taught elementary school for several years while pursing vocal studies on the side. After winning a prestigious operatic competition in 1961, he built his reputation as he performed throughout Europe. No less a personage than Dame Joan Sutherland brought him onstage with her in Miami in 1965, but tonight's New York debut carries him to another level. Known for his bravura style and magnetic personality, Pavarotti has an illustrious career until his death in 2007.

NOVEMBER
24

1963 In a nation cloaked in grief, people gather at their televisions to watch the procession carrying JFK's flag-draped coffin from the White House to the Capitol. But before it begins, NBC switches live to the basement of the Dallas jail where detectives are escorting suspected killer Lee Harvey Oswald to an armored truck. Out of the crowd, a man in a dark suit aims a pistol and fires. Oswald gasps, grimaces, grabs his side, and falls. Pandemonium erupts, witnessed live by millions of stunned viewers. "He's been shot!" shouts NBC correspondent Tom Pettit. "Lee Oswald has been shot!" And so the national nightmare spirals even deeper. "Violence has not yet subdued its appetite," says CBS's Charles Collingwood. The networks repeat the shooting in slow motion, over and over. With that grotesque spectacle on everyone's minds, TV returns to the procession moving somberly towards the Capitol. Along marches riderless horse Blackjack, sword strapped to the saddle and boots reversed in its stirrups in the ancient tradition of Tamerlane and Genghis Khan. "Ceremony," says Collingwood, "is man's built-in reaction to tragedy."

NOVEMBER 25

1960

Premiering today, the day after Thanksgiving, Edward R. Murrow's landmark CBS documentary *Harvest of Shame* has its intended effect. Americans are shocked at the plight of previously invisible migrant farm workers and their bone-wearying work, dirt-cheap pay, and squalid living conditions. "We used to own slaves," says narrator Murrow, quoting a migrant-hiring farmer. "Now we just rent them." The following January, though, after taking a government job at the US Information Agency, the pioneering journalist tries—unsuccessfully—to prevent an airing of the exposé in England, arguing that it was intended for only a domestic audience. Many decry his two-faced stance, and British tabloids can't resist piling on. "If Murrow builds up America as skillfully as he tore it to pieces last night," says one writer after the show airs, "the propaganda war is as good as won."

ONE-HIT WONDERS

On November 25, 1967, the Strawberry Alarm Clock rang up their only real hit, the nonsensically psychedelic "Incense and Peppermints." A sampling of other one-hit wonders of the decade:

1960: "Alley-Oop" (The Hollywood Argyles); "You Talk Too Much" (Joe Jones); "Stay" (Maurice Williams & the Zodiacs)

1961: "Mother-in-Law" (Ernie K-Doe): "I Like It Like That" (Chris Kenner); "Who Put the Bomp" (Barry Mann)

1962: "Hey! Baby!" (Bruce Channel); "Rhythm of the Rain" (The Cascades); "Sukiyaki" (Kyu Sakamoto); "Sally, Go Round the Roses" (The Jaynetts)

1964: "Popsicles and Icicles" (The Murmaids); "We'll Sing in the Sunshine" (Gale Garnett); "Ringo" (Lorne Greene); "Tobacco Road" (Nashville Teens)

1965: "The Boy from New York City" (The Ad Libs); "The Birds and the Bees" (Jewel Akens); "Liar, Liar" (The Castaways); "Everyone's Gone to the Moon" (Jonathan King)

1966: "Lies" (The Knickerbockers); "Dirty Water" (The Standells); "They're Coming to Take Me Away, Ha-Haaa!" (Napoleon XIV); "Winchester Cathedral" (New Vaudeville Band)

1967: "We Ain't Got Nothin' Yet" (Blues Magoos); "Come on Down to My Boat" (Every Mother's Son); "Let It All Hang Out" (The Hombres); "Pata Pata" (Miriam Makeba)

1968: "Reach out of the Darkness" (Friend & Lover); "Angel of the Morning" (Merrilee Rush); "Fire" (The Crazy World of Arthur Brown)

1969: "Something in the Air" (Thunderclap Newman); "Love Can Make You Happy" (Mercy); "In the Year 2525" (Zager & Evans); "My Pledge of Love" (Joe Jeffrey Group)

NOVEMBER 26

1966 Teens rioting tonight near LA's Sunset Strip inspire Stephen Stills of Buffalo Springfield to write "For What It's Worth," one of the most remembered protest songs of the '60s. Only the kids aren't protesting the Vietnam War or social injustice, as so many mistakenly come to believe. No, they're fighting for their right to party. Neighbors have long complained about huge, rowdy crowds congregating after hours outside Pandora's Box, a tiny ramshackle club. Baton-swinging police move in to enforce a curfew, making wholesale arrests, and the city eventually closes the club down. The melees also inspire a quickie exploitation film, *Riot on Sunset Strip*, but it's the Buffalo Springfield folk-rock tune—"There's somethin' happening here, what it is ain't exactly clear..."—that endures.

HIGH SOCIETY, BAD BEHAVIOUR

The British press has always reveled in reporting the latest lavish events and goings-on amongst the royalty and upper-crust society. Beginning in late 1963, the society pages began covering major pop stars—but the news was often rather, shall we say, unseemly. The Rolling Stones, unsurprisingly, tended to dominate. Here are a few gems:

• Mick Jagger is fined ten pounds at Tettenhall, Staffordshire, for driving without insurance. His solicitor explains in court that the Rolling Stones are "not long-haired idiots, but highly intelligent university men." (Nov. 26, 1964)

• Jagger, Bill Wyman, and Brian Jones are each fined five pounds for urinating against the wall of a filling station "without taking steps to conceal this act." (July 22, 1965)

• Jagger and Keith Richards appear in court after a raid of one of Richards' parties turns up marijuana and amphetamines. They are charged with offences under the Dangerous Drugs Act, on the same day that Jones was arrested at his flat in Courtfield Road, South Kensington, and charged with possessing fifty grains of cannabis. "After being released on 250 pounds bail," one paper notes, "the pop star was driven away from the court in a new silver-grey Rolls-Royce." (May 10, 1967)

NOVEMBER
27

1962

Playing the famed "chitlin' circuit," the inaugural Motown Revue opens tonight in Tallahassee, Florida. Begun the previous month at the Howard Theater in Washington, DC, the star-studded show features Motown acts like the Supremes (well before their hit-making prime), Little Stevie Wonder, the Marvelettes (right), the Temptations, the Contours, and top draws the Miracles and Mary Wells. Motown runs a tight ship—in this case, a battered bus—packing in its young charges. "Every few days we'd stop at a cheap motel to bathe and wash some clothes," says the Supremes' Mary Wilson. "Compared to sleeping sitting up on a hard bus seat, being able to lie on any mattress was heaven." Coming from the gritty streets of Detroit, the performers get an eye-opening view of segregated America—in many arenas, blacks can sit only in the balconies. But the traveling show spreads the gospel of the Motown sound to true believers everywhere.

NOVEMBER
28

1966 The soiree of the century lives up to its advance billing. Truman Capote's masked, celebrity-filled Black and White Ball captivates New York City—and the world— tonight at the Plaza Hotel. "It was always shimmering," says producer David Merrick. "It was never still, nor was there a static moment." Frank Sinatra hobnobs while his new wife, Mia Farrow, dances all the fast numbers with Bennett Cerf's son, Christopher....Norman Mailer argues loudly over Vietnam with politico McGeorge Bundy....Lauren Bacall dances with choreographer Jerome Robbins....And presiding over it all in a receiving line until nearly midnight stand Capote and his honored guest, Katharine Graham, publisher of the *Washington Post*. With much embracing and air kissing they greet the 500+ carefully se- lected guests, whom Capote describes as "international types, lots of beautiful women, and ravishing little things." When a staffer asks movie producer Darryl Zanuck to identify himself upon his arrival, Zanuck huffily replies, "If you don't know, you shouldn't be here."

NOVEMBER
29

1969 It began as a throwaway song by a nonexistent group, and wound up an enduring pop cultural anthem. Such is the strange saga of "Na Na Hey Hey Kiss Him Goodbye," dashed off in a single evening by producer Paul Leka as a purposely bad B side that would force disc jockeys to play the A tune he preferred. But Fontana Records had other ideas, and the song quickly catches fire. Today it enters the Top 5 on its way to a two-week stay at #1. Exiting the studio that night, Leka notices steam pouring out of a manhole cover. So the name of the group, which he quickly assembles in light of the single's success, becomes Steam. A forgettable follow-up barely cracks the Top 50, and Steam soon dissipates. But a few years later, when the Chicago White Sox organist plays it at Cominsky Park as an opposing team's pitcher is being replaced, the fans catch on and gleefully start belting out the chorus. And it's "nah nah nah nah, nah nah nah nah" forevermore.

NOVEMBER
30

1968 Deejays often move to jobs behind the scenes, helping to create the types of records they used to play. Upstart DJ Sylvester Stewart took a more involved, circuitous route. He started as a writer and producer on hits like the Beau Brummels' "Laugh, Laugh," then attended a radio broadcasting school and became a popular San Francisco jock known as Sly Stone. His radio gig embraced 360 degrees of an ever-changing music scene, and after spinning discs by the likes of James Brown and Jimi Hendrix he decided to make his own kind of music. Tapping old friends and siblings, he formed Sly and the Family Stone. Their debut single, "Dance to the Music," taught the world some new math: R&B + rock = funk. Today the band releases a song that simplifies the message of racial equality to the level of nursery rhymes and double-dutch: "Everyday People."

DECEMBER

DECEMBER 1

1969 Is there a draft in here? As the first Selective Service lottery in twenty-seven years unfolds today in a conference room deep in Washington, DC, 850,000 young men hold their collective breath. From a big glass jar, Representative Alexander Pirnie (R-NY) pulls out the first blue capsule. It's the luck of the draw, and somebody has to step up first: the unlucky birthday is September 14, followed by 365 more days. Of the fifty-six young men scheduled to draw capsules, representatives from Michigan, Alaska, and Washington, DC, refuse. Not so one of the sons of America's heartland, as blond Jonathan Crawford pauses before drawing his quota to proclaim, "The youth of Indiana are proud to participate." The whole affair takes about ninety minutes, presided over by retiring Selective Service director General Lewis B. Hershey, a WWI veteran who never served in combat.

DECEMBER 2

1965 Yes Virginia, there is a USS *Enterprise*. But the ship doesn't gallivant about the galaxy, helmed by *Star Trek*'s Captain James T. Kirk. Rather, it's the world's first nuclear-powered aircraft carrier, launched in 1962 and dubbed the Big E. Its first mission was participating in the naval blockade of Cuba during the Cuban missile crisis, preventing Soviet ships from reaching the island nation. Fortunately for all sides, no battle ensued. That happens today, nearly three years later, when the Big E becomes the first nuclear-powered ship to engage in combat. Off the coast of Vietnam, it launches bomber aircraft that complete 125 sorties, dropping 167 tons of bombs and rockets on suspected Viet Cong supply lines and bases.

DECEMBER 3

1967

Have a heart. South African cardiac surgeon Christiaan Barnard performs the world's first heart transplant today. The nine-hour operation, conducted with a thirty-person team, saves the life of a fifty-five-year-old diabetic man—but only for eighteen days. Nevertheless, Barnard's pioneering surgery ushers in a new era in medicine that offers new hope to terminal patients and concurrently catapults him to global fame. He graces the cover of *Time* magazine, and the *Guinness Book of World Records* lists him for receiving the most fan mail on earth. He becomes a jet-setting, oft-photographed celebrity who embarks on affairs with Gina Lollobrigida, Sophia Loren, and other beauties. Yet at work he's always pragmatic. His next transplant lives for nineteen months, and another for twenty-four years. "Suffering isn't ennobling," he says. "Recovery is."

DECEMBER 4

1963

As the Beatles' popularity soars, companies inundate manager Brian Epstein with solicitations to manufacture Beatles merchandise, from aprons to wigs. He enlists his solicitor, David Jacobs, who unfortunately knows as little about licensing as Epstein. Today Jacobs taps Nicky Byrne, a blustery jack-of-all-trades, who forms Seltaeb ("Beatles" spelled backwards). Byrne offers an absurd 10 percent to the Beatles' side as a starting point for negotiations, but Jacobs' firm doesn't take much notice. It blithely signs the contract, a move that will cost the Beatles an estimated $100 million during their peak. "When it dawned on Brian what had happened, it started to make him physically ill," says Peter Brown, author of Beatles bio *The Love You Make*. Epstein later hires US celebrity attorney Louis Nizer, who embarks on a legal odyssey that eventually ends Byrne's sweetheart deal.

DECEMBER 1963
5

Despite a twenty-five-year age gap, suave Cary Grant and mischievous Audrey Hepburn make a charming couple in *Charade*, opening today. Their sharp repartee ("I don't bite, you know, unless it's called for"—Hepburn) in a smart script, plus gay Parisian settings and a sprightly Henry Mancini score, make director Stanley Donen's Hitchcock-style film a huge box-office hit. Its producers, mindful of the recent assassination of JFK, make one last-minute edit— dubbing in the word "eliminate" for "assassinate." Everyone's favorite gamine, Hepburn, charms wherever she goes, while classy co-star Grant has his share of admirers. "I'm getting older too, dear," says actress Grace Kelly. "The only one who isn't is Cary Grant."

DECEMBER
6

1964 Cartoon and live-action specials have entertained kids at Christmastime for years, but tonight something else is coming to town: stop-motion animation. CBS debuts *Rudolph the Red-Nosed Reindeer* on *General Electric's Fantasy Theater*, and an annual holiday treat is born. Hosted by affable Burt Ives, the holiday adventure stars poor ostracized Rudolph and his pal Hermey, an elf who wants to become a dentist. Pursued by the Abominable Snowmonster, they flee to the Island of Misfit Toys, meet prospector Yukon Cornelius, and eventually return to save Christmas. The puppets with "no strings attached" and the songs by Johnny Marks (writer of the original "Rudolph") are instant hits with kids—so much so that the producers later give the same treatment to another Christmas classic, *Santa Claus Is Coming to Town*, though *Rudolph* reigns as the longest-running holiday special, repeating every Christmas since.

HELL ON TURF

After the peace and love of the Woodstock Festival in August, the other shoe dropped on December 6, 1969, when the Altamont music festival proved to be an extremely bad trip. The free show at a speedway in Livermore, California, had 300,000 attendees and plenty of alcohol and drugs (soft and heavy) to go around. Ill advisedly, security was provided by Hell's Angels brandishing pool cues, beer bottles, and tire irons. The mood got ugly fast, and skirmishes started breaking out, with and without Angels. After Ike and Tina Turner opened and Santana performed, Jefferson Airplane took the stage, and when lead singer Marty Balin tried to keep an Angel from beating a fan, he got knocked out himself. The Flying Burrito Brothers and Crosby, Stills, Nash, and Young performed next, then the fashionably late, headlining Rolling Stones took the stage, by then crowded with roadies and journalists anxious to avoid the ugly crowd. While they played "Under My Thumb," a young black man approached, waving a gun. He shot wildly, and an Angel (later acquitted in court) stabbed and stomped him to death. Not knowing what happened but eager to scram, the Stones finished and left via helicopter. The grisly killing lives on in *Gimme Shelter*, the Stones' documentary that was being shot by Albert and David Maysles. Three more people died at Altamont, two trampled to death in their sleeping bags and one drowned in a drainage ditch.

DECEMBER 7 1964

While the movie *The Sandpiper*—which features another onscreen coupling between Elizabeth Taylor and her on-again, off-again leading man, Richard Burton—was being filmed, most of it was shot along California's Big Sur coast, leading Frank Sinatra to call it "Liz and Dick's beach blanket party." But they finished by filming some interiors in Paris, which is where Taylor throws a wrap party today and has her handbag stolen. It's a rather inauspicious omen for the star-powered soap opera, which also stars Eva Marie Saint and Charles Bronson. Director Vincente Minnelli's film doesn't make many waves at the box office, though it picks up an Oscar and a Grammy for "The Shadow of Your Smile," a song that Tony Bennett later records in its most-remembered version.

DECEMBER 8

1967

Mrs. Robinson, the critics love you more than you will know. Today the LA press gets a sneak peek at *The Graduate*, which will open nationwide next week. Newcomer Dustin Hoffman delivers a star-making performance in the title role of angst-ridden Benjamin Braddock, which was previously rejected by Warren Beatty and Burt Ward (Robin in *Batman*). Robert Redford also read for the part, but the producers realized his smoldering good looks and magnetic charm wouldn't fit the naiveté of a character who embarks on an affair with Mrs. Robinson (Anne Bancroft), the wife of his father's business partner. Bancroft's seductress role entrances critics and viewers alike, as *The Graduate* goes on to become the year's top-grossing film. With its pungent, anti-establishment feel and spot-on music by Simon & Garfunkel, the film wins director Mike Nichols the Oscar—the only time in the '60s that the winner for Best Picture (*In the Heat of the Night* this year) doesn't also take the statue for Best Director.

DECEMBER 9

1965

Poor Charlie Brown can never seem to do anything right. But another Charlie, *Peanuts* creator Charles Schulz, nails it his first time out, in tonight's *A Charlie Brown Christmas*. Initially, CBS executives have little faith. They dislike its slow pace and swinging jazz score in lieu of traditional Christmas music; its use of real kids, rather than trained actors for the voices; and, most worrisome of all, its closing recitation of a long biblical passage. Good grief, are they ever wrong.

Nearly half the country tunes in, enamored by the gentle tale and snappy sounds—especially "Linus and Lucy," a bouncy instrumental to which the gang dances enthusiastically, by composer Vince Guaraldi (who also scored with the similarly timeless "Cast Your Fate to the Wind"). The overwhelming audience reaction guarantees more future *Peanuts* specials, though this original returns each and every December thereafter.

DECEMBER 10

1961 On Human Rights Day, Amnesty International lights its first candle at the church of St.-Martin's-in-the-Fields, London. "Better to light a candle than curse the darkness" is the motto of the nascent human rights organization co-founded by left-leaning British lawyer Peter Benenson. Its first meeting earlier in the year attracted delegates from Belgium, England, France, Germany, Ireland, Switzerland, and the US. "Open your newspaper," says Benenson, "any day of the week, and you will find a report from somewhere in the world of someone being imprisoned, tortured, or executed because his opinions or religion are unacceptable to his government." Amnesty International aims, with success, to be a thorn in the side of those governments, and goes on to groundbreaking— and prisoner-freeing—work that results in a Nobel Peace Prize.

GOODBYE, SWEET SOUL

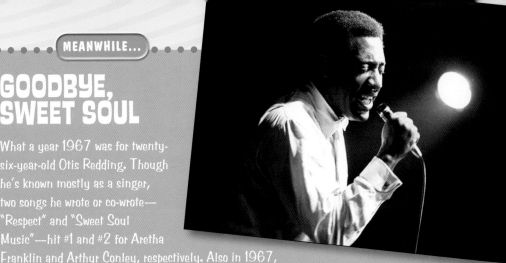

What a year 1967 was for twenty-six-year-old Otis Redding. Though he's known mostly as a singer, two songs he wrote or co-wrote— "Respect" and "Sweet Soul Music"—hit #1 and #2 for Aretha Franklin and Arthur Conley, respectively. Also in 1967, Redding toured England twice, enhancing his already considerable reputation there, and won an award for top male vocalist from the influential music mag *Melody Maker*. Back stateside, he delivered an electrifying Monterey Pop Festival set that exposed his raw R&B sound to a whole new audience. ("This is the love crowd, right?" he playfully teased the hippie-heavy crowd before breaking into "I've Been Loving You Too Long.") In early December, Redding was in the studio recording a peaceful, laid-back ballad, but on December 10, 1967, his private plane crashed into a lake near Madison, Wisconsin, en route to a concert, and he died tragically. Pallbearers at his funeral included R&B singers Joe Tex, Joe Simon, Johnnie Taylor, Solomon Burke, Percy Sledge, Don Covay, and Sam Moore (of Sam and Dave). The ballad "(Sittin' On) The Dock of the Bay" became his biggest hit, winning two Grammy awards and reigning at #1 for four weeks.

DECEMBER 11

1961 Once upon a time, singing with a big band often proved a steppingstone to becoming a talk show host. Dinah Shore started with Xavier Cugat, while a young Merv Griffin sang with the Freddy Martin Orchestra. Today on KYW in Cleveland, Mike Douglas, singer on the Kay Kyser orchestra's #1 record "Ole Buttermilk Sky" back in 1946, debuts his afternoon talk show. The genial host opens each episode with a musical number, and before long his easygoing song-and-chat fest goes national. It relocates to Philadelphia, then Los Angeles, and becomes the first daytime talk show to win an Emmy. Famous moments over the years include a surprise reunion of Lucille Ball and her *I Love Lucy* co-star Vivian Vance; a duet (ironically, "United We Stand") by Cher and ex-hubby Sonny; and six ex-Tarzans clad in loincloths. But perhaps the most intriguing feature of its two-decade run is the rotating weekly guest co-hosts, none more memorable than John Lennon and Yoko Ono in 1972.

DECEMBER
12

1969 The big break for a new Bond: Connery is out, Lazenby in. For the first and last time, George Lazenby stars as suave agent 007 in Ian Fleming's *On Her Majesty's Secret Service*. Still, the franchise doesn't miss a beat, with its usual globe-trotting, hair-raising adventures. To offset the unknown, rugged Aussie lead, the producers cast Diana Rigg, hot off her run as lithe Emma Peel in ABC's *The Avengers*. She famously catches the elusive gold ring, not just bedding but wedding the peripatetic secret agent—though not for long. The James Bond juggernaut rolls on, with Sean Connery (see Dec. 21) returning for the next movie (*Diamonds Are Forever*) before Roger Moore, having ended his duties on *The Saint,* signs on for the next seven 007 adventures starting with *Live and Let Die*.

DECEMBER
13

1965 It'll be ten years before Judy Collins asks to "Send in the Clowns," but don't bother—they're already here. *A Thousand Clowns*, a faithful film adaptation of the Broadway comedy, premieres today with Jason Robards Jr., reprising his stage role as a freewheeling slacker (long before that term was invented). A semi-employed television writer, he's threatened with losing the custody of his young nephew (Barry Gordon) unless he takes a full-time job, a sort of catch-22 that will destroy his non-conformist lifestyle. "Romantic crackpotism," says critic Pauline Kael of the audience-pleasing film that garners four Oscar nominations, including Best Picture. Martin Balsam takes home its only trophy, however, for Supporting Actor.

DECEMBER 1964

14

With that unmistakable blonde bouffant and those achy, powerhouse vocals, Dusty Springfield makes a big impression on both sides of the Atlantic. First noticed singing lead on the Springfields' "Silver Threads and Golden Needles," she embarks on a solo career after the group breaks up. Her intense, soul-inspired sound delivers a string of hits, including "Wishin' and Hopin'" and "You Don't Have to Say You Love Me." "It's marvelous to be popular," she says, "but foolish to think it will last." Today, on a tour of South Africa, Springfield sings before a non-segregated audience—an act of disobedience that gets her deported the next day. She doesn't miss a beat, singing and touring and hosting a television special next year in her native England featuring visiting Motown bands. Springfield later releases the masterful, R&B-tinged album *Dusty in Memphis*, which includes the Top 10 hit "Son of a Preacher Man." Her career rises and falls; some twenty years later she reappears at #2 with the Pet Shop Boys, contributing to "What Have I Done to Deserve This?"

DECEMBER
15

1962 His dead-on impersonation of President Kennedy makes standup comedian Vaughan Meader an overnight sensation. Enlisting an ensemble cast, he records *The First Family*, a good-natured parody of life at the White House. Today it tops the album charts, where it reigns for an astonishing three months, selling more than seven million copies. Even the president enjoys the act, once playfully telling an interviewer, "I listened to Mr. Meader's record and, frankly, I thought it sounded more like Teddy than it did me—so now *he's* annoyed." Meader records a follow-up, and others, including George Segal, Joan Rivers, and Buck Henry, release a parody of Russia's Khrushchev family. But the laughter—and, effectively, Meader's career—ends with JFK's assassination.

COMEDY ON RECORD

While Vaughan Meader led the pack for a short stretch in the '60s, other comedians delivered their share of laughs on vinyl. Allan Sherman, one-time comedy writer for Jackie Gleason and creator of *I've Got a Secret*, scored big with his homesick camper yarn, "Hello Muddah, Hello Fadduh!", and three #1 comedy albums beginning with *My Son, The Folk Singer*. Deadpan comedian Bob Newhart, in his pre-TV days, reigned with *The Button-Down Mind of Bob Newhart*. Comedian Bill Dana took his Latino character creation to new heights with *José Jimenez—The Astronaut*. And Tom Lehrer mined a topical, increasingly political brand of humor with songs from his hit television series that became a hot album, *That Was the Year That Was*.

DECEMBER
16

1969 Turning the age-old "dumb blonde" joke on its ear, Goldie Hawn today makes a huge leap from television's *Rowan and Martin's Laugh-In* to the big screen. In her second movie, the giggly, often painted and bikini-clad sketch show star snags the role of (what else?) the ditzy girlfriend in the romantic comedy *Cactus Flower*, a role played on Broadway by Brenda Vaccaro. "Goldie can really act," reports *Time* magazine, as surprised as most by the winning performance of the former can-can dancer at the 1964 World's Fair in New York. The Oscars agree, awarding twenty-four-year-old Hawn the Best Supporting Actress trophy. She quickly jumps into a successful movie career as both actor and producer in a run of well-received roles, including Steven Spielberg's *The Sugarland Express*, *Shampoo*, *Private Benjamin*, and more. Off-screen she hooks up with longtime companion Kurt Russell, who leaves behind his boyish Disney roots (*The Travels of Jaimie McPheeters*) for a solid film career of his own.

A SLEEK SHEIK

A swelling score, a sweeping panorama, a stunning performance: director David Lean's *Lawrence of Arabia*, a big-budget, 70mm period piece brimming with action and adventure, was shot on location throughout the Middle East, North Africa, and Europe. Opening December 16, 1962, it became an instant classic, catapulting blue-eyed Irish stage actor Peter O'Toole to sudden stardom. Based loosely on the life of mythical adventurer T. H. Lawrence, the blockbuster biopic also featured a heavyweight supporting cast, including Anthony Quinn, Jose Ferrer, and Omar Sharif. Critic Roger Ebert called it "a bold, mad act of genius," but Bosley Crowther (see Oct. 3) disagreed, dubbing it "just a huge, thundering camel-opera." The film swept seven Oscars, including Best Picture, Director, Cinematography and Editing, and might have won another had the producers remembered to submit it for costume design.

> **❝ If Peter O'Toole had been any prettier, it would have been 'Florence of Arabia.' ❞**
> —playwright Noel Coward

DECEMBER 17

> **❝ Although there was no Oscar for his biggest picture— the larger than life *Zorba*—it's the Quinn performance that's brain-burned in most people's memory banks. Critics are forever flinging it back at him, neither fairly not flatteringly. ❞**
>
> —Harry Haun

1964 Anthony Quinn (of Mexican/Irish descent) becomes forever associated today with the Greek isles as he delivers his signature performance as *Zorba the Greek*. Shot on location in Crete, the film features Quinn as an earthy, larger-than-life patriarch with a soft spot for dancing and romancing. Mikis Theodorakis' theme song, "Sirtaki," also assumes enduring status as a popular wedding party song and dance. The movie goes on to win three Oscars—but not for Quinn, who loses in a strong field to Rex Harrison (*My Fair Lady*). Five years later, a far different "Z" emerges from Greece—Costa-Gavras' gripping political thriller Z, which actually shoots in Algeria since a military dictatorship then rules in Greece. *Zorba*, meanwhile, later gets several Broadway musical treatments—first from veteran producer Harold Prince (*Fiddler on the Roof*, *Cabaret*), then in a revival that reunites Quinn and his Oscar-winning co-star, Lila Kedrova.

DECEMBER 18 1961

King of the jungle and—as of today— also the charts. "The Lion Sleeps Tonight," based on a traditional South African folk song called "Wimoweh," pounces to the #1 spot. Its unlikely singers are a lily-white New York group, the Tokens. They'd tried their new version with lyrics at an audition for RCA Records several months ago, updating the 1939 Zulu lullaby that had been recorded previously by both Miriam Makeba and American folkies the Weavers. The doo-wop harmonies of the Tokens never grace the Top 10 again, though members go on to produce hits for others, including the Chiffons' "He's So Fine," Dawn's "Knock Three Times," and Robert John's version of "The Lion Sleeps Tonight," which hits #3 in 1972.

DECEMBER 19 1964

In his obscenity-laced nightclub appearances, controversial comedian Lenny Bruce rails against the system—and the system doesn't like it one bit. Targeted by the police and the self-appointed guardians of morality, he's repeatedly stalked, harassed, and arrested. Even the press gives him a hard time, with one reporter calling him a "reputed comedian" and another complaining that his act "takes off on wild and frequently disgusting flights." Arrested at a Greenwich Village cafe last summer, Bruce gets support at his latest trial from artists and writers, including Woody Allen, James Baldwin, Bob Dylan, Jules Feiffer, and Dorothy Kilgallen—but it doesn't help. A Manhattan court sentences him to four months for giving obscene performances, and fines the club's owner $1,000. Newspapers today report that his appeal has been denied, but Bruce remains unrepentant and unbowed 'til he dies of a drug overdose in 1966 (see Aug. 3). He later receives a posthumous pardon.

DECEMBER 20 1962

Popular, smiling singer Andy Williams welcomes heavyweight guests Bette Davis and Debbie Reynolds to tonight's episode of his NBC variety series, *The Andy Williams Show*. The house band, the New Christy Minstrels, provides their usual smooth backup—but not for long. For also on tonight's bill is a bubbly "youthful barbershop harmony group from Ogden, Utah" doing a couple of upbeat numbers. The Osmond Brothers quickly become regulars, beginning a long, steady rise to the top. Occasionally joined by younger siblings, the group welcomes six-year-old brother Donny the next year. Still, it'll be almost a decade before they bust onto the charts with their lone #1 hit, "One Bad Apple." Like that other singing family, the Jackson 5, to whom they draw comparisons, the Osmonds get most of their solo success from Donny—just as Michael Jackson breaks out to massive post-family fame.

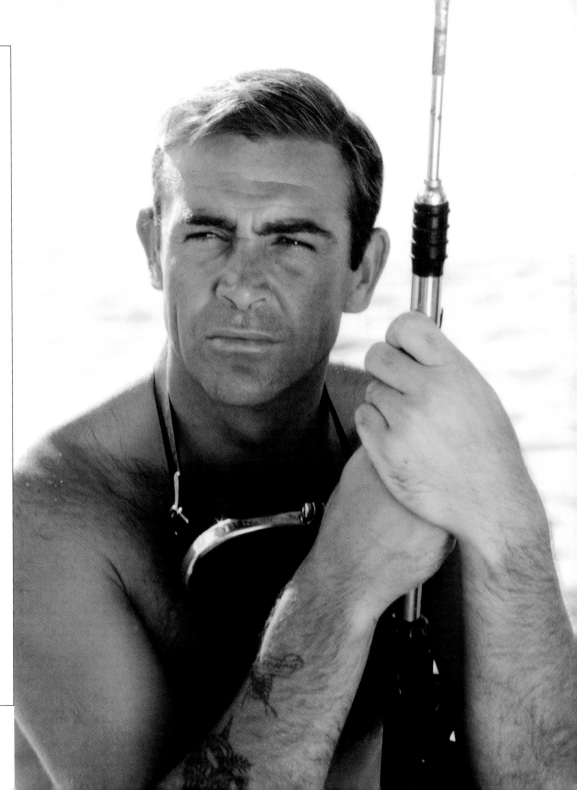

DECEMBER
21

1965 Producer Albert "Cubby" Broccoli originally wanted to make *Thunderball* the first James Bond flick. But legal problems between 007 creator Ian Fleming and a co-writer resulted instead in *Dr. No* opening the film franchise in 1962. Today *Thunderball* crashes onscreen, with Sean Connery again playing the ultra-suave British secret agent. "Sean Connery," writes film critic David Denby, "[is] a scoundrel in gentlemen's clothes." The film rakes in a record $140 million internationally and triggers a spate of spy-themed movies and TV series in both the US and UK. And its influence isn't only limited to entertainment—the underwater Caribbean scenes contribute to a resurgence of scuba diving, just as last year's *Goldfinger* boosted sales of vodka martinis (shaken, not stirred, of course).

DECEMBER
22

1967 The newsreel flickers and goes out today as television's success claims another victim. The black-and-white newsreels, a mainstay of news communication for the masses, had preceded motion pictures in movie theaters for more than half a century. The last of the five competitors, Universal Newsreel, ends its run today; the others—News of the Day, Warner-Pathe, Paramount News, and Fox Movietone News—had all gone dark before now. Ed Herlihy, the familiar, resounding voice of Universal for a quarter-century, says, "The most trying moment for me was the assassination of President Kennedy. When I saw his picture on the film, I burst into tears. They all walked out and left me alone."

DECEMBER
23

1966 For decades, Theodor Geisel (a.k.a. Dr. Seuss) has entertained and enthralled kids and parents alike with instant classics like *The Cat in the Hat* and *Green Eggs and Ham*. Tonight, *How the Grinch Stole Christmas!* becomes his first animated TV special, thanks to animator Chuck Jones (of Bugs Bunny, Wile E. Coyote, and Daffy Duck fame). A perfect fit, extols critic Leonard Maltin: "[Jones] had a subtlety and a grace, and a fondness for verbal wit that matched his facility for verbal humor, even slapstick." Former Frankenstein Boris Karloff lends an ominous but humorous tone to the lead character, while Thurl Ravenscroft (the voice of Tony the Tiger whose Frosted Flakes are ggggreat) contributes "You're a Mean One, Mr. Grinch" in his trademark baritone. The Grinch's efforts to stop Christmas from coming to the Whos in Whoville have the opposite effect: the show's stunning success on CBS ensures a Christmastime return to Whoville and primetime TV year after year.

DECEMBER 24

1960 "Shop Around" by the Miracles enters the Top 40 today en route to #2—the first million-seller for budding Motown Records. The song is an interesting case of art imitating life. Before signing with the label, the group had only limited success with songs like "Bad Girl" and "Got a Job," an answer to the Silhouettes #1 hit "Get a Job." Apparently Smokey Robinson, the group's songwriter and lead singer, and Motown founder Berry Gordy have to, well, shop around before finding the perfect record. Find it they do with Robinson's "Shop Around," based on advice his mother had given him while growing up. An initial bluesy version doesn't quite work, so savvy producer Gordy has the group record a snappier, upbeat version that puts Motown on the map.

DECEMBER 25

1962 Harper Lee won the Pulitzer Prize for her stunning first novel, *To Kill a Mockingbird*, about racism dividing a small Southern town. Today the motion picture adaptation premieres, with an Oscar-winning turn by Gregory Peck as Lincolnesque small-town lawyer Atticus Finch. A widowed father, he makes a principled, unpopular stand defending a black man falsely accused of raping a white woman. Also featuring a memorable debut by Robert Duvall as a spooky neighbor, the movie wins Horton Foote an Oscar for Adapted Screenplay. A close friend of Truman Capote, Lee wrote the novel before she accompanied him to Kansas during his research for *In Cold Blood*. She never writes another novel.

DECEMBER 26

1968 Today *Monterey Pop*, D.A. Pennebaker's up-close and personal documentary about the Monterey International Pop Festival, debuts in theaters, bringing back the one-of-a-kind spirit of the three-day festival that had kicked off the Summer of Love in 1967. The eclectic lineup included newcomers the Who, ever-dynamic Janis Joplin with Big Brother & the Holding Company, and wild man Jimi Hendrix, who set his guitar afire during "Wild Thing." All of the performers (with the exception of sitar-player Ravi Shankar) played for free—a sign of the passionate times. *Monterey Pop* isn't the only immortalization of the event. "Monterey," by Eric Burden and the Animals, anoints Brian Jones of the Rolling Stones ("His majesty, Prince Jones, smiled as he moved among the crowd") even though his band didn't even play.

DECEMBER 27

> ❝ **Brando in *Mutiny on the Bounty* simply took charge of everything. You had the option of sitting and watching him, or turning your back on him.** ❞
>
> —Director Lewis Milestone

1962 There's been trouble in paradise (Tahiti, that is, where the movie filmed), but today it's all sunny skies as Hollywood's latest remake of *Mutiny on the Bounty* rides high as the nation's top-grossing film. Marlon Brando, miscast as master's mate Fletcher Christian (portrayed in earlier, better versions by Errol Flynn and Clark Gable), has filled the gossip pages with tales of misbehavior and gluttony on the set. Critics are kinder to Trevor Howard as Captain Bligh, whose tyrannical leadership is the basis for the real-life mutiny that occurred nearly 175 years ago. Disgusted co-star Richard Harris refuses to film a final scene with Brando, who also usurps the power of replacement director Lewis Milestone. Pilloried by the press, Brando watches his career slip noticeably in the aftermath (though he'll be nominated for a Golden Globe for his next film—the appropriately titled *The Ugly American*). A decade of clunkers ensues until his Phoenix-like return as Don Corleone in *The Godfather*.

DECEMBER 28

1961 Playwright Tennessee Williams strikes again, bringing the smoldering *Night of the Iguana* to Broadway. Bette Davis detours from her Hollywood career to play a two-bit hotelier who lusts after a visiting tour guide leading a troubled group of tourists. This being Williams, their one-night stop will certainly turn into a one-night stand, but for whom? Though tonight's debut doesn't generate the heat of earlier multi-award winners like *A Streetcar Named Desire* or *Cat on a Hot Tin Roof*, it nevertheless delivers a trademark mix of promiscuity and problems. Hollywood quickly comes calling, with John Huston directing a 1964 movie adaptation that stars Richard Burton, Deborah Kerr, Ava Gardner, and Sue Lyon. Filming with such a volatile cast, Huston presents each co-star with a gold-plated derringer, loaded with bullets bearing the names of the other stars.

DECEMBER 29

1965 Filming begins today at Shepperton Studios in England on *2001: A Space Odyssey*, filmmaker Stanley Kubrick's eagerly awaited sci-fi epic. Kubrick had previously holed up with renowned author Arthur C. Clarke in New York's Chelsea Hotel, hashing out a screenplay based on Clarke's short story "The Sentinel." The film, which won't reach theaters for another two and a half years, tackles controversial themes like human evolution, artificial intelligence, and extra-terrestrial life. Upon its release many critics carp, but Roger Ebert awards it four stars, saying it "succeeds magnificently on a cosmic scale." That's the prevailing opinion in later years, too, for what's considered one of cinema's greatest achievements—though it wins only a single Oscar, for its unprecedented special effects.

DECEMBER 30

1963 Can a grown man dressed like a condiment bottle win thousands of dollars or a new car? Sure, if he's holding a sign that says "I'd relish a deal with you, Monty." Such is the stuff of *Let's Make a Deal*, a loud, frenetic game show that debuts this afternoon on NBC. Host/producer Monty Hall wheels and deals with outrageously attired contestants (the better to attract the host's attention, of course). These zany folks often risk all by opting to trade up, though their hunches often lead to trading down, for no one knows what prizes lurk behind the numbered doors (wo)manned by lovely model Carol Merrill. The series later jumps to ABC and a primetime berth, a testament to its wacky ability to deliver the ratings, and it survives in various incarnations for almost thirty years.

DECEMBER 31

1964 And he's off! Daredevil Englishman Donald Campbell breaks the world's water speed record today, zipping along at more than 276 mph in his speedboat, *Bluebird,* on a lake in Australia. His wife, one of several hundred spectators, dives in and swims out to embrace her record-setting hubby. Back in July, Campbell had broken the land speed record in a specially designed car that topped 403 mph. Combined with today's achievement, Campbell becomes the only person to break both the land and water speed records in the same year—a feat not equaled since. "I never thought we had the chance of a snowball on the desert of cracking it today," says an ecstatic Campbell. Trying to break the record two years later, he's killed when his jet-powered boat catapults into the air and breaks apart upon landing on the water. Portrayed by Anthony Hopkins in a 1988 BBC movie, the speed demon's body won't be recovered until 2001.

Film

Oscar Winners

1960

Picture . . . . *The Apartment*

Actor . . . . Burt Lancaster (*Elmer Gantry*)

Actress . . . . Elizabeth Taylor (*Butterfield 8*)

Supporting Actor . . . . . . Peter Ustinov (*Spartacus*)

Supporting Actress . . . . Shirley Jones (*Elmer Gantry*)

Director . . . . Billy Wilder (*The Apartment*)

Adapted Screenplay . . . . Richard Brooks (*Elmer Gantry*)

Original Screenplay . . . . . I.A.L. Diamond, Billy Wilder
(*The Apartment*)

1961

Picture . . . . *West Side Story*

Actor . . . . Maximilian Schell
(*Judgment at Nuremberg*)

Actress . . . . Sophia Loren (*Two Women*)

Supporting Actor . . . . . . George Chakiris (*West Side Story*)

Supporting Actress . . . . Rita Moreno (*West Side Story*)

Director . . . . Jerome Robbins and Robert Wise
(*West Side Story*)

Adapted Screenplay . . . . Abby Mann (*Judgment at Nuremberg*)

Original Screenplay . . . . . William Inge (*Splendor in the Grass*)

1962

Picture . . . . *Lawrence of Arabia*

Actor . . . . Gregory Peck (*To Kill a Mockingbird*)

Actress . . . . Anne Bancroft (*The Miracle Worker*)

Supporting Actor . . . . . . Ed Begley (*Sweet Bird of Youth*)

Supporting Actress . . . . Patty Duke (*The Miracle Worker*)

Director . . . . David Lean (*Lawrence of Arabia*)

Adapted Screenplay . . . . Horton Foote (*To Kill a Mockingbird*)

Original Screenplay . . . . . Ennio De Concini, Pietro Germi,
Alfredo Giannetti (*Divorce—Italian Style*)

1963

Picture . . . . *Tom Jones*

Actor . . . . Sidney Poitier (*Lilies of the Field*)

Actress . . . . Patricia Neal (*Hud*)

Supporting Actor . . . . . . Melvyn Douglas (*Hud*)

Supporting Actress . . . . Margaret Rutherford (*The V.I.P.s*)

Director . . . . Tony Richardson (*Tom Jones*)

Adapted Screenplay . . . . John Osborne (*Tom Jones*)

Original Screenplay . . . . . James R. Webb (*How the West Was Won*)

1964

Picture . . . . *My Fair Lady*

Actor . . . . Rex Harrison (*My Fair Lady*)

Actress . . . . Julie Andrews (*Mary Poppins*)

Supporting Actor . . . . . . Peter Ustinov (*Topkapi*)

Supporting Actress . . . . Lila Kedrova (*Zorba the Greek*)

Director . . . . George Cukor (*My Fair Lady*)

Adapted Screenplay . . . . Edward Anhalt (*Becket*)

Original Screenplay . . . . . S.H. Barnett, Peter Stone,
Frank Tarloff (*Father Goose*)

1965

Picture . . . . *The Sound of Music*

Actor . . . . Lee Marvin *(Cat Ballou)*

Actress . . . . Julie Christie *(Darling)*

Supporting Actor . . . . . . Martin Balsam *(A Thousand Clowns)*

Supporting Actress . . . . Shelley Winters *(A Patch of Blue)*

Director . . . . Robert Wise *(The Sound of Music)*

Adapted Screenplay . . . . Robert Bolt *(Doctor Zhivago)*

Original Screenplay . . . . . Frederic Raphael *(Darling)*

1966

Picture . . . . *A Man for All Seasons*

Actor . . . . Paul Scofield *(A Man for All Seasons)*

Actress . . . . Elizabeth Taylor
(Who's Afraid of Virginia Woolf?)

Supporting Actor . . . . . . Walter Matthau *(The Fortune Cookie)*

Supporting Actress . . . . Sandy Dennis
(Who's Afraid of Virginia Woolf?)

Director . . . . Fred Zinnemann *(A Man for All Seasons)*

Adapted Screenplay . . . . Robert Bolt *(A Man for All Seasons)*

Original Screenplay . . . . . Claude Lelouch, Pierre Uytterhoeven
(A Man and a Woman)

1967

Picture . . . . *In the Heat of the Night*

Actor . . . . Rod Steiger *(In the Heat of the Night)*

Actress . . . . Katharine Hepburn
(Guess Who's Coming to Dinner)

Supporting Actor . . . . . . George Kennedy *(Cool Hand Luke)*

Supporting Actress . . . . Estelle Parsons *(Bonnie and Clyde)*

Director . . . . Mike Nichols *(The Graduate)*

Adapted Screenplay . . . . Stirling Silliphant
(In the Heat of the Night)

Original Screenplay . . . . . William Rose
(Guess Who's Coming to Dinner)

1968

Picture . . . . *Oliver!*

Actor . . . . Cliff Robertson *(Charly)*

Actress . . . . (tie) Katharine Hepburn
(The Lion in Winter)

Barbra Streisand *(Funny Girl)*

Supporting Actor . . . . . . Jack Albertson *(The Subject Was Roses)*

Supporting Actress . . . . Ruth Gordon *(Rosemary's Baby)*

Director . . . . Carol Reed *(Oliver!)*

Adapted Screenplay . . . . James Goldman *(The Lion in Winter)*

Original Screenplay . . . . . Mel Brooks *(The Producers)*

1969

Picture . . . . *Midnight Cowboy*

Actor . . . . John Wayne *(True Grit)*

Actress . . . . Maggie Smith
(The Prime of Miss Jean Brodie)

Supporting Actor . . . . . . Gig Young
(They Shoot Horses, Don't They?)

Supporting Actress . . . . Goldie Hawn *(Cactus Flower)*

Director . . . . John Schlesinger *(Midnight Cowboy)*

Adapted Screenplay . . . . Waldo Salt *(Midnight Cowboy)*

Original Screenplay . . . . . William Goldman
(Butch Cassidy and the Sundance Kid)

Top 25 Movies

Most-watched films based on box-office receipts.

1. *2001: A Space Odyssey*
2. *The Absent-Minded Professor*
3. *The Alamo*
4. *The Apartment*
5. *Butch Cassidy and the Sundance Kid*
6. *Cleopatra*
7. *Doctor Zhivago*
8. *Exodus*
9. *Funny Girl*
10. *The Graduate*
11. *Guess Who's Coming to Dinner*
12. *Guns of Navarone*
13. *It's a Mad, Mad, Mad, Mad World*
14. *The Jungle Book*
15. *Let's Make Love*
16. *Mary Poppins*
17. *My Fair Lady*
18. *One Hundred and One Dalmatians*
19. *Psycho*
20. *Solomon and Sheba*
21. *The Sound of Music*
22. *Spartacus*
23. *Suddenly, Last Summer*
24. *Swiss Family Robinson*
25. *West Side Story*

Television

Emmy Winners

1960

Drama . . . . *Playhouse 90* (CBS)

Comedy. . . . . *Art Carney Special* (NBC)

Actor. . . . . Robert Stack, *The Untouchables* (ABC)

Actress . . . . Jane Wyatt, *Father Knows Best* (CBS)

1961

Drama . . . . *Macbeth*, *Hallmark Hall of Fame* (NBC)

Comedy. . . . . *The Jack Benny Show* (CBS)

Actor. . . . . Raymond Burr, *Perry Mason* (CBS)

Actress . . . . Barbara Stanwyck, *The Barbara Stanwyck Show* (NBC)

1962

Drama . . . . *The Defenders* (CBS)

Comedy. . . . . *The Bob Newhart Show* (NBC)

Actor. . . . . E.G. Marshall, *The Defenders* (CBS)

Actress . . . . Shirley Booth, *Hazel* (NBC)

1963

Drama . . . . *The Defenders* (CBS)

Comedy. . . . . *The Dick Van Dyke Show* (CBS)

Actor . . . . E.G. Marshall, *The Defenders* (CBS)

Actress . . . . Shirley Booth, *Hazel* (NBC)

1964

Drama . . . . *The Defenders* (CBS)

Comedy. . . . . *The Dick Van Dyke Show* (CBS)

Actor. . . . . Dick Van Dyke, *The Dick Van Dyke Show* (CBS)

Actress . . . . Mary Tyler Moore, *The Dick Van Dyke Show* (CBS)

1965

(a poorly received one-year experiment with different categories)

Outstanding Program . . . *The Dick Van Dyke Show* (CBS)

Outstanding Program . . . *The Magnificent Yankee* (NBC)

Outstanding Program . . . *My Name is Barbra* (CBS)

Outstanding Individual Achievement . . . . Lynn Fontanne, *The Magnificent Yankee* (NBC)

Outstanding Individual Achievement . . . . Alfred Lunt, *The Magnificent Yankee* (NBC)

Outstanding Individual Achievement . . . . Barbra Streisand, *My Name is Barbra* (CBS)

1966

Drama . . . . *The Fugitive* (ABC)

Comedy. . . . . *The Dick Van Dyke Show* (CBS)

Actor Drama. . . . . Bill Cosby, *I Spy* (NBC)

Actress Drama . . . . Barbara Stanwyck, *The Big Valley* (ABC)

Actor Comedy . . . . Dick Van Dyke, *The Dick Van Dyke Show* (CBS)

Actress Comedy. . . . . . . Mary Tyler Moore, *The Dick Van Dyke Show* (CBS)

1967

Drama . . . . *Mission: Impossible* (CBS)

Comedy. . . . . *The Monkees* (NBC)

Actor Drama. . . . . Bill Cosby, *I Spy* (NBC)

Actress Drama . . . . Barbara Bain, *Mission: Impossible* (CBS)

Actor Comedy . . . . Don Adams, *Get Smart* (NBC)

Actress Comedy. . . . . . . Lucille Ball, *The Lucy Show* (CBS)

1968

Drama . . . . *Mission: Impossible* (CBS)

Comedy. . . . . *Get Smart* (NBC)

Actor Drama. . . . . Bill Cosby, *I Spy* (NBC)

Actress Drama . . . . Barbara Bain, *Mission: Impossible* (CBS)

Actor Comedy . . . . Don Adams, *Get Smart* (NBC)

Actress Comedy. . . . . . . Lucille Ball, *The Lucy Show* (CBS)

1969

Drama . . . . *NET Playhouse* (NET)

Comedy. . . . . *Get Smart* (NBC)

Actor Drama. . . . . Carl Betz, *Judd for the Defense* (ABC)

Actress Drama . . . . Barbara Bain, *Mission: Impossible* (CBS)

Actor Comedy . . . . Don Adams, *Get Smart* (NBC)

Actress Comedy. . . . . . . Hope Lange, *The Ghost and Mrs. Muir* (ABC)

Top 25 Television Shows

The most-watched shows of the decade based on Nielsen ratings.

1. *The Andy Griffith Show*
2. *Batman*
3. *Ben Casey*
4. *The Beverly Hillbillies*
5. *Bewitched*
6. *Bonanza*
7. *Candid Camera*
8. *The Dick Van Dyke Show*
9. *Family Affair*
10. *The Fugitive*
11. *Gomer Pyle, U.S.M.C.*
12. *Green Acres*
13. *Gunsmoke*
14. *Have Gun Will Travel*
15. *Hazel*
16. *The Jackie Gleason Show*
17. *The Lucy Show*
18. *Mayberry R.F.D.*
19. *Perry Mason*
20. *Petticoat Junction*
21. *Rawhide*
22. *The Real McCoys*
23. *The Red Skelton Show*
24. *Rowan & Martin's Laugh-In*
25. *Wagon Train*

Grammy Award Winners for Record of the Year

1960 . . . . *The Theme From "A Summer Place,"* Percy Faith

1961 . . . . *Moon River*, Henry Mancini

1962 . . . . *I Left My Heart in San Francisco,* Tony Bennett

1963 . . . . *The Days of Wine and Roses,* Henry Mancini

1964 . . . . *The Girl From Ipanema,* Stan Getz/Astrud Gilberto

1965 . . . . *A Taste of Honey,* Herb Alpert & the Tijuana Brass

1966 . . . . *Strangers in the Night*, Frank Sinatra

1967 . . . . *Up, Up and Away,* The 5th Dimension

1968 . . . . *Mrs. Robinson*, Simon & Garfunkel

1969 . . . . *Aquarius/Let the Sunshine In,* The 5th Dimension

Top 25 Songs

Most popular songs, based on total points earned during chart runs on *Billboard* and *Cashbox*. (In the 1960s, there was no universal measure of record sales or radio airplay.)

1. "The Twist," Chubby Checker (1960, 1962)
2. "Hey Jude," the Beatles (1968)
3. "I'm a Believer," the Monkees (1967)
4. "I Want to Hold Your Hand," the Beatles (1964)
5. "Tossin' and Turnin'," Bobby Lewis (1961)
6. "The Theme from 'A Summer Place,'" Percy Faith & His Orchestra (1960)
7. "I Heard It Through the Grapevine," Marvin Gaye (1968)
8. "Aquarius/Let the Sunshine In," the 5th Dimension (1969)
9. "Are You Lonesome Tonight?", Elvis Presley (1960)
10. "I Can't Stop Loving You," Ray Charles (1962)
11. "To Sir With Love," Lulu (1967)
12. "Love Is Blue," Paul Mauriat (1968)
13. "Big Girls Don't Cry," the Four Seasons (1962)
14. "Sugar Shack," Jimmy Gilmer and the Fireballs (1963)
15. "Sugar, Sugar," the Archies (1969)
16. "It's Now or Never," Elvis Presley (1960)
17. "The Ballad of the Green Berets," SSgt. Barry Sadler (1966)
18. "Daydream Believer," the Monkees (1967)
19. "Ode to Billie Joe," Bobbie Gentry (1967)
20. "Honey," Bobby Goldsboro (1968)
21. "Big Bad John," Jimmy Dean (1961)
22. "In the Year 2525," Zager and Evans (1969)
23. "People Got to Be Free," the Rascals (1968)
24. "Hello, Dolly!", Louis Armstrong (1964)
25. "(I Can't Get No) Satisfaction," the Rolling Stones (1965)

Academy Award Winners for Best Song

1960	"Never on Sunday," *Never on Sunday*
1961	"Moon River," *Breakfast at Tiffany's*
1962	"The Days of Wine and Roses," *The Days of Wine and Roses*
1963	"Call Me Irresponsible," *Papa's Delicate Condition*
1964	"Chim Chim Cher-ee," *Mary Poppins*
1965	"The Shadow of Your Smile," *The Sandpiper*
1966	"Born Free," *Born Free*
1967	"Talk to the Animals," *Doctor Dolittle*
1968	"The Windmills of Your Mind," *The Thomas Crown Affair*
1969	"Raindrops Keep Fallin' on My Head," *Butch Cassidy and the Sundance Kid*

About the Authors

Three months after Bob Dylan electrifies the crowd and his music at the Newport Folk Festival (see July 25), junior high student **Harvey Solomon** and two pals attend their first Dylan concert: acoustic, intermission, electric. Extraordinary. So begins a lifelong interest in music and the arts. After college he tops the masthead at a publisher producing millions of monthly cable TV programming guides. But the muse favors freelance over full-time employment, so he embarks on an itinerant literary life: hundreds of media-related articles for trades from *Adweek* to *Variety*, and newspapers from the *Boston Globe* to the *Los Angeles Times*. Answering Hollywood's siren call, he writes for *Law & Order* and options a screenplay. He even braves choppy corporate waters, writing speeches and scripts and such. About the only writing he doesn't attempt, thank God, is poetry.

Rich Appel hears Little Peggy March's "I Will Follow Him" (see April 27) and decides what he's going to do with the rest of his life. Unfortunately, there are no executive search firms targeting kindergarteners (these days it's a different story). So Appel takes a more obvious career route: spending the next forty years listening to radio, watching television, and reading *Weekly World News*, all the time making notes in preparation for a book like the one you're holding right now. During this period, he also finds time to get a couple of fancy college degrees, win a nationwide rock 'n' roll trivia contest, and find work as a radio DJ, nightclub performer, media and record company researcher, album liner notes writer, editor of radio/music e-zine *Hz So Good*, and salesman for the Craftmatic automatic adjustable bed. Says Appel, "At least I sleep at night."

Photography Credits